این غزل شطحــست و قوالش منم
وین سخن حقست و بـرها نش تـویی

عطار

This song is an ecstatic word, and I am its singer;
and this word is true, for You are its proof.

`Attar`

SUNY Series in Islam
Seyyed Hossein Nasr, Editor

At a time when so much attention is concentrated upon the role of Islam on the stage of contemporary history, it is important to focus upon the roots and sources of Islam and the spirituality which has infused it over the ages and which has been and remains its perennial fountainhead of energy and rejuvenation. In this series, under the general editorship of Seyyed Hossein Nasr, works of a scholarly nature which at the same time treat the spiritual aspects of the Islamic tradition will be made available to the English-speaking public. Some of these books concern the Islamic religion itself, others its inner dimension as contained in Sufism, and yet others the intellectual teachings of those schools which have been intertwined with and are inseparable from Islamic spirituality and which in fact represent a most important expression of this spirituality. It is hoped that in this way the series will provide a more in depth knowledge of Islam and the Muslim peoples at a moment when broad and yet profound knowledge of the Islamic tradition has become so necessary for the contemporary world.

WORDS OF ECSTASY
IN SUFISM

Carl W. Ernst

State University of New York Press
ALBANY

Published by
State University of New York Press, Albany

Printed in the United States of America

For information, address State University of New York
Press, State University Plaza, Albany, N.Y., 12246

Library of Congress Cataloging in Publication Data

Ernst, Carl W., 1950-
  Words of ecstasy in Sufism.

  (SUNY series in Islamic spirituality)
  Bibliography: p.
  Includes index.
  1. Sufism. I. Title. II. Series.
BP189.6.E76 1984   297'.42   84-113
ISBN 0-87395-917-5
ISBN 0-87395-918-3 (pbk.)

10   9   8   7   6   5   4   3   2   1

Contents

Preface and Acknowledgments

This study is designed to introduce a little known body of mystical literature, its various interpretations, and its repercussions in the Islamic society in which it flourished. In its present form, this is a revised version of my doctoral thesis (Harvard University, 1981). Although this book is based on specialized research, its subject matter raises questions of wider' significance in the history of religion, such as the nature of extra-scriptural revelation, the problem of understanding mystical experience from verbal descriptions, and the relationship between mysticism and the law in a legally-oriented tradition such as the Islamic one. While a certain amount of knowledge about Islam is presupposed here, I trust that the general reader with an interest in mysticism will find the subject sufficiently congenial, despite its exotic dress. The tradition of ecstatic expressions in Sufism, which is the main subject of this book, has fascinated religious thinkers in the Islamic world for centuries. It is to be hoped that, through this publication in the Islamic Spirituality Series, a new audience will come to appreciate this often surprising and daring form of mystical expression, the ecstatic sayings of the Sufis. I am grateful to Professor S. H. Nasr for including this study in the series.

Writing this book would have been impossible without the help of many people, who assisted me in a variety of ways. In particular, I want to thank Professor Annemarie Schimmel of Harvard, who advised me closely throughout my thesis work, and who provided an outstanding example of teaching and scholarship. Among the many others at Harvard

vii

who assisted me in vital ways, I want to thank Professors Wilfred Cantwell Smith, Wheeler M. Thackston, Jr., Wolfhart Heinrichs, William A. Graham, John Carman, Jane I. Smith, Dr. Michelle de Angelis, and Dr. A. Kevin Reinhart. I am grateful also to Professors Bruce Lawrence of Duke University, K. A. Nizami of Aligarh Muslim University, Herbert Mason of Boston University, Eric Voegelin of Stanford University, L. Carl Brown of Princeton University, and the late Paul Nwyia of the Sorbonne.

Institutions are also indispensable to this kind of work. I would like to make a special acknowledgement to the Center for the Study of World Religions at Harvard University, its staff and residents, for crucial support, both moral and material, throughout my graduate studies. Part of the research for this study was supported by a Fulbright-Hays Grant for Doctoral Dissertation Research Abroad, and by a Foreign Language Area Studies Grant. Many libraries cooperated generously in making available books and manuscripts, including the Middle Eastern Department of Widener Library, Harvard; the Andover-Harvard Library, Harvard Divinity School; the Maulana Azad Library, Aligarh; and the British Museum, London. Clerical assistance was funded by a grant from the Faculty Research Committee of Pomona College; I would like to thank typists Frances Homans, Michael Radiloff, Denise Bruce, and Mary Breuner for their diligent work, and the staff of the Seaver Computer Center for their assistance.

There is no room to mention all the friends who helped in important ways, in Cambridge, in Oregon, in London, in India, and in Claremont; they all have my gratitude. I would like particularly to thank my parents, Mr. and Mrs. William R. Ernst, for their unfailing support through the years. Special thanks go to Alice and David Duncan and to Kathryn O'Brien. Most of all, I want to thank my wife Judy, an astute critic and editor, to whom this is dedicated with love and respect.

Abbreviations

Akhbar   al-Husayn ibn Mansur. *Akhbār al-Hallāj. Recueil d'oraisons et d'exhortations du martyr mystique de l'Islam.* Edited and translated by Louis Massignon and Paul Kraus. Études Musulmanes, IV. 3rd ed. Paris, 1957.

Diwan   — — —. *Le Dîwân d'al-Hallâj.* Edited and translated by Louis Massignon. 2nd ed. Paris, 1957.

EI[1]   *The Encyclopaedia of Islam.* Edited by Th. Houtsma et al. 4 vols. plus Supplement. Leiden, 1913–1938.

EI[2]   *The Encyclopaedia of Islam.* Edited by H. A. R. Gibb et al. New ed. Leiden, 1960–.

Essai   Massignon, Louis. *Essai sur les origines du lexique technique de la mystique musulmane.* Études Musulmanes, II. 2nd ed. Paris, 1968.

GAL, GALS   Brockelmann, Carl. *Geschichte der arabischen Litteratur.* 2nd ed. 2 vols. and 3 supplementary vols. Leiden, 1937–49.

GAS   Sezgin, Fuat. *Geschichte des arabischen Schrifttums.* Leiden, 1967–.

*Luma`*  al-Sarráj al-Ṭúsí, Abú Naṣr Abdallah ibn `Alì. *The Kitáb al-Luma` fi'l-Taṣawwuf* (*sic*). Edited by Reynold Alleyne Nicholson. "E. J. W. Gibb Memorial" Series, XXII. London, 1963.

Pages – – –. *Pages from the Kitāb al-Luma`*. Edited by A. J. Arberry. London, 1947.

Passion Massignon, Louis. *La Passion de Husayn ibn Mansûr Hallâj, martyr mystique de l'Islam exécuté à Baghdad le 26 mars 922.* Étude d'histoire religieuse. 2nd ed. 4 vols. Paris, 1975.

q. qamari, i.e., lunar Islamic calendar.

Quatre textes Massignon, Louis, ed. *Quatre textes inédits, relatifs à la biographie d'al-Hosayn-ibn Manṣoūr al Hallaj* (*sic*). Paris, 1914.

Qur. *al-Qur'an al-Karim.* Beirut, 1394. Cited by *surah* and *ayah* in my translation, unless otherwise noted. Commentaries on particular verses are indicated by *in Qur.*

SEI *The Shorter Encyclopaedia of Islam.* Edited by H. A. R. Gibb and J. H. Kramers. Leiden, 1961.

sh. shamsi, i.e., solar Islamic calendar.

Sharh Ruzbihan Baqli Shirazi. *Sharh-i Shathiyat.* Edited by Henry Corbin. Bibliothèque Iranienne, 12. Tehran, 1966.

Shaybi al-Shaybi, Kamil Mustafa, ed. *Sharh Diwan al-Hallaj.* Beirut, 1393/1973.

Tawasin, ed. Massignon al-Hallaj, al-Husayn ibn Mansur. *Kitâb al-Tawâsîn.* Edited by Louis Massignon. Paris, 1913.

Tawasin, ed. Nwyia – – –. *Kitāb al-Ṭawāsīn.* Edited by Paul Nwyia. Mélanges de l'Université Saint-Joseph, vol. 47. Beirut, 1972.

Transliteration of Persian and Arabic

ء	,	ر	r	ف	f	ای	a
ب	b	ز	z	ق	q	و	u
پ	p	ژ	zh	ک	k	ی	i
ت	t	س	s	گ	g	‒	a
ث	th	ش	sh	ل	l	‒	u
ج	j	ص	s	م	m	‒	i
چ	ch	ض	z	ن	n	ﻪ	-ah
ح	h	ط	t	و	w	‒و	aw
خ	kh	ظ	z	ه	h	‒ی	ay
د	d	ع	'	ی	y		
ذ	dh	غ	gh	آ	a		

Introduction

Sufism is a mystical tradition that is Qur'anic and Muhammadan. Historically, the term denotes a vast spiritual enterprise, carried out in many lands that differ widely in culture and language, but are unified by the spiritual authority of the Qur'anic revelation and the example of the Prophet Muhammad. Essentially, however, Sufism is a path of mystical life, which begins with the soul's conversion, or turning, towards God. The end of this path is human perfection in union with God. The foregoing is a brief description of a process that cannot be encompassed by any theoretical account, no matter how long. Yet it has been with words — both brief phrases and lengthy treatises — that the Sufis have attempted to evoke this mysterious transformation of human qualities into divine ones.

"Sufism" is the modern English word used to translate the Arabic *tasawwuf*, which is a verbal noun meaning the act or process of becoming a Sufi. Thus it is not, as the English word implies, an "ism" or theory, but rather a living experience and a quest for perfection. This path has been followed by individuals of widely different temperaments and characters, and consequently exhibits a wide variety of approaches. Stern asceticism, loving surrender to God, rigorous self-scrutiny, vast cosmic speculations, poetic outpourings, political activism, even deliberate unconventionality — these are some of the forms that Sufism has taken and articulated in ways appropriate to particular historical situations. It is important to remember, however, that Sufism as an internal process is only partly revealed by the doctrinal, literary, and institutional deposits it has left in history. Over eight centuries ago, one Sufi observed that

"Today Sufism is a name without a reality, though it used to be a reality without a name."[1] We will do well to take seriously this warning of the elusiveness of Sufism.

It is sometimes suggested that Sufism has always existed. This is, in a sense, true, insofar as in every community there have always been those who seek the inner dimension of existence, and who strive for some glimpse of the eternal, however it be conceived. Thus it is not accidental that there are remarkable similarities between Sufis and Christian mystics, Taoists, Buddhist monks, and yogis. Yet to lump all these "mystics" together on the basis of an abstract theory is to overlook the spiritual orientation peculiar to each, which opens up a distinctive (though comparable) range of potentialities that are only fully intelligible in terms of a given historical tradition. A simplistic view of mysticism also fails to deal with the remarkable variety of types and levels of spirituality within any tradition. Nineteenth-century European scholars, in a mistaken search for doctrinal "influences," sought to find the "sources" of Sufism in Neoplatonism, eastern Christianity, or Buddhism. This approach, which consistently misinterpreted the lasting power of the spiritual irruption that took place through Muhammad, saw Sufism as an exotic foreign growth incompletely grafted onto the stock of intolerant and rigid Semitic monotheism. This is far from the case, and indeed reflects mostly the persistence in Europe of medieval anti-Islamic biases, racial prejudices, and the positivistic ideologies of the day. Though Sufism is comparable to the mystical aspects of other religous traditions, its practical basis and distinctive characteristic is the repetition, contemplation, and internalization of the divine word of the Qur'an, and the imitation of Muhammad as exemplar and Perfect Man.

How, then, is this inner process related to the external data of revelation? This problem has been perennial in Islamic civilization, and it can be formulated, for our purposes, as the problem of the tension between the spirit and the letter (cf. 2 Cor. 3:6 ff.). This tension produced, on the one hand, a Sufi exegesis of the Qur'anic text, in which they sought to avoid the shackles of literalism. It brought forth, on the other hand, a host of new voices among the mystics, whose inspiration or private revelation needed to be harmonized with the word of God as publicly revealed in the Qur'an. The Islamic dispensation rests upon a foundation of religious and legal practice, in which obeying the divine law is much more important than creed or doctrine. Mystical experience and spiritual freedom thus exist in tension with the letter of the law as well as with the literal sense of scripture. While most Sufis insisted on the external law as the prerequisite and correlative of the inner path, their devotional life was enriched by experiences and practices unaccounted for in strictly legal interpretations of Islam. While mysticism in itself in no way implied rejection of the divine law, its inner freedom inevitably brought it into conflict with a human legalism that would have reduced inspiration to formula.

The focus of this study is the nature, significance, and impact of inspired expression in Sufism. Ecstatic expressions (*shathiyat*) constitute a pivotal problem for the understanding of Sufism. Post-scriptural inspiration is ambiguous; for the mystic it can be the key to divine revelation, but to outsiders it can be a blasphemous parody of scripture. The most famous ecstatic expressions, Abu Yazid al-Bistami's "Glory be to Me!" and Hallaj's "I am the Truth," have indeed been the cause of both insight and outrage over the centuries. Popular imagination has always associated the execution of Hallaj with his saying "I am the Truth"; this has given rise to a kind of historiography of martyrdom in which the mystic's expressions inevitably collided with the revealed law. The relationship between the spirit and the letter, in any case, has given rise to ambiguity. This very ambiguity has led some of the mystics to express their state in terms that paradoxically placed them outside the community of the faithful. The tension between the spirit and the letter could, and did, grow to an unendurable pitch, leading Hallaj (d. 309/922)* to say, "I became infidel to God's religion, and infidelity is my duty, because it is detestable to Muslims."[2] In the same mood, Hallaj counselled a disciple, "May God veil you from the exterior of the religious law, and may he reveal to you the reality of infidelity. For the exterior of the religious law is a hidden idolatry, while the reality of infidelity is a manifest gnosis."[3] This should not be misunderstood as a deliberate rejection of God or the Islamic faith, nor as any kind of secularism or nihilism. To impose such a superficial modern ideology on a mystical paradox would be absurd. Ecstatic sayings need to be interpreted in terms of the mystical vocabulary of the times. From this perspective, Hallaj's saying points to the limitations of rigid legalism just as it underlines the controversial nature of mystical gnosis. Though at first sight difficult to interpret, nonetheless the ecstatic sayings on faith and infidelity offer an intriguing perspective on the whole problem of inspired speech. As a kind of self-reflective statement, they describe all human formulations as shot through with duality, and thus define the limitations of mystical expression. Even today, the foremost Persian lexicon, the *Lughat Namah,* defines *shath* as "'certain words resembling infidelity, which are uttered by the Sufi in overpowering ecstasy."[4] To clarity the relationship between mystical experience and infidelity will be one of the most difficult as well as fascinating tasks of this study.

The attempt to understand these typical ecstatic utterances separates itself into three related subjects that constitute the parts of this book:

---

*All dates are given according to the Islamic *hijri* calendar, followed by a solidus (/) and the equivalent date in the Gregorian Christian calendar.

first, the literary genre of *shathiyat* in Sufism, considered in its historical development and in its principal topics and forms of expression; second, the ecstatic sayings on faith and infidelity and their interpretation in Sufism; third, the problem of the spirit and the letter in Sufism, which illustrates the legal and dogmatic repercussions of mysticism in Islamic society. This is followed by a conclusion that compares *shathiyat* to mystical speech in other religious traditions, to establish a basis for evaluating the significance of ecstatic expressions.

Although students of Islam have long recognized the importance of *shathiyat*, most have been content to allude to it in passing. Louis Massignon's classic *Essai sur les origines du lexique technique de la mystique musulmane* was focussed on the writings of Hallaj "as most clearly exhibiting . . . the crucial question of mysticism: the experiential phenomenon of *shath*, the sign of transforming union."[5] Massignon remained preoccupied, however, with other problems, above all, the fate of Hallaj. Although he was the first to sketch the outline of the problem of interpreting *shath*, he never attempted a sustained analysis of it.[6] More recently, Paul Nwyia, in a study of Sufi Qur'an exegesis that extended the work of Massignon, recognized *shath* as the pinnacle of mystical experience; here, where the speaker becomes united to the divine word and renounces deceptive language, Nwyia finds the source of "the authentic language . . . of experience" in Arabic.[7] But aside from a few highly insightful passages on this subject, Nwyia, like Massignon, devoted most of his time to introducing and explicating the unpublished writings of individual Sufis. Other scholars of Sufism, such as R. A. Nicholson and Hellmut Ritter, have only mentioned this problem in brief. It is still too early to attempt an exhaustive study of *shathiyat*, since many essential texts, such as the great Sufi Qur'an commentaries of Sulami and Ruzbihan Baqli, have yet to be published in critical editions. But with Henry Corbin's edition of Ruzbihan's *Commentary on Ecstatic Expressions (Sharh-i Shathiyat)* in 1966, enough material is now available to permit a general analysis.

I have chosen to center this investigation on the "classical" period of Sufism, from the third/ninth to the sixth/twelfth centuries, in Iraq and Iran, a choice which requires some justification. In its earliest period, Sufism began to emerge as a distinctive movement formed of the ascetic and devotional aspirations of early Islam. Pious Muslims in the first generations of the new Islamic society had increasingly turned away from the worldliness of the caliphal court. The ascetic Hasan of Basra had warned his listeners to abandon the wealth of the world and prepare for judgment, at the very moment when the caliph's armies were conquering Spain, the Indus valley, and Transoxania. This call was echoed in eastern Iran, where Ibrahim ibn Adham, the prince of Balkh, renounced his throne and gave up the world. Other figures like Rabi`ah of Basra mitigated this austerity; she expressed her unconditional and selfless love for God in a way that imprinted the stamp of genuine mysticism on early Sufism.

The classical period with which we are concerned began with the great Sufis of the third/ninth century, Dhu al-Nun of Egypt, the Iranian Abu Yazid al-Bistami, and the members of the Baghdad school, such as Abu al-Husayn al-Nuri, Abu Sa`id al-Kharraz, and Junayd. This period saw an outburst of creativity in Sufism, based on minute examination of internal spiritual states and extended speculation on moral, legal, and philosophical subjects. In the realm of *shath*, however, the dominant figure was of course Hallaj, who more than any other found in this divine speech his "mystical vocation," as Massignon put it. Hallaj's martyrdom, which necessarily increased the controversy over *shathiyat*, caused many Sufis either to adopt conservative legalistic positions or to engage in deliberate esotericism. In subsequent generations, inspired speech continued to play an important role in the elaboration of Sufism, as in the work of Abu Nasr al-Sarraj, but the *Sharh-i Shathiyat* of Ruzbihan Baqli is the single most important treatise on the subject. It is, as Corbin observed, "a veritable Summa of Sufism, studied from the characteristic viewpoint of *shath*," and an essential source for any future history of Sufism.[8] One other interpreter of Hallaj will be crucial for the interpretation of the ecstatic sayings on faith and infidelity: this is `Ayn al-Qudat al-Hamadani, who was executed in 525/1131. In his treatise *Tamhidat*, he has given a lengthy discussion of the mystical concept of true infidelity that became definitive for many later Sufis. Ruzbihan's work reflects the accumulated wisdom of the Baghdad school of Sufism as well as that of Ibn al-Khafif in Shiraz, thus uniting the traditions of Iraq and southern Iran. `Ayn al-Qudat summarizes the outlook of the Sufis of northern Iran, especially as represented by his master Ahmad al-Ghazali, brother of the famous theologian. In choosing Hallaj, and his two interpreters Ruzbihan and `Ayn al-Qudat, we have selected figures representative of the major Sufi schools of this period, who were responsible for the dominant formulations of *shathiyat* in general and the ecstatic expressions on faith and infidelity in particular.

The authors selected are also appropriate examples to take in studying the problem of the spirit and the letter in Sufism. A historical examination of Sufi trials (Nuri, Hallaj, `Ayn al-Qudat) will afford the opportunity of testing the popular notion that mystical sayings inevitably conflict with Islamic law. The historiography of martyrdom in Sufism has understandably obscured the political and social causes of the Sufi trials, in order to highlight the religious issues. Bringing out the essentially political nature of these so-called heresy trials will make it easier to understand how, in other circumstances, outspoken mystics like Ruzbihan could have lived wholly untroubled by such inquisitions. In addition, an analysis of contemporary heresiographic and legal literature will permit a more balanced view of the status of ecstatic savings in Islamic law.

The spirit of *shath* flourished during this classical period of Sufism, but in subsequent centuries the social and theoretical elaboration of Sufism tended to cast *shathiyat* into more formal literary and philosophical molds. By the sixth/twelfth century, Sufism was taking on the form of public orders extending into all levels of society, partly as a response to the decay of the social order as manifested in the decline of the caliphate. Distinctive orders arose in different cultural areas such as Central Asia and India, reflecting the particular character of each region. Persian mystical poetry inherited the classical ecstatic expressions as literary *topoi*, which continually recur in the delicate allusive forms that give Persian Sufi poetry its texture and density. This is above all true of the poetry of Farid al-Din `Attar, whose lyrics contain innumerable symbolic references to mystical infidelity. When the theoretical outlook associated with the Andalusian master Ibn `Arabi came to dominate the intellectual expression of Sufism, *shathiyat* became mere allegories for the subtle doctrines of Ibn `Arabi's school. After this time, inspired speech became a conventional rhetorical device.

Thus the period and the authors in question can serve as the basis for a general and introductory survey of ecstatic expressions in Sufism and their repercussions, with special regard to the topic of faith and infidelity. This study does not pretend to completeness; an exhaustive inquiry into *shathiyat* would require a comprehensive collection of the literature of early Sufism, much of which is still unpublished, and it would entail in particular a thorough analysis of Sufi Qur'an commentaries. Nevertheless, I hope that the present book will achieve its goal of introducing the literature of *shath* in its religious and historical context. Despite the intrinsic difficulty and even obscurity of this subject, it remains a fascinating monument to the aspirations of the human spirit. *Shath* raises questions of universal scope regarding human-divine relationships, and it offers testimonies that pose extraordinary challenges for conventional religious notions. As Gerardus van der Leeuw said, "We can never understand God's utterance by means of any purely intellectual capacity; what we can understand is only our own answer."[9] This study is an attempt at recovering the meaning of a particular variety of human response to the word of God. If it can succeed in making this religious phenomenon accessible to modern readers, and if it will throw some light on the problem of reconciling spiritual experience with the larger historical tradition, it will have served its purpose.

Part I

ECSTATIC EXPRESSIONS
IN SUFISM

A.

The Literature and Theory of Ecstatic Expression

1. CLASSICAL SUFISM UP TO RUZBIHAN

For Sufis, the phenomenon of *shath* as a mode of speech with God must seek its origin, ultimately, in the experience of the Prophet Muhammad. The Qur'an is the word of God, which has been internalized to form the basis of the mystical vocabulary of Sufism.[1] The model for *shath* is especially to be looked for in the Divine Saying (*hadith qudsi*), the extra-Qur'anic revelations in which Muhammad reported what God said to him. It was the view of Louis Massignon that many of the Divine Sayings were not authentic reports going back to Muhammad, but were the results of the experiences of the early mystics, who circulated these sayings publicly in the guise of *hadith*, before the standardization of the *hadith* corpus.[2] The recent researches of William A. Graham have shown that this is not necessarily the case. Most of the Divine Sayings can be found in the canonical collections of *hadith*.[3] In these canonical *hadith*, there are some that emphasize the possibility of close contact between man and God: "The Prophet said, 'God says: "I fulfill My servant's expectation of Me, and I am with him when he remembers Me. . . . "'"[4] Other sayings stress the importance of love (*mahabbah*). ". . . I heard the Apostle of God say: 'God said: "My love belongs by right to those who love one another in Me, to those who sit together (in fellowship) in Me. . ."'"[5] The most famous of these Divine Sayings is the saying on supererogatory worship (*hadith al-nawafil*), which expresses an experience in which the worshipper feels the divine presence so strongly

9

that his volition is taken up by God, and all his actions are performed by God. The essential section is the following: "And My servant continues drawing nearer to Me through supererogatory acts until I love him; and when I love him, I become his ear with which he hears, his eye with which he sees, his hand with which he grasps, and his foot with which he walks."[6] The importance of this Divine Saying for Sufism can scarcely be overestimated. It "forms one of the cornerstones of mystical teaching in Sufism."[7] As the word of God to the Prophet, this saying stands as a constant reminder of the possibility of union with God through devotion.

As far as we can tell, the first major development of the concept of divine speech was the work of the sixth imam of the Shi`ah, Ja`far al-Sadiq (d. 148/765). Respected for his piety and wisdom by all Islamic sects, Ja`far was regarded especially highly by the Sufis, who took his Qur'an commentary as the basis for their growing body of mystical Qur'anic literature. In his exegesis of the theophany experienced by Moses on Mt. Sinai, Ja`far found the key to the nature of divine speech in the words by which God identified Himself. According to Ja`far, when God said to Moses, "I am I, your Lord (*inni ana rabbuka*)" (Qur. 20.12), Moses then realized that

> it is not proper for anyone but God to speak of himself by using these words *inni ana*, "I am I." I was seized by a stupor (*dahsh*), and annihilation (*fana'*) took place. I said then: "You! You are He who is and who will be eternally, and Moses has no place with You nor the audacity to speak, unless You let him subsist by your subsistence (*baqa'*) and You endow him with Your attribute." . . . He replied to me: "None but I can bear My speech, none can give me a reply; I am He who speaks and He who is spoken to, and you are a phantom (*shabah*) between the two, in which speech (*khitab*) takes place."[8]

One of the striking things about this comment is that it reveals selfhood as an exclusively divine prerogative. Only God has the right to say "I." This important point would later be stressed by Sufis such as Abu Sa`id al-Kharraz (d. 279/892) and Abu Nasr al-Sarraj (d. 378/988).[9] A further aspect of Ja`far's comment that greatly influenced Sufism was the use of the terms "annihilation (*fana'*)" and "subsistence (*baqa'*)," which refer to the disappearance of the human ego and the manifestation of the divine presence. This would later be articulated by the Sufi Dhu al-Nun (d. ca. 246/859), who was the first Sufi editor of Ja`far's Qur'an commentary.[10] Finally, Ja`far interprets Moses' experience of the divine speech as an event occurring within the consciousness of a human being. One must agree with Nwyia that Ja`far has described

> precisely that which the Sufis designate by the technical term of *shath* or theopathic locution. Moses heard in himself the *inni ana rabbuka*, Bistami will say *subhani* (glory be to Me!), and Hallaj, *ana al-haqq* (I am the

Truth), but the phenomenon is the same: in none of these cases is the subject of the sentence either Moses, Bistami, or Hallaj, but it is God who speaks by and through the human consciousness.[11]

Although he does not use the term *shath*, Ja`far has described this phenomenon in a way that will remain archetypal for later Sufis.

The first widely quoted author of ecstatic sayings was Abu Yazid al-Bistami (d. 261/875), the Persian ascetic and mystic (known as Bayazid in Iran), who is most famous for his phrase, "Glory be to Me! How great is My Dignity!" He did harsh penances for many years, and then began to express his spiritual experiences in a most daring language. He spoke of the annihilation of the self, but he also described the experience of ascent into the presence of God, comparable to the heavenly ascension (*mi`raj*) of Muhammad.[12] The great Sufi master of Baghdad, Abu al-Qasim al-Junayd (d. 298/910), gathered and discussed many of Bayazid's sayings in a work called *Tafsir al-Shathiyat* ("Commentary on the Ecstatic Expressions"). Junayd's approach was apparently based on sobriety (*sahw*), as opposed to the intoxication (*sukr*) that he saw in Bayazid, but he regarded Bayazid's sayings as significant data of the mystical life. In some instances, he indicated that Bayazid's sayings did not emerge from the highest level of mystical experience. The largest collection of Bayazid's sayings is the *Kitab al-Nur min Kalimat Abi Yazid Tayfur* ("The Book of Light from the Sayings of Abu Yazid Tayfur"), compiled by al-Sahlaji (d. 476/1082-3) on the basis of reports going back to Bayazid's descendants. This book has been edited by `Abd al-Rahman Badawi under the title *Shatahat al-Sufiyah*.[13] Junayd himself is credited with a number of ecstatic sayings, despite his sobriety. Junayd's commentary, and many of Bayazid's sayings, would not have survived without the valuable work of Abu Nasr al-Sarraj (d. 378/988). A native of Tus in Khurasan, Sarraj was widely travelled, and was an authoritative master in Sufism and law. He compiled his *Kitab al-Luma` fi al-Tasawwuf* ("The Book of Glimmerings on Sufism") as a guide to all aspects of Sufism, designed to show that Sufism was completely in accord with the principles and ordinances of Islam. The last of the twelve sections of this book is entitled "The Commentary on Ecstatic Expressions, and Words that are Externally Found Repulsive, Though they are Internally Correct and Well-founded." This section incorporates Junayd's comments on Bayazid, as well as sayings of Shibli, Nuri, Wasiti, and other early Sufis.

Sarraj has developed a very interesting theory of *shath* and the conditions for understanding it. His discussion, which is the earliest treatment of its kind, deserves to be considered here at some length. In the following passage he gives the etymology and definition of the term, and describes its essential features:

If a questioner asks the meaning of *shath*, the answer is that it means a strange-seeming expression describing an ecstasy that overflows because of its power, and that creates commotion by the strength of its ebullience and overpowering quality. This is shown by the fact that *shath* in Arabic means "movement". . . . The flour-sifting house is called "the shaking house (*al-mishtah*)" because they shake the flour so much, above the place where they sift it, and sometimes it spills over the edges from so much shaking. Thus *shath* is a word derived from movement, because it is the agitation of the intimate consciences of the ecstatics when their ecstasy becomes powerful. They express that ecstasy of theirs by an expression that the hearer finds strange — but he will be led astray to his perdition by denying and refuting it when he hears it, and he will be safe and sound by avoiding its denial and by searching out the difficulty in it by asking someone who really knows it. This is one of its characteristics: have you ever noticed that when a great deal of water is flowing in a narrow stream, it overflows its banks? It is then said, "The water *shataha* (overflowed) in the stream." Therefore when the ecstasy of an aspirant becomes powerful, and he is unable to endure the assault of the luminous spiritual realities that have come over his heart, it appears on his tongue, and he expresses it by a phrase that is strange and difficult for the hearer, unless he be worthy of it and have widely encompassed the knowledge of it. And that, in the language of those who are familiar with technical terminology, is called *shath*.[14]

This is a learned and sophisticated description that presents a number of concepts central to the understanding of *shath*. The sense of the overflowing and spilling over of a powerful experience is the basic connotation of this term. Yet Sarraj also stresses the component of knowledge in *shath*. It is essential that the enquirer ask one "who really knows it (*ya`lamu `ilmahu*)," one who has "widely encompassed the knowledge of it (*mutabahhiran fi `ilmiha*)." Evidently the ecstasy (*wajd*) and its strange-seeming expression are by no means devoid of intellectual content, although the determination of this content may be difficult.

Sarraj goes on to explain the kind of knowledge that is stressed in Sufism, and the place it holds relative to the other branches of Islamic knowledge. He articulates four kinds of knowledge: first, the knowledge of the sayings of the Prophet; second, the knowledge of religious law and ordinances; third, the knowledge of analogy, theory, and disputation, which protects the faith against innovations and error; fourth, and highest of them all, the knowledge of spiritual realities, stations, acts of piety, abstinence, and contemplation of God.[15] This last branch of knowledge is what we call Sufism. Just as in any other kind of knowledge, says Sarraj, one must always go to the experts in that particular science when there is a problem to be solved, so in questions of spiritual realities one must approach the appropriate experts, the Sufi masters, in order to understand properly their sayings on this subject. For this reason, "it is inappropriate for anyone to think that he encompasses all knowledge, lest he err in his opinion of the sayings of the elect, and anathematize them and charge them with heresy (*yukaffirahum wa yuzandiqahum*), when he is devoid of experience in their states and the stations of their spiritual realities and their actions."[16] It is from a clearly established theretical position that Sarraj formulates the relation of mystical experience to the standard Islamic religious sciences, and he does so in order to defuse serious accusations that have been brought against Sufis in the past. He further points out that the Sufis are frequently learned in the traditional fields of jurisprudence, *hadith*, and disputation, in addition to their own speciality, while this is not true of the experts in those fields.

Finally, Sarraj elaborates more on the stages of spiritual development at which *shathiyat* are likely to occur:

> *Shath* is less frequently found among those who are perfected, since the latter are fully established in their spiritual realities (*ma`anihim*). It is only one who is at a beginning stage who falls into *shath*, one whose goal is union with the ultimate perfection.[17]

Sarraj here contrasts the self-possession of the perfected soul with the soul that is overpowered and cannot refrain from expressing *shathiyat*. He considers this an experience of novices, at least in theory. There will be occasion to question this judgement later on; if, after all, Bayazid's utterances were only the result of immature experiences, why did Junayd and Sarraj consider them worthy of comment? Junayd's explanation of Bayazid's statements is referred to as a *tafsir*, a word usually reserved for commentaries on the Qur'an. If the view of *shathiyat* as characteristic of the beginner is inconsistent with Sarraj's real position, it may well be that his explanation is intended to offer a ready excuse in cases where otherwise heresy would be suspected. Furthermore, Sarraj ultimately derives the *shath* of Bayazid from the celebrated Divine Saying on supererogatory worship (*hadith al-nawafil*), as it obviously implies some sort of approximation to union with God.[18] Yet Sarraj's caution kept him from mentioning Hallaj's ecstatic expressions in his discussion of *shathiyat*, although he elsewhere refers to Hallaj's execution. Evidently Sarraj deliberately avoided reference to the controversial "I am the Truth" of Hallaj, in what is admittedly an apologetic work.

Other writers of this era also discussed *shath*. One of them was Abu Sa`d al-Khargushi (d. 406/1015) a pious Sufi of Nishapur who devoted himself to building hospitals and caring for the sick. His lengthy work *Tahdhib al-Asrar* ("The Refinement of Consciences") evidently has some reference to *shath*, but it remains in manuscript and has not been accessible to me. According to Arberry, Khargushi favored sobriety over intoxication, so he may have been cautious about approving ecstatic utterances.[19] The eminent Sufi biographer Abu `Abd al-Rahman al-Sulaı̇ni (d. 412/1021) also referred to *shath* briefly, but in the main copied the views of Sarraj.[20]

A restrained view of *shath* is given by Abu Hamid al-Ghazali (d. 505/1111), who devoted a couple of pages to the subject in his massive encyclopedia *Ihya' `Ulum al-Din* ("Revival of Religious Sciences"). There Ghazali showed his great concern about the possibility of misinterpreting these sayings. Ghazali distinguishes two kinds of *shath*. The first kind consists of

> broad, extravagant claims (made) in passionate love of God Most High, in the union that is independent of outward actions, so that some go to the extent of claiming unification, rending of the veil, contemplative vision (of God), and oral conversation (with God). Then they say, "We were told such-and-such, and we said such-and-such." In this they resemble al-Husayn ibn Mansur al-Hallaj, who was crucified for uttering words of this kind, and they quote his saying, "I am the Truth."

Ghazali goes on to say that this kind of talk is very dangerous to the common people, because they lose their chance for salvation, since they think that a purified soul that has attained spiritual states can dispense with required actions. Ghazali concludes from this that "the killing of him who utters something of this kind is better in the religion of God than the resurrection of ten others." The other kind of *shath* is that which is unintelligible to the listener, regardless of whether it is merely confused babbling or something which the speaker comprehends but cannot articulate properly. Since this is bound to be interpreted *ad lib.*, it is not permissible to express such things publicly. Ghazali concludes by quoting sayings from Jesus, to the effect that one should not cast pearls before swine. In this exposition, Ghazali's main concern is to prevent ordinary people from being misled by difficult or strange sayings, even though he implicitly regards them as valid for those who can understand. In the most mystical sayings, however, he sees a real danger of antinomianism.[21]

The next author of importance for the study of *shath* is `Ayn al-Qudat Hamadani (d. 525/1131). He was a brilliant and audacious writer; his sayings and his untimely execution will be studied in detail in parts II and III. Although he pronounced many ecstatic sayings, especially in his Persian writings, he only devoted a few pages to the theoretical explanation of *shath*, in his *Shakwa al-Gharib* ("Stranger's Lament"), composed during his final imprisonment. His explanations are very similar to those of Sarraj, and he also refers to the Divine Saying on supererogatory worship as the archetype of *shath*.[22]

While Sarraj in his *Kitab al-Luma`* devoted some forty pages, about one-tenth of the book, to a discussion of *shathiyat*, in *Sharh-i Shathiyat* of Ruzbihan Baqli we have a complete treatise filling six hundred pages in the edition of Henry Corbin. Ruzbihan Baqli Shirazi (d. 606/1209) is the pre-eminent authority on *shath* in Sufism, so that in Iran he is known as *Shaykh-i Shattah*, "Doctor Ecstaticus."[23] His spiritual lineage goes back to Ibn al-Khafif (d. 372/982), one of the last confidants of Hallaj before his execution. Ruzbihan is the most important interpreter of Hallaj; he not only preserves many significant sayings and interpretations of Hallaj, but also brings his own original vision to bear on the subject. He originally composed his commentary on ecstatic sayings as a treatise in Arabic entitled *Mantiq al-Asrar fi Bayan al-Anwar* ("The Language of Consciences explaining their Illuminations"), and it was primarily devoted to Hallaj, with other sayings added for completeness. At the request of his disciples, he translated the book into Persian under the title *Sharh-i Shathiyat* ("Commentary on Ecstatic Expressions"), increasing the volume of the book substantially by giving accounts of his own experiences.[24] This work is an extraordinarily rich exposition of the spiritual life, although the idiosyncrasies of style in the *Sharh* are such that "it would be an exaggeration to say that the Persian is much clearer than the Arabic original," as Corbin dryly remarks.[25] Yet this work has a strange and fascinating beauty. As Annemarie Schimmel observes,

> What so profoundly impresses the reader in Ruzbihan's writings . . . is his style, which is at times as hard to translate as that of Ahmad Ghazzali and possesses a stronger and deeper instrumentation. It is no longer the scholastic language of the early exponents of Sufism, who tried to classify stages and stations, though Baqli surely knew these theories and the technical terms. It is the language refined by the poets of Iran during the eleventh and twelfth centuries, filled with roses and nightingales, pliable and colorful.[26]

The work is composed on roughly chronological lines. After a long introduction on the aims and theories of this commentary, Ruzbihan describes the origins of *shath* in the theophanic elements of the Qur'an and *hadith*. Then, after discussing the *shathiyat* of the Prophet's companions, Ruzbihan gives a total of 192 ecstatic expressions of forty-five different Sufis, from Ibrahim ibn Adham (d. ca. 174/790) to Abu Sa'id ibn Abi al-Khayr (d. 440/1049). A number of these authors are scarcely known to history, and these are usually represented here by only one or two sayings. Among the most prominent authors are Abu Bakr al-Wasiti (d. ca. 320/932) and Abu al-Hasan al-Husri (d. 371/981), each with over a dozen sayings, while special emphasis is given to the twenty-two sayings of Abu Bakr al-Shibli (d. 334/945) and the thirty-one sayings of Bayazid. Yet the place of honor is reserved for Hallaj. Forty-five of his sayings are commented on, as well as his twenty-five spiritual *hadith* (the *Riwayat*), and the composite book known as the *Kitab al-Tawasin*. Thus one-third of the *Sharh-i Shathiyat* is devoted to Hallaj. In terms of completeness, it may be pointed out that Ruzbihan did not apparently have access to the works of some Sufis from north-western Iran or Transoxania. He never refers to the Sufi martyr `Ayn al-Qudat Hamadani, whose work shows such strong parallels to his own. As for sources, it is clear that Ruzbihan was thoroughly familiar with the *Kitab al-Luma`* of Sarraj. He not only borrowed from Sarraj a number of technical explanations and commentaries on individual *shathiyat*, but also drew on him for some twenty-eight quotations from five different authors.

In the introduction to his book, Ruzbihan has given an eloquent description of his purpose in clarifying the words of the saints, so that those who do not comprehend will refrain from the error of persecuting the saints;

> When I bent my head in contemplation and read in the famous books of the leaders in gnosis, I recognized the disparities in their states through their sayings. It was clear to me that the subtleties and allusions of those who are rooted in gnosis are bestowed by the states that come upon them, and I saw that the understanding of that knowledge is difficult. Language becomes manifest in the form of *shathiyat* particularly for those intoxicated ones who are drowned in the waves of eternity, on account of the thundering clouds experienced in the moment of profound sighs, in the reality of overwhelming raptures. From each of their words, a world of learned men is filled with consternation. The deniers have drawn forth the sword of ignorance from the scabbard of envy, and from foolishness are wielding it themselves. . . . God's jealous ones cried out from the wombs of the hidden world, "O witness of secrets and niche of lights! Free the holy spirits from denial by the bankrupt, show forth the long past of those who kill and crucify in sacrifice! Say the secret of the *shath* of the lovers, and the expression of the agitation of the intoxicated, in the language of the people of the inner reality and the outer law! Say every subtlety in the form of knowledge connected with a spiritual state, and the guidances of Qur'an and *hadith*. (Say all this as) a subtle and marvellous commentary . . ."[27]

Ruzbihan is inspired to write upon the difficulties of *shathiyat* in terms of his knowledge of the spiritual experiences from which they derive, though they are incomprehensible and frightening to the learned religious scholars. Therefore he is called upon to reveal the connection between the inner reality and the outward law, to explain the knowledge (`*ilm*) inherent in the spiritual states, and to show its conformity with the data of revelation enshrined in the Qur'an and *hadith*.

One can see the extent to which Ruzbihan is moved by the persecutions and martyrdoms suffered by the prophets and the saints by the fact that he devotes chapters three and six to a recitation and litany of "the persecution of the folk," as he describes it. Dwelling on the inevitable sufferings of those who are close to God, he makes it clear that uttering incomprehensible spiritual sayings, and being oppressed by those who do not possess the inner knowledge or science of it, are both part of the destiny of the lovers of God. After proceeding through several chapters that describe the virtues and attainments of "the men of *shath*," Ruzbihan once again shows what an important position Hallaj has in this science of *shath*:

> The sole object of all this is the commentary (*tafsir*) of the *shathiyat* of Hallaj, that I might remove the occasion for refutation, and comment upon his enigmas in the language of the religious law (*shari`at*) and the spiritual reality (*haqiqat*). The quality of his sayings is stranger than all others, just as his deeds were stranger than all others, since he mostly speaks in terms of "I-ness (*ana'iyat*)." The path to his spiritual reality became incomprehensible in the sight of the imperfect. We are removing the murky doubts from the clear face of reality. Know that that dear one had fallen into "essential union (Pers. `*ayn-i jam`*)." He was drowned in the limitless ocean of eternity, pure ecstasy overcame him. He entered into that sea with the quality of creaturehood, and he departed with the character of lordship. From the depth of that ocean he brought forth the pearls of everlastingness. None saw, and none heard, for some said he was a magician, and some said he was a conjurer, some said he was mad, and some said he was a heretic. Few said that he was truthful. Yes, some who were ignorant spoke thus (in condemnation), but since it is the prophetic norm (*sunnah*), prophets are called magician and conjurer.[28]

As in the case of Sarraj, part of the purpose of Ruzbihan's work is apologetic, as it attempts to remove the basis for criticism by externalists; this is to be accomplished by demonstrating that the *shathiyat* are in conformity, not only with the spiritual reality (*haqiqat*) revealed in a mystical state (*hal*), but also with the religious law (*shari`at*), which is applicable to all of the faithful. Another interesting feature is the characteristic application of the epithet "strange" (*gharib*) to Hallaj, who was frequently termed *al-`alim al-gharib*, or "Doctor Singularis" as Massignon translated it. More importantly, Ruzbihan is here introducing several technical terms that are crucial to his interpretation of the Hallajian *shathiyat*. First is the term *ana'iyat* ("I-ness"), which is the form of the word favored by Ruzbihan; Hallaj uses the term *aniyah*, while later writers use the term *ananiyah*.[29] The problematic nature of the ego in an intense confrontation with God is probably the most sensitive topic raised by the *shathiyat* of Hallaj and Bayazid. When the contemplative is experiencing annihilation of his ego and direct converse with God, it is a very delicate question, from moment to moment, as to the actual identity of the speaker. A second important term here is "essential union (`*ayn al-jam`*)," which was used by Junayd to describe the state of Bayazid. According to Ruzbihan, this term does not have the *odium theologicum* of the term "incarnationism (*hulul*)," and he often uses the synonym "unification (*ittihad*)."[30] The basic import of these terms is that the most important topic of *shathiyat* is the possible union of the human with the divine, which is the question of the nature of selfhood.

In the chapter devoted to the meaning of the term *shath*, Ruzbihan begins with the lexicographical example already given by Sarraj, of the mill-house where grain is sifted by shaking. He continues to follow Sarraj's lead, but adds enough of his own interpretation to make a full translation worthwhile:

> Then in the vocabulary of the Sufis, *shath* is derived from the agitations of the intimate consciences of their hearts. When ecstasy becomes strong and the light of manifestation becomes elevated in the inmost part of their consciences, by the quality of the annunciation and revelation and strengthening of the spirits illuminated by the inspiration that appears in their intellects, it stirs up the fire of their longing for the eternal Beloved. They reach the vision of the seraglio-curtain of Majesty, and they are moving in the world of beauty. When they see the objects of contemplation in the hidden, and the secrets of the hidden of the hidden, and the mysteries of greatness—intoxication enters in upon them unasked, the soul enters into ebullience, the consciousness enters into commotion, the tongue enters into speech. Speech comes forth from the ecstatic, from his incandescent state (*hal*) and from his spirit's exaltation, regarding the science of the stations (*maqamat*). The outward form of it is symbolic (*mutashabih*). It is an expression the words of which are found to be strange. When others do not understand the inner aspect through the outward forms, and they do not see the method of it, they are led astray to denial and refutation of the speaker.[31]

This description contains basically the same elements found in Sarraj's definition, already quoted, of the overflowing of ecstasy into speech, and the necessity of having the true knowledge or science (`*ilm*) of inner experience in order to understand *shath*. Ruzbihan adds a certain stress on the differentiation of inner experiences, referring to the state (*hal*) and the stations (*maqamat*) of the path, while at the same time transforming this into a characteristically poetic invocation by his series of balanced clauses.

One of the most striking aspects of Ruzbihan's interpretation is his assimilation of *shathiyat* to the expressions in the Qur'an and *hadith* known as enigmatic utterances (*mutashabihat*). Certain verses of the Qur'an, particularly those that symbolically describe God in physical terms (hand, face, sitting on the throne), cannot be taken literally without anthropomorphism. In the following passage, Ruzbihan follows a method of symbolic exegesis whereby the enigmatic sayings of the Qur'an, *hadith*, and *shath* are seen as revelations of the divine Attributes and Names, while the actions of the Prophet Muhammad serve as a perfect mirror for those Attributes. For the common people, it is necessary to accept the divine origin of these sayings without asking why. Only for the elect is it permissible to delve into interpretation, for they possess knowledge (`ilm`), a knowledge that by its very nature is esoteric.

> If God gives assistance to an insightful person, so that his insight hits the mark, he restrains his tongue from denial and does not inquire into the allusions of *shath*. He has faith in their (the saints') truthfulness in symbolic speech. He escapes from the calamity of denial, because their *shath* is symbolism (*mutashabih*) like the symbolism of the Qur'an and *hadith*. Know that the principle of the unvarying *shath* (i.e., the Qur'an) is in the Attributes; it is the symbolism of the Attributes. In the word of the Messenger (i.e., *hadith*), displaying the secrets of the revelations of the Attributes occurs through the form of actions . . . When the ocean of eternity rolled back from the shore of non-existence, it displayed the pearls of the Attributes and Qualities and Names in an unknown guise. From the pleasure of passionate love, the loquacity of his lover's soul became agitated by the overwhelming fragrances of love. From the ocean of symbolism, he cast forth the *shathiyat* of love.
>
> Both divine and prophetic symbolism come as a testing for the faithful of the community, so that they confess to the outward aspect and do not examine the inward aspect, so that they do not fall into anthropomorphism, imagination, or agnosticism regarding the Attributes, by a denial of symbolic meanings. It is not right for the common people to discuss the investigation of symbolic meanings of exegesis (*ta'wil*). They recite the verse, "They will say, 'Our God, we had faith'" (Qur. 23.109). In the same way, they have no share in the symbolism of *hadith* except faith. The saints, (on the other hand, are referred to in the verse) "and none knows the exegesis of it save God and those rooted in knowledge" (Qur. 3.7). For others there is faith, but for them there is gnosis in the problems of symbolism.[32]

As Ruzbihan reveals, the esoteric principle of knowledge looks to this Qur'anic verse 3.7 for its support. The usual reading of this text is quite different; a period is generally placed after "God," so that the full verse reads: "And those with error in their hearts follow the symbolic part, desiring dissension and desiring its exegesis, but none knows the exegesis of it save God. And those who are firmly rooted in knowledge say, 'We have faith in it . . .'" Ruzbihan's reading was, however, supported by one of the earliest Qur'an scholars, Mujahid (d. 104/722).[33] This verse was in fact widely used to support the esoteric principle of knowledge. The Andalusian philosopher Ibn Rushd (Averroes) maintained that the common people must necessarily read this verse with the period in the middle, so that for them, only God knows the interpretation; the elect must read this verse without the period, since their knowledge is demonstrably in accord with the truth.[34] In the same way Ruzbihan insists that the saints have a gnosis that entitles them to interpret the symbolic sayings in Qur'an, *hadith*, and *shath*.

In summarizing his theory of *shath*, Ruzbihan introduces the key terms in his vocabulary of mystical union. Essential union (`*ayn al-jam*`), a classical term used by Junayd, is now presented in company with "the clothing of the human with the divine (*iltibas*)."

The principles of symbolism in *shath* are from three sources: the source of the Qur'an, the source of *hadith*, and the source of the inspiration of the saints. But that which comes in the Qur'an is the mention of the Attributes and the isolated letters, and that which is in *hadith* is the vision of the clothing of the human with the divine (*iltibas*). That which is in the inspiration of the saints is the Qualities of God in the form of the clothing of the human with the divine. This takes place in the station of passionate love and the reality of unification, in gnosis and unknowings (*nakirat*), in divine ruses (*makariyat*). The proclamation of the Attribute belongs to those who are "rooted in knowledge" (Qur. 3.7), for their station is the contemplation of eternity. The deserts on which their paths lie are too hot for conventional wayfarers, who have no aptitude for the comprehension of the enigmas of the symbolism of the Attributes. God's *shath* is that symbolism which proclaims essential union (Pers. `*ayn-i jam*`) and the clothing of the human with the divine Attributes in the station of passionate love; in that station is the knowledge (`*ilm*`) which was God's qualification in pre-eternity. With that (*shath*) He discourses to the famous among His lovers . . .[35]

This passage reveals the breath-taking scope that *shath* has assumed in the mysticism of Ruzbihan. With an authority that follows directly upon that of God and the Prophet, the saints' status and utterances must be accepted by the faith of the generality of believers. This, in effect, makes of the *shathiyat* of the saints a supplementary canon, formed by the uninterrupted contact that God maintains with the elect. The clothing of humanity with divinity, first enacted on the primordial Adam, is manifest in the form of Muhammad, and is created anew, by God's grace, in the saints. Love and unification are equated with "gnosis and unknowings . . . (and) divine ruses," an intriguing combination that is discussed below. After invoking once again the Qur'anic sanction for esoteric knowledge, Ruzbihan effortlessly unites the concepts of essential union, clothing with divinity, and the primordial "knowledge" that was God's in pre-eternity. All these together are nothing but the *shath* of God, by which He converses with His lovers. Ruzbihan's theoretical discussion of the nature of the *shath* does not necessarily solve any problems. Rather, it evokes profound mysteries, which, by their very nature, are resistant to analysis. He does, nonetheless, provide intimations and allusions (*isharat*) that point to the goal of this difficult path.

2. LATER DEVELOPMENTS

In later Sufism, there is nothing to compare with Ruzbihan's treatment of *shathiyat*, either in scope or profundity. Still, it may be of interest to give some details on authors who make some reference to the topic in later times.

There is an anonymous manuscript in the British Museum, dated to the eighth/fourteenth century and deriving from North Africa, with the simple title *Aqwal al-A'immah al-Sufiyah* ("Sayings of the Sufi Leaders"). This bulky and badly copied treatist quotes from many of the early Sufi masters, and contains a section on "the ecstatic expressions of the folk (*shathiyat al-qawm*)," occupying some five pages and containing fourteen sayings, some not known from other sources. Of interest is Ibn al-Khafif's definition of *shath*: "It is that which overflows from ecstasy and seems strange in speech." This work quotes the *Kitab al-Luma`* several times, and gives sayings from Husri, Junayd, Hallaj, Wasiti, and Shibli. The author has put together in several places the response of one Sufi to the saying of another, usually in the form of a criticism or an attempt to outdo the other saint. Of special interest regarding Hallaj is a previously unknown fragment, "(The) witness sees Him in the essence of His spiritual realities, and he does not see anything that is dependent on His qualities besides Him." One of Hallaj's poems is given in a longer version than previously known, and in the biographical section a completely new poem by Hallaj can be found, on the meaning of union and separation. One of the sayings quoted is, interestingly, a *hadith* of the Prophet, in which Muhammad boasts of his superiority to Moses. This treatise sheds no new light on the nature of *shath*, but it is valuable for the several pieces it adds to the corpus of *shathiyat*.[36]

Around the end of the sixth/twelfth century the word *shath* occurred in an interesting non-Sufi context, in an Isma`ili text from the Assassin fortress of Masyad in Syria. This text contains a juxtaposition of *shath* with the esoteric interpretation (*ta'wil*) brought by one of the supreme charismatic leaders in the Isma`ili hierarchy, who was known by the title "the Foundation (*al-asas*)." In a description of the divine inspiration (*ta'yid*) that springs forth from the Foundation's esoteric interpretation, it is said, "The knowledge of inspiration (`ilm al-ta'yid*) flowed forth (*shataha*) from it." This is an exegesis of Qur. 9.40, the flood of Noah, and here *shataha* is the esoteric synonym for *fara*, "gushed."[37] Since this "knowledge of inspiration" is, in Isma`ili doctrine, only vouchsafed to the highest representative of God to mankind, the imam or his surrogate, the use of the verb *shataha* here indicates the overflow of the most sublime spiritual knowledge. As we may infer from Marshall

G. S. Hodgson's analysis, this is an instance in which the Isma'ilis used terms derived from Sufism as part of a tendency toward mystical interpretation of apocalyptic symbolism.[38] This does not add greatly to our knowledge of *shath*, but it does show that even to non-Sufis the term had associations with esoteric interpretation and mystical knowledge.

The tradition of *shathiyat* became somewhat fossilized in Sufism after Ruzbihan. The theosophical teaching of Ibn 'Arabi (d. 638/1240) stood on the foundation of early Sufism, but advanced towards a vast system of complex ideas expressive of universal theophany throughout all degrees of existence. Ibn 'Arabi and his disciples, who were known as the school of "the unity of existence (*wahdat al-wujud*)," knew the term *shath*, but it did not figure prominently in their doctrine. Ibn 'Arabi seems to have considered *shath* as a vain self-indulgence, the product of uncontrolled and subjective ecstasy.[39] By now, however, Sufis were expected to produce such expressions as a matter of course. The historian al-Dhahabi noted that Ibn 'Arabi did not employ *shath* in his writings, but still he supposed that Ibn 'Arabi must have done so privately in states of intoxication.[40] As the school of Ibn 'Arabi became dominant in Sufi thought, *shathiyat* tended to become bland and trite expressions, concocted at leisure, which summarized the theories of the *wujudi* school. Thus *shath* tended to fall into a literary and theoretical pattern.

Nevertheless, we do find echoes of the classical view of ecstatic expressions in the Islamic east, particularly in India. Sharaf al-Din ibn Yahya Maneri (d. 782/1381) was an eminent Sufi in Bihar, who wrote numerous letters and whose discourses were collected in many volumes. In one of his conversations, he described *shath* as "expansiveness in speech with utter disregard (of the consequences)," and he followed Ghazali in distinguishing two kinds, the mystical claim and the unintelligible utterance. In spite of his theoretical disapproval of uttering *shath*, Maneri admitted, "We have said such things," and he clearly had great sympathy for Hallaj.[41] A slightly later Indian Sufi, Sayyid Nur Qutb-i 'Alam of Pandua in Bengal (d. 817-8/1415), referred to Ruzbihan's *Sharh-i Shathiyat* by name, although he did not discuss the contents in any detail.[42] Nur Qutb-i 'Alam probably learned of Ruzbihan's work from his fellow-Sufi in Bengal, Ashraf Jahangir Simnani (d. 829/1425), an emigre from central Asia. Simnani thought very highly of Ruzbihan, whose theory of love he discussed in one of this letters, and he also wrote a Qur'an commentary along the lines of Ruzbihan's great compendium *Ara'is al-Bayan*.[43] On the subject of *shathiyat*, Simnani has a general discussion in his collected discourses, but his is a fairly modest presentation, which cautiously deems it better not to interpret or approve these sayings before the common people. Simnani does mention, however, a seance held in Gujarat, during which he and another Sufi burst into *shathiyat*.[44]

Another writer on *shathiyat* from this period was Adhari of Isfarayin (d. 836/1432-3). A poet in the service of the Timuri princes, he travelled widely and spent some years in India at the court of Ahmad Bahman Shah in Gulbarga. While there, at the request of his friends he wrote *Jawahir al-Asrar*, a literary treatise on the symbolic expressions employed in Persian poetry and prose. In this work he commented on a number of *shathiyat*, with a perspective (derived from his master Shah Ni'mat Allah Wali) that stressed the views of Ibn 'Arabi, as modified by 'Ala' al-Dawlah Simnani. Concerning *shath* he says, "Many things like this are in the Qur'an and *hadith*, but at that level they are not called *shath* but the confession of God's unity (*tawhid*)."[45] Nonetheless, Adhari interprets each saying as a metaphysical epigram, yet at the same time regards them all as the products of uncontrolled intoxication. Though his method of interpretation is somewhat haphazard, his collection is an interesting one. The most unusual feature of Adhari's work is the inclusion of a saying from the fourth caliph, 'Ali: "I am the time of times, I am the cause of causes, I am the face of God toward which you turn, I am the side of God on which you rely (?). I come from God into a place, but when I am pious, then I am He."[46] This remarkable saying, derived from the chief authority of Shi'ism, is an illustration of the convergence of the *hadith* of the Shi'i imams and the *shathiyat* of the Sufis.

A clear continuation of Ruzbihan's work is found in the work of Mughul crown prince and Sufi, Dara Shikuh (d. 1069/1659). Son of Shahjahan and Mumtaz Mahal, Dara was a gifted scholar who preferred mysticism to politics. He became attracted to two masters of the Qadiri order in Lahore, Mian Mir and his successor Mulla Shah. Dara wrote biographical works on Sufism as well as theoretical treatises and poetry, and he is known for his work on the Persian translation of the Upanishads. When Dara read Ruzbihan's *Sharh-i Shathiyat*, he found it to be a precious mine of the sayings of the early Sufis, but the commentary, he felt, was difficult and "fatiguing."[47] Therefore he decided to produce an abridgement that would give the sayings, with only the briefest comments, and at the same time bring the collection up to date by quoting the ecstatic utterances of the Sufis who had lived after Ruzbihan. Dara Shikuh's work, begun in 1062/1650 under the title *Hasanat al-'Arifin* ("Fine Words of the Gnostics"), is in a sense a popularization. He only retained the barest sense of the theory of *shath*, which he interpreted as a simplified form of Ibn 'Arabi's philosophy. Still, his goal was similar, in that he wanted to refute the attacks that ignorant jurists have made on Sufis (Dara, we may note, was anything but a lover of traditionalism; he defined paradise as the place where there are no *mullas*). Dara included in his own work nearly fifty of the *shathiyat* from Ruzbihan's collection, in one instance with a reading that corrects a corruption in our text of Ruzbihan.[48] Dara drew on various sources to augment the anthology, mainly the *Nafahat al-Uns* of ʿAbd al-Rahman Jami (d. 898/1492), who was also an admirer of Ruzbihan. Dara also used Ruzbihan's Qur'an commentary, of which he had commissioned a Persian translation. The last third of the book concerns Sufis known personally to Dara, and well-known Indian religious figures, such as Kabir and the pandit Baba Lal Das. These contemporary notices are very detailed biographical sketches, and they contain interesting material on some otherwise unknown figures. No longer is Hallaj the central figure, as for Ruzbihan; now Dara's masters, Mian Mir and Mulla Shah, are the most important speakers of *shathiyat*. As far as the understanding of *shath* is concerned, though, this is a somewhat disappointing production. Dara's general assumption is that all famous Sufis must have uttered at lest one good saying that can be called a *shath*, and that all such sayings tend to express the oneness of existence, according to the view of Ibn ʿArabi. It is interesting to note that, when Dara's friends asked him why he had uttered no *shath*, he replied, "My *shath* is that all of the *shathiyat* are mine."[49] Since the number of Sufis quoted in the book amounts to ninety-nine, it is tempting to speculate that Dara is likening his *shath* to the unknown one-hundredth "Greatest Name" of God, which unifies the ninety-nine known Names.

These are the literary legacies of *shath*. The term continued to be used, but in a somewhat artifical literary ways. In 1086/1675, the Meccan shaykh Ibrahim al-Kawrani (d. 1101/1688-9) gave a formal defense of a *shath* uttered by one of his Javanese disciples, Hamzah al-Fansuri: "God Most High is our self and our existence, and we are His self and His existence." This saying, far from being ecstatic, is a simple formulation of Ibn ʿArabi's theory of oneness of existence. ʿAbd al-Ghani al-Nabulusi (d. 1140-1/1728) wrote another defense of this saying in 1139/1727, and it is again an exposition of the theory of Ibn ʿArabi.[50] In 1151/1738, an otherwise obscure Indian Sufi named ʿAziz Allah of Bijapur compiled the *Durr-i Maknun*, a collection of *shathiyat* combined with moral and religious advice, and arranged by topic. As with Dara's collection, its chief interest lies in the *shathiyat* uttered by later Indian Sufis. Though it offers no new critical perspective, it deserves a more extended treatment than we can give here.[51] We even see the word *shath* being used to describe an "ascension" poem written by a thirteenth/nineteenth century Sudanese Sufi, which is recited annually at the celebration of the birth of the Prophet.[52] Such self-conscious literary and theoretical productions seem far removed from the early ecstatic utterances.

B.

Topics and Forms
of Expression

Ecstatic expressions, we are told, are sayings that derive from ecstasy. The Sufi interpreters maintain that the sayings in some way describe the original ecstasy, although this description can only be comprehended by one who knows the state from actual experience. Those who are not graced with the knowledge (*'ilm*) that God grants to the elect must seek out the interpretation of a qualified master. Since I do not, for the purposes of this study, claim any sort of esoteric knowledge, I therefore approach the study of *shathiyat* through the authoritative works of Ruzbihan and Sarraj. Their general definitions and approaches have been given, and now it will be appropriate to consider the principal topics of *shathiyat*. First, and most important, is the nature of selfhood, divine and human. Second is transcendence of the created, expressed as "the isolation of the eternal from the temporal," which is the way to unification. Third is the paradoxical stress on "unknowing" as the only way to reach real knowledge. Following the discussion of these topics is a consideration of the unusual and provocative forms of expression in *shathiyat*, variously interpreted as divine madness, perception of the divine presence in nature, and saintly boasting. The final section deals with the nature of *shath* as a testimony to the reality and presence of God.

1. SELFHOOD

Probably the most important topic of early *shathiyat* was, as Ruzbihan pointed out, the question of selfhood, or in his terminology,

"I-ness (ana'iyat)." Over one third of the nearly two hundred shathiyat in Ruzbihan's collection are spoken in the first person, making some statement about the nature and experience of the self. Bayazid and Hallaj are most prominent in speaking on this subject. In a particularly condensed saying, Bayazid said, "My 'I am' is not 'I am,' because I am He, and I am 'he is He.'"[53] Sahlaji gives a fuller version of the same saying, which may be paraphrased as follows: "My 'I' is not the human 'I,' it is the divine 'I.' Since my 'I' is He, I am 'he is He.'"[54] This saying reports on an experience of deification that the Sufis codified under the phrase, "he is He (huwa huwa)." This phrase stands for the doctrine of God's gift of divine qualities to the primordial man in the pre-creational state.[55] Bayazid is not asserting that his ordinary ego is God; he says that the only real identity is God, and that God is the only one who has the right to say "I am." Just as with Ja'far al-Sadiq's exegesis of the Sinai theophany, the ego-consciousness of the human disappears under the impact of the divine "I am I, your Lord." Bayazid's "I" has been replaced with the divine "I," and therefore he says, "I am He; I am 'he is He.'" In another saying, Bayazid indicates that his first presentiments of this union came through the abandonment of a spiritual practice that he had followed for years: "For thirty years I was hidden from God. My absence from Him was my recollection (dhikr) of Him. When I refrained (from dhikr), I saw Him in every state, to such a degree that it was as if I were He."[56] In this case Bayazid alludes to a state of quasi-identification with God, after his abandonment of the recollection of the name of God, a practice which for him must still have had ego-connections. In both these instances one may point to the elimination of the ego as the prerequisite for experiencing the divine self.

If the boundaries of the human ego are breached, then it is understandable that there should be fluctuation in the perception of the "I." Is one's identity lost forever, or is it replaced by the divine? The same issue occurs in the story of the man who came looking for Bayazid and knocked on his door. Bayazid said, "Who do you want?" The man answered, "I am looking for Bayazid." Bayazid replied, "For thirty years Bayazid has been looking for Bayazid and has not seen him, so how will you see him?"[57] In another saying, made perhaps after his thirty years of incredible austerities, Bayazid addressed God thus: "You were a mirror for me, and then I became the mirror."[58] This metaphor is one of the fundamental symbols in mystical literature throughout the world; the mirror held up to the divine reality denotes the purified conscience that reflects the form of the real self without obscurity or distortion.

As to how this "mirror" appears to the rest of creation, we can see from this famous saying: "He took me up and set me before Him. He said, 'Bayazid! My creatures desire to see You.' I said, 'Array me in Your oneness and clothe me with Your selfhood, and bring me to Your unity, so that when Your creatures see me, they will see You. There it will be You, and I will not be there.'"[59] Later mystics will call this the clothing with divine selfhood (*iltibas*). Bayazid has also presented transformation of identity in the opposite image of a snake shedding its skin: "I shed my self (*nafsi*) as a snake sheds its skin, then I looked at myself, and behold! I was He (*ana huwa*)."[60] A remarkable variety of images conveys the sense of radical transformation of selfhood.

Hallaj has also given many subtle comments on identity in his *shathiyat*. In one place he said, "I wonder at You and me. You annihilated me out of myself into You. You made me near to Yourself, so that I thought that I was You and You were me."[61] The complete poem from which Ruzbihan translated these lines conveys Hallaj's intense awareness of God's presence in all of his thoughts and moods. Hallaj seems to refer here to an imagined union, and Ruzbihan explains it as the fancy (*wahm*) born of human weakness as it contemplates the All, and he adds, "The intoxicated speak in this way frequently, even though they know that the Essence of divinity is unattainable by the created."[62] If there was still any ego left in him, he was not sufficiently purified of self, and must undergo complete self-negation. In a bolder metaphor, Hallaj said, "My spirit mixes with your spirit, in nearness and in distance, so that I am You, just as You are I."[63] This is actually a truncated version of a poem in the *Diwan*, which is even more remarkable in its imagery: "Your spirit was mixed in my spirit, just like wine and clear water, and if something touches You, it touches me, for You are I in every state."[64] In another poem transmitted by Ruzbihan, Hallaj put it thus: "Praise be to Him whose humanity manifested the secret of the splendor of His radiant divinity, and who then appeared openly to His people, in the form of one who eats and drinks!"[65] These verses have been criticized, not only by the Hanbali jurist Ibn Taymiyah but also by Hallaj's friend Ibn al-Khafif, because they seemed to imply a semi-Christian doctrine of incarnatin (*hulul*).[66] Ruzbihan explains, however, that Ibn Khafif either did not realize that these verses were by Hallaj (whom he revered as "a divine master"), or he was thinking of the effect of this verse on the externalists, whose inner conviction is weak. The Sufis understand this verse as an allusion to the station of clothing with the divine (*iltibas*), and they hold that this poem describes the primordial man, the eternal *logos* of Muhammad, as the manifestation of divine qualities.[67]

Another controversial *shath* of Hallaj was a letter by him, produced at one of his trials, which began, "From the Compassionate, the Merciful, to so-and-so . . ." When he was charged with claiming divinity for himself, he replied, "No! But this is essential union (Pers. `ayn-i jam`). None understands this but the Sufis."[68] In this case Hallaj used the term "essential union" to identify the spiritual state that was the source of this letter. In another poem, Hallaj said,

Is it You or I? That would be two gods in me;
   far, far be it from You to assert duality!
The "He-ness" that is Yours is in my nothingness

forever;
my "all" added to Your "All" would be a
    double disguise.
But where is Your Essence, from my vantage point
    when I see You,
since my essence has become plain in the
    place where I am not?
And where is Your face? It is the object of
    my gaze,
whether in my inmost heart or in the glance
    of my eye.
Between You and me there is an "I am" that
    battles me,
so take away, by Your grace, this "I am"
    from in between.[69]

Here Hallaj expressed the passionate desire to be ravished out of his selfhood, and made empty, to become a fit dwelling for the pure spirit that will speak through him.

Other Sufis have further touched upon the subject of selfhood, although rarely with the piquancy of the sayings of Bayazid and Hallaj. Junayd said,

> I was in three states. I was in one state in which, if everything in heaven and earth wept for me on account of my bewilderment, it would be no wonder. I was in another state in which, if I wept for everything in heaven and earth on account of their hiddenness from God and their striving with Him, it would be no wonder. I was in another state in which I saw nothing but the quality of eternity and might and will and dominion and decree. I contemplated primordiality and finality. Then I became hidden from the all, and annihilated from the all, and I became subsistent in the all.[70]

Junayd has summarized his experience in another saying, "When the devotee is annihilated in terms of his own attributes, he finds perfect subsistence."[71] Junayd was reluctant to speak openly of deification, but his formulation of "annihilation (*fana'*)" and "subsistence (*baqa'*)" points in this direction.

2. TRANSCENDENCE OF THE CREATED—"UNIFICATION IS THE ISOLATION OF THE ETERNAL FROM THE TEMPORAL"

Probably the most typical feature of Islamic mysticism is the assertion of the divine unity. The term *tawhid*, "making one," "unification," or "affirming the oneness (of God)," is the central concept of Islamic theology as well. In Sufism, *tawhid* denotes equally the affirmation in speech of God's unity, and the existential realization of that unity. The classic formulation of *tawhid* is Junayd's: "Unification is the isolation of the eternal from the temporal."[72] This is a way of negation. Perfect unity in isolation can be expressed only by rejecting all concepts tied to the world of multiplicity. Its existential implication, for the way to approach the divine unity, is a radical purification from all worldliness. Junayd's formulation of *tawhid* is the way of transcendence, and it expresses the underlying basis of many *shathiyat* that emerge from the longing for union. Junayd's contemporary Abu Muhammad al-Ruwaym (d. 303/915) gave a definition of *tawhid* that subtly presents the dialectic of annihilation and subsistence: "*Tawhid* is the effacement of the characteristics of humanity and the stripping bare of divinity."[73] According to Sarraj, the first part of this statement, "effacement of the characteristics of humanity," means "the transformation of the character of the soul, because it pretends to lordship by regarding its own actions, as when the creature says 'I'; but none says 'I' save God, for selfhood (*aniyah*) belongs to God." The second part of the definition, "the stripping bare of divinity," Sarraj glosses as "the isolation of the eternal apart from temporalities," which is Junayd's definition.[74] Transcendent unity existentially merges with divine selfhood, though we may keep them conceptually distinct.

Transcendence of the created is an unceasing movement of the soul, going beyond every aspect of creation. When Hallaj was asked to define Sufism, he said, "When you become obliterated, you arrive at a place in which nothing is obliterated or confirmed. . . It is the divine erasings and effacements. . . . It is inexpressible."[75] In a more theological vein, Hallaj said, "Insofar as the Names of God are comprehended, they are (mere) names. But insofar as they are True (or: insofar as they are God, *haqq*), they are reality."[76] Here he is stressing that the divine reality is beyond the created form of the Names as we understand them. One must go beyond the names of all created things. When Bayazid was asked, "What is the Greatest Name?" he replied, "Make your heart free from everything that is less than God. Then utter whatever name you want, and in a moment you will fly from the east to the west. . ."[77]

Other sayings concern the transcendence of space and time. Abu Bakr al-Shibli (d. 334/945) said, "O people! I go to a place beyond which there is no beyond. I go to the south and the north, to a place beyond which there is no beyond. Everything that I saw after that I could see in one hair of my little finger."[78] In a satirical mood Abu al-Hasan al-Husri (d. 371/981) once asked, "Where are the lovers who claim, 'We are the lovers of God' whose name is mighty? Tell me, when did you see Him? And in what place did you see Him? And in what assembly did you see Him, that you might become friendly with Him?"[79] Regarding the transcendence of time, Shibli also said, "Pass beyond a thousand years of the past and a thousand years of the future. Behold them! It is the present — and do not be deceived by phantasms!"[80]

Other sayings suggest the transcendence of the human nature inherited from Adam. Husri said, "Come with me and pass beyond me and my affliction; you are not of the children of Adam, whom He created with His hand, and in whom He breathed His spirit, and before whom He brought the angels to bow down. He commanded him one thing, and he disobeyed that command. When the first of the bottle is dregs, what will the last be like?"[81] According to Ruzbihan, Husri was urging his disciples to overcome their human nature by reaching the primordial state of perfection prior to their creation. For Junayd, too, the doctrine of *tawhid* implied a return to the pre-creational state.[82]

In the religious sphere, *shathiyat* point to a rejection of absorption in the outward forms of ritual. Abu al-Hasan al-Muzayyin (d. 328/939) said, "God has occupied with His service and obedience all those who turn away from the contemplation of God."[83] This does not imply that one should abandon the customary religious practices, but that one should pray as if one sees God directly; mechanical prayer is inferior to contemplation. In one of Bayazid's surprising anecdotes, he said, "I performed seven circumambulations around the Ka'bah. Then I said, 'God! You removed every veil that was between You and me.' Then a voice came from above the Ka'bah, saying, 'Bayazid! There is no veil between lovers.'"[84] Bayazid had feared that the ritual would become a veil between him and God, but God assured him that this was not the case. In another version, we read, "I was circumambulating the House (the Ka'bah) seeking Him; but when I was united with Him, I saw the House circumambulating me."[85] Again, Husri pointed out the limited nature of religious rites in themselves, in his saying, "We want to be in prayer without prayer, in fasting without fasting. Obedience is a custom that reality obliterates."[86] These sayings point in the direction of the Hallajian doctrine of "the eclipse of intermediaries (*isqat al-wasa'it*)," according to which ritual practices are of secondary importance to those who have attained the goal of those practices. This relativism was suspicious in the eyes of jurists, who saw in it a threat to the religious tradition. From the viewpoint of *shath*, however, all such actions have a created character, which must be transcended along with everything else. Husri's saying does not imply abandonment of prayer and fasting, but a search for the reality toward which ritual is directed.

The Sufis were quite definite about pointing out the relativity of the various stages of the inner spiritual path, which must be clearly separated from the ultimate goal of that path. One of the most famous examples of this is Bayazid's account of a visionary experience that in the end he rejected utterly.

I entered into His oneness and became a bird, whose body was of unity and whose wings were of everlastingness. Then I kept flying in the atmosphere of quality for ten years, so that I was in an atmosphere like that a hundred million times. I kept on flying until I entered the plain of primordial eternity, and in it I saw the tree of unity. Then (says Sarraj) he described its earth and its root and its branches and its limbs and its fruits, and then he said: Then I looked, and I knew that all this was a cheat.[87]

Junayd's comment on this abridged version is that it does not reveal the highest sort of experience, and while it is on the true path to the reality of the knowledge of unity, all is not what it seems. The visions of bodies, trees, and so forth, mean that in this case Bayazid was looking on things other than God.[88] Ruzbihan, on the other hand, regards this account as indicative of a process of spiritual realization, culminating in an experience of absolute annihilation. In Ruzbihan's version, Bayazid ate of the fruit of this heavenly tree, which Ruzbihan at one point equates with the burning bush of Mt. Sinai. This fruit conferred on Bayazid the subsistence that follows annihilation, and clothed him with the garment of the true knowledge that confounded him in unknowing. Ruzbihan placed considerable importance on this *shath*, even quoting it in his commentary on the heavenly tree in Qur. 14.24-5. In his explanation of Bayazid's vision, Ruzbihan includes a sort of personal re-enactment of it, in the first person. This is another example of Ruzbihan's technique of attempting to regain the original experience behind each ecstatic saying.[89] According to both Junayd and Ruzbihan, Bayazid's narrative should be interpreted as the realization of the relativity of certain astonishing visionary experiences.

Some Sufis showed a disdain for any seemingly special experiences. Bundar ibn Husayn (d. 353/964) said, "Although each of you may want a lofty abode, I want the station of worship (`ubudiyat*) to be active in me."[90] He pursues devotion rather than spiritual states. There are also numerous sayings that criticize the individual states (*ahwal*) of the path, since these are not goals in themselves, but merely way-stations. Husri, alluding to the state of fear (*khawf*), said, "Fear of God is a defect."[91] In the same way Wasiti said, "There are four stations that are not conducive to knowledge: asceticism (*zuhd*), reliance on God (*tawakkul*), satisfaction (*rida'*), and submission (*taslim*)."[92] Yusuf ibn Husayn al-Razi (d. 303/916) has vividly expressed a similar notion: "If honesty and sincerity were two slaves, I would sell them, and if fear and hope knocked on the door of my soul, I would not open the door for them."[93] The point is that all states and stages on the path are relative, and necessarily pertain to the realm of the created; the goal of the true seeker must always be to transcend these stages.

The speakers of *shathiyat* not only critize the traditional stages of the Sufi path, but also make disparaging statements about the special practices that had become current in Sufi circles at this time. In reference to the practice of listening to music (*sama`*) for the purpose of inducing ecstasy, Abu Bakr al-Kattani (d. 322/934) said, "For those acquainted with reality, audition (*sama`*) is through revelation and vision."[94] In other words, engaging in a performance of *sama`* is only involvement with the created unless sublimated by mystical experience. Sahl al-Tustari (d. 238/896) made a similar remark about the practice of recollection of God (*dhikr*) through invocation of the divine Names: "Recollection by the tongue is nonsense, and recollection by the heart is prompting of the devil (*waswasah*)."[95] Here again, the practice as an act in itself is condemned. Ruzbihan observes that this applies to the heedless reflection of a creature, whose vocal recollection is a faint temporal imitation of God's pre-eternal self-recollection ("pre-eternal" translates *azali*, "eternal without beginning"). As for the silent recollection, in the case of one who is absent from God, this is similar to mentioning other people behind their backs![96] Anticipating many critiques of pseudo-Sufism by eminent later Sufis, Abu al-Khayr al-Tinati (d. 343/954) remarked, "I looked into hell, and I saw that most of the inhabitants of hell wore patched frocks and carried water-bags."[97] Those who wear only the outward regalia of Sufism are thus condemned as the worst of hypocrites. Finally, Shibli in one of his most memorable sayings indicated how the very striving for transcendence, to the extent that it is the effort of a limited creature, necessarily creates a false duality: "Sufism is idolatry, since it is the safeguarding of the heart from seeing any other (than God), and there is no other."[98] The quest for the transcendent unity is uncompromising, for that unity is inviolable.

3. KNOWLEDGE AND UNKNOWING

There are a number of sayings in Ruzbihan's collection that describe with considerable subtlety the nature of knowledge, its limitations, and how to overcome them. The fundamental saying on this subject from the viewpoint of *shath* is attributed to the companion of the Prophet, Abu Bakr al-Siddiq, in these words: "Inability to attain comprehension is (true) comprehension."[99] It is difficult to tell when this saying may first have come into circulation. A version of this saying is credited to Sahl al-Tustari, who said, "Glory be to Him, of Whose gnosis men have attained naught but (the knowledge) that they are incapable of knowing Him." Hallaj referred to this saying in his critical review of all theories of knowledge, the *Bustan al-Ma`rifah* ("Garden of Gnosis").[100] Prior to Ruzbihan, the saying has been quoted in one form or another by Hujwiri

(d. ca. 465/1072) and `Ayn al-Qudat (d. 525/1131).[101] Sufis have consistently interpreted this saying as a *via negativa* comparable to the Christian version of the negative path, as formulated in the *Mystical Theology* of Dionysius, the *De Docta Ignorantia* of Cusanus, and the anonymous *Cloud of Unknowing*. It is a mystical interpretation of the Socratic paradox, that the wisest man is he who knows that he knows nothing.[102]

The negative path is strange and difficult, and it may be worthwhile to review the basic character of this *via negativa* teaching here before proceeding further. Dionysius' *Mystical Theology* begins with a description of the divine dark into which Moses had to enter in order to meet God. In this interpretation of the Sinai theophany, all human knowledge consists of inadequate symbolizations of the incomprehensible God. As the purified Moses approaches the place where God dwells, the divine presence

> plunges the mystic into the Darkness of Unknowing, whence all perfection of understanding is excluded, and he is enwrapped in that which is altogether intangible and noumenal, being wholly absorbed in Him who is beyond all, and in none else (whether himself or another); and through the inactivity of all his reasoning powers is united by his highest faculty to Him who is wholly unknowable; thus by knowing nothing he knows That which is beyond his knowledge.[103]

All human knowledge, in comparison with that of God, is seen as ignorance. It is only by unknowing, the systematic transcendence of all limited knowledge, that one can approach the unknowable divine being. The divine dark, a blindness caused by excess of light, is the paradoxical formulation of the contemplation of transcendence. Unknowing became a central concept in Christian mysticism after Dionysius, and it also formed a part of the Sufi outlook, not because of any direct historical influence, but because it is the answer to a riddle posed in both traditions.

It is instructive to examine Ruzbihan's commentary on this saying:

> The depth of the inaccessibility of the eternal exists from the point of view of the comprehension of the temporal, and the impotence (`ajz) of the temporal, in relation to the eternal. Otherwise, how would the essence of knowledge come about from impotence in knowledge? . . . But the realization of this particular *shath* lies in the fact that he (Abu Bakr) makes impotence in knowledge the cause of knowledge. Indeed, when the seeker of the goal becomes annihilated in his seeking through the quality of impotence, he becomes one who comprehends himself. Then subsistence (*baqa'*) brings him into the Essence (`ayn), so that subsistence may be subsistent. He sees himself, and gives of himself to Him. When the knower takes on the qualities of the Known, he recognizes the Known by the Known. One would say that he has attained reality, so much happiness does he see through knowledge and travelling in subsistence. Otherwise it

would be a delusion (*makr*) that the temporal has reached the eternal, for the temporal with the eternal is impossible. Do you not see how when the cavaliers of "I cannot count Thy praise" came on the foot (*qadam*) of eternity (*qidam*), they said, "Know thyself!"[104]

The subtleties of this passage are striking, and the fluidity of Ruzbihan's style is at once the delight and the despair of the translator. A few points, however, seem to emerge. First of all, Ruzbihan states that there is a vast chasm separating the temporal from the eternal, which is demonstrated by the fact that the created and time-bound knower can discern no end to the depth of eternity. The existence of a duality is also evident in the difference between real knowledge and the present lack of that knowledge. If this gap did not exist, no one would experience the movement from ignorance to knowledge. Yet real knowledge does occur, on every level from the sensible to the mystical. The secret of mystical knowledge is that it can only be attained when one in the condition of creaturely ignorance realizes fully the nothingness of his condition. This somehow clears the stage for the manifestation of the real. The manifestation of reality makes it appear that a creature has attained to knowledge of the divine, though this is, literally speaking, impossible. The creature has been annihilated, and the reality has remained; the knower has received the qualities of the Known, in a way that transforms the very nature of knowledge. After this remarkable exhibition of the dynamics of annihilation and subsistence, Ruzbihan seals his account with a characteristically poetic outburst, culminating in the famous *hadith* of the prophet, "I cannot count the praise that is Yours; You are just as you praised Yourself!"[105] The Prophet's confession of unknowing illustrates the state of one who has emptied himself completely before God, in order to behold the infinite. And Ruzbihan explicitly assimilates the prophetic confession to the Socratic "know thyself."

When unknowing becomes the prerequisite for the attainment of real knowledge, it follows that any limited form of worldly knowledge must be rejected. Perception is dualistic by its very nature, and the self-consciousness of the ego is wily enough to pervert any seemingly straightforward recognition, unless one is sufficiently purified. Wasiti said, "Thoughts about one's intention are a denial of the beloved; how can one have regard for his own intention, when he has attained the intended spiritual realities?"[106] Commenting on the dualistic nature of perception and thought, Shibli also said, "Gazing is infidelity, thought is idolatry, and allusion is delusion."[107] Ja`far al-Hadhdha' (d. 309/922) remarked, on the subject of contemplation, "If you look (`ayan kuni), you are a heretic. If you become a witness, you become astonished, but it is astonishment within astonishment, and desert upon desert."[108] Here he is distinguishing between the theory that God may be seen with outward vision (*mu`ayanah*), which is equivalent to heresy, and the experience of witnessing God (*mushahadah*) in the heart. The inner witnessing of God brings one to the realization of one's own nothingness. This realization finds expression in the characteristic image of the desert, symbolic of the emptiness of unknowing.

Unknowing is a strange subject that leads to strange explanations. Wasiti boasted, "I sought God in clarity, but found Him in obscurity."[109] Abu Yahya al-Shirazi described the relation of knowledge to wonderment (*hayrat*) in these terms:

> Wonderment has a beginning, and an end. Between the two wonderments knowledge is revealed. When men reach learning and tradition and authority, however, they do not pass into reality, because of their understanding and the proofs of their sciences. Beyond that (knowledge), wonderment within wonderment becomes manifest, and one never comes out of that wonderment.[110]

This saying alludes to the deadlock of positive knowledge that leads to a recognition of ignorance, and the subsequent opening up to greater realities that is described as intensified astonishment. The connection of unknowing with annihilation becomes apparent in Husri's saying, "The 'learning (*ilm*)' with which we are concerned requires the denial of everything that is learned and habitual, and the effacement (*mahw*) of everything that is caused. Everything that becomes manifest becomes effaced."[111] Hallaj had earlier summed up this polarity in a minimal formulation: "Knowledge is concealed within unknowing, and unknowing is concealed within knowledge."[112] In his treatise *Mashrab al-Arwah* ("The Spirits' Font"), which is devoted to a description of one thousand and one spiritual states, Ruzbihan has given another definition of unknowing: "Unknowing is the obliteration of the eye of the inner consciousness from the comprehension of the reality of the Essence and the Attributes."[113] It is, in effect, an overloading of the normal avenues of perception, and it so stuns the normal dualistic apprehension that an unmediated contact with the divine Attributes may take place.

The meaning of unknowing can be seen further in a striking passage from the *Tawasin* of Hallaj (VII.3), in which Iblis (Satan) speaks of the four "No's" that he uttered before God: "Thus, No, and No, and No, and No! And I remained in the first No, then I was cursed in the second No. I was cast into the third No, but what have I to do with the fourth?" According to Ruzbihan, these four negations represent denial (*nafy*), repudiation of God (*juhud*), prohibition (*nahy*), and unknowing (*nakirah*). Iblis went through the first three negations, but his refusal to bow down before Adam resulted in his being cursed by God: "I did not enter the No of unknowing, because 'knowledge' of unification 'is concealed within unknowing.' I was veiled by these No's from the gnosis (*irfan*) of unknowing and the unknowing of gnosis."[114] Iblis was thus prevented from seeing the deification (unification) of Adam, because, secure in the pride of his own knowledge, he had refused to submit to unknowing. Here Hallaj has been playing with the grammatical meaning of *ma'rifah* and *nakirah* as signifying not only knowledge (gnosis) and ignorance (unknowing), but also the definite noun and the indefinite noun in Arabic grammar.[115] The definite noun, of which one has knowledge (*ma'rifah*), is preceded by the definite article *al-*, the Arabic letters *alif* and *lam*, thus conferring ordinary existance on the noun. To deny the existence of something, one uses the word "no" (just the reverse, *la* or *lam-alif*) as a generic negation, followed by the noun in the indefinite (*nakirah*). If the excessively literal Iblis had grasped the full meaning of negation, he could have followed the path of transcendence to its ultimate conclusion: "The beginning (of the path) is symbolizations (of the divine Attributes, *mutashabihat*), and there are clearly beheld visions in the symbolizations. The end (of the path) is unknowings, because of the holy manifestation of the Attributes (which cannot be comprehended directly except by unknowing)."[116]

4. MADNESS, AUDACITY, AND BOASTING

So far the discussion of *shathiyat* has dwelt on extremely subtle and abstract subjects—identity, transcendence, unknowing—but there is another side to the phenomenon of *shath*. There are many examples of *shath* expressed, not through speech, but through action, and in addition, there are sayings that are rude, violent, and shocking, hardly the sort of thing one expects of respectable mystics.

There is one class of such audacious acts that falls under the heading of apparent madness or loss of consciousness of one's surroundings. For instance, Abu al-Husayn al-Nuri on one occasion received a large inheritance. He proceeded to throw the money into the Tigris, crying, "My friend, you thought to deceive me with this much!"[117] Critics blamed Nuri for his insane wastefulness, but Ruzbihan praised him for his self-possession in eliminating a veil between him and God; Nuri had deliberately counted out the coins one by one before throwing them away. It is likely that Nuri was addressing God as the friend who had attempted to deceive him thus, for God lays many a ruse (*makr*) for the unsuspecting. Another example, more understandable as a case of being overwhelmed by ecstasy, is that of Hisham ibn 'Abdan al-Shirazi, who refrained from food, drink, and prayer for a year; ecstasy is considered an excuse for not performing obligatory prayers, by analogy with madness.[118] The story of Abu Sahl al-Baydawi gives a rather different twist to the problem of ecstasy. His disciple in attendance was a farmer, and since it was time for him to water the crops, he was in a quandary

whether to desert his entranced master or let his crop fail. The master op-
portunely emerged from ecstasy and told the disciple to go attend to his
fields.[119] Another interesting story concerning actions during ecstasy is
the tale of Abu Bakr al-Tamistani. Once while wandering he fell in with a
band of drunken thieves, who were having a music party. Because of the
intensity of his delight in the music, which increased his ecstasy, the
thieves derived such benefit that they all repented from their evil way of
life.[120] Shaykh Ibrahim al-A`raj, imam of the great mosque of Shiraz,
one day during prayer had a conceited thought about the fact that he was
the imam. In contrition, he began at once to walk on his hands in front of
the first line of worshippers, much to their amusement, and he never
acted as imam again.[121] These incidents are all the sort of thing that a
madman might have done. Like the madman, the ecstatic who is unconscious of the world is not responsible for his actions. People who
acted in this way were considered to be holy fools, and they could say the
most outrageous things, even insult God, without being punished.[122]

Another class of audacious actions is that inspired by an overwhelming sense of the divine presence in nature. Some of the mystics who had
this experience expressed it by addressing God in whatever form they saw
or heard Him. Theologians considered the resulting utterances to be
evidence of belief in the incarnation of God in bodies. Here are a few examples: "They called Abu al-Gharib (al-Isfahani) an incarnationist
(*hululi*), because when clear water was trickling over a lawn, he laughed
sweetly with the lip of love, from the ebullition of love; he alluded to
'essential union (Pers. `ayn-i jam`).'"[123] Wasiti explained this by producing another *shath*, saying, "Sometimes existence laughs with the mouth
of power, with the mouths of the Lord." Other instances of hearing the
voice of God in nature are mentioned in the cases of Abu Hamzah al-
Isfahani, who responded with "Here am I, Lord (*labbayk*)!" to the
bleating of al-Muhasibi's sacrificial goat, and Nuri, who made the same
reply to the barking of a dog.[124] According to Ruzbihan, these sayings
derive from the state of essential union, and are really on the highest level
of *shath*.

The surprising quality of these actions of *shath* is matched by the
audacious and aggressive nature of some of the sayings. A perfect example of this is the encounter between Hallaj and `Ali ibn Sahl in Isfahan.
`Ali was sitting with a circle of his followers, when Hallaj approached
and sat down in front of him, saying, "You, shopkeeper! You speak of
gnosis, while I am alive? Between sobriety and ravishment (*istilam*) there
are seven hundred steps that you do not know or even scent." `Ali replied
to him, "You should not be in a town where Muslims live." Although
Hallaj did not understand these words, since `Ali spoke in Persian, the
message must have been clear. Having been advised that his life was in
danger, Hallaj left town that night.[125] Ruzbihan sees in this a reflection
of the divine jealousy, for a *hadith* has it that "if the hidden saints (*abdal*)

became aware of one another, some would hold the others' blood as licit." The misunderstandings of Moses and Khidr (Qur. 18.60–82) are also examples of holy persons not seeing eye to eye. Further, the two men exemplify the two widely separated states to which Hallaj alluded, sobriety (ʿAli) and intoxication (Hallaj).[126] Another such encounter took place in Shibli's assembly, when a man fainted in apparent ecstasy. Shibli commanded that the man be thrown into the Tigris, saying, "If he is sincere, he will escape, like Moses, and if he is a liar he will drown, like Pharaoh."[127] The man evidently survived his ordeal; Shibli found him the next day working in his smithy, and when he passed Shibli a piece of red-hot iron with his bare hand, Shibli calmly took it and tucked it into his sleeve. Ruzbihan concludes, "This action is from the jealousy of gnosis, and jealousy is an attribute of God. . . . This wrangling (*munaqarah*) of the prophets and saints is exemplary (*sunnah*)."[128] Sometimes this rivalry extended retrospectively, and included deceased saints. Wasiti said, "They all died in delusion, up to Bayazid, and he also died in delusion."[129] Likewise Shibli said, "If Abu Yazid were here, he could become Muslim with the aid of our children."[130] These are all examples of divine jealousy, which makes the lover give himself wholly to the Beloved, without admitting any thought of others.

In some cases, the audacity of *shath* even turns against the role of the Prophet. Bayazid heard someone saying, "All creatures will be under the banner of Muhammad!" He replied, "My banner is greater than the banner of Muhammad!"[131] Ruzbihan explains this as Bayazid's being filled with the light of divine manifestation after abandoning the two worlds; he speaks with the presumptuousness of the servant of a great king, who identifies himself with his master. Once Hallaj was accused of pretending to prophethood. He said, "Shame on you! You make so little of my worth!"[132] The implication of this remark is that it would be beneath his dignity for Hallaj merely to claim to be a prophet; it is he, after all, who said, "I am the Truth." The audacity of this saying goes so far beyond the bounds of propriety that even Ruzbihan handles it gingerly, reminding the reader of Hallaj's praises of Muhammad in the *Tawasin*, and mentioning Hallaj's discussion with the Christians of Jerusalem, in which he declared himself a humble follower of Muhammad. Some cases of audacity verge on the grotesque, as in Shibli's saying, "God has some servants who could extinguish the fires of hell by spitting into hell."[133]

The audacity of *shath* is also, of course, directed against God. Abu al-Hasan al-Kharaqani represented himself as having wrestled with God, in a story reminiscent of Jacob's: "One morning I went out, and God came before me. He wrestled with me and I wrestled with Him. I continued wrestling with Him until He threw me down."[134] Bayazid even treated the divine word with contumely. Once when he heard the call to prayer, "God is great," he said, "I am greater than He!"[135] In the same way, when he heard the verse, "Surely thy Lord's assault is terrible" (Qur.

85.12, trans. Arberry), Bayazid replied, "By His life! My assault is more terrible than His!"[136] Hellmut Ritter has discerned in these sayings of Bayazid the experience that Ruzbihan calls *iltibas*, being clothed with divinity: "He is then clothed with the qualities of God, and he sometimes feels this clothing with the qualities of God more vividly than the qualities of the transcendent God, who is spoken of in the Koran and in the call to prayer."[137] Sometimes the more daring *shathiyat* of this type have been too much for later Sufis to accept. Bayazid's statement, "I set up my tent over against the cupola (over the throne of God)," was considered by al-Harawi as infidelity according to the *shari`ah* and distance from God according to the *haqiqah*.[138]

These audacious and aggressive sayings are not without precedent in Islamic literature. We can find the rhetorical basis for this audacity in the ancient boasting-contest (*mufakharah*) of the pre-Islamic Arabs. In these contests, poets would lavishly praise the honor of their own tribes and heap abuse on their opponents, in a ritual performance that had a distinctly religious (or socio-religious) character. According to Bichr Farès, in this kind of sacred feud, "the individual forces are stimulated to the extent of bringing about a complete transfiguration of the individual."[139] The similarity between this pagan vaunting-match and the wrangling (*munaqarah*) of the saints is too obvious to be denied. In fact, the moderate Sufi author Abu al-Najib al-Suhrawardi (d. 563/1168) corroborates this in his widely used manual of conduct for Sufi novices, *Adab al-Muridin*. In the lengthy section on the dispensations (*rukhas*) or permissible deviations from the rules, Suhrawardi says the following:

> Among the (dispensations) are boasting and publicizing one's claim (to spiritual states). In this matter, their standard is that one should intend to publicize the bounties of God, who is exalted above it. "Indeed speak of the bounty of your Lord" (Qur. 93.11). That is (permissible) in the raptures of a spiritual state or in a boasting-contest (*mufakharah*) with an adversary.[140]

Suhrawardi goes on to quote magnificent boasts made by the Prophet in a state of expansion, and he recalls an incident in which the poet Hassan ibn Thabit, on behalf of Muhammad, triumphed over the Banu Darim tribe in a boasting-match. It is precisely the same sort of phenomenon that we see in the *shathiyat* contests of the saints, when one outrageous statement is outdone by the next.

If we can believe the biography of Ruzbihan, the sober Suhrawardi got a strong dose of this type of behavior when the two men met in Medina. They got into a debate on the subject of the relative merits of the sober wayfarer and the enraptured saint as models for imitation. The argument grew heated, as Suhrawardi challenged the younger man's sanity (Suhrawardi was thirty-two years older), and Ruzbihan was overcome by a spiritual state. He said, "May God hide my state from you! I am stan-

ding on the mountain-top, and you are sitting on the flat ground!"
He then marched off alone into the desert. Three nights later, Suhrawardi
had a dream in which the angel Gabriel made clear to him that Ruzbihan's
status was far beyond that of all the saints of the age. On Ruzbihan's
return, Suhrawardi found him listening to music. Before Suhrawardi
could say a word, Ruzbihan told him, "Unless they show you Ruzbihan's
state from heaven, they will not make you acknowledge us a second
time." Ruzbihan then caught him up in the dancing and the weeping,
presumably this time to reveal this state to him directly and not through a
dream.[141] While this story is partly a hagiographic glorification of Ruzbihan by his descendants, it gives an authentic picture not only of the attitudes of the two Sufis, but also of the form that this boasting frequently
took.

Was this an authentic form of spiritual behaviour? Ibn `Arabi
thought it was a self-indulgence. He said, "Ecstatic expressions indicate
one's degree relative to God by following the path of pride (fakhr). That
is done by likenesses and images. God forbid that His people get mixed
up with likenesses or start boasting! For this reason shath is a frivolity of
the carnal soul . . ."[142] Yet in Ruzbihan's mind, wrangling (munaqarah)
was a prophetic norm to be followed as part of the imitation of the Prophet's example. It was not a personal expression, but a formal and stylized
ritual, in which divine inspiration revealed itself by boasting. Doubtless
this sort of ritual activity could be abused, but in theory Ruzbihan's view is defensible. Beyond this, the explanations presented here
have also stressed the influence of the divine Attribute of jealousy and
the overwhelming effect of being clothed with divine selfhood. In a suggestive remark, Hallaj pointed out how love creates intimacy with God in
the innermost layer of the heart. "Love (mahabbat) is from the seed (habbat) of the heart. The seed of the heart is its pith (lubb), the pith is the
locus of the subtlety (latifah), the subtlety is the place of God, and the
place of God is dalliance (tamalluq) with Him."[143] It is also, one suspects,
the freedom of this intimate relationship with God that confers on the
lover the liberty to speak as he wills.

5. TESTIMONY

Beyond these interesting forms of expressing shath—apparent
madness, audacity, and boasting—the most powerful shath is expressed
in the form of testimony to the continuing activity of God. There are
several texts from Hallaj and Bayazid that emphasize the theme of
testimony and that show once again the importance of selfhood and

transcendence in *shath*. During the final trial of Hallaj, the following interrogation took place:

> When they wanted to put Husayn ibn Mansur to death, the jurists and the learned men were summoned for that purpose, and they brought him out (of prison) and introduced him into the presence of the sultan (i.e., the wazir Hamid). They then questioned him, and proposed a problem (which he should solve); he said, "Proceed." So they said to him, "What is the proof (of the existence of God)?" He said, "The proof is the graces (*shawahid*) with which God clothes the sincere ones, by which He draws souls toward Him, leading (them) to acceptance (of Him)." And they replied unanimously, "This is the language of the heretics (*ahl al-zandaqah*)!" And they indicated to the sultan that he be put to death.[144]

In the view of Massignon, this passage represents Hallaj's doctrine of mystical grace, by which God reveals His existence in the hearts of men. Massignon has pointed out that *shahid* (plural *shawahid, shuhud*) can mean a legally qualified witness, a grammatical proof-text, or "a living being full of grace (generally a human being), who proves God by the style of his speech or . . . by the qualities of his countenance."[145] Taken in the latter sense, the *shawahid* that prove God are gifts of grace experienced by the saints, who testify to mankind; through these graces, souls are drawn to God. Ruzbihan glosses *shawahid* as *ayat*, "signs" or "miracles," alluding to the verse, "clear signs (*ayat*) in the breasts of those to whom knowledge was given" (Qur. 29.49).[146] The condemnation of this "theory of the witness" as heresy is understandable, given the severe anti-anthropomorphism of the dominant doctrine of that time (see part III).

Another important text, "the crucial, essential piece of the Hallajian dossier," is the last recorded prayer of Hallaj.[147] This particular passage is so rich and so striking that a full commentary would carry us too far afield. What does one make, for example, of Hallaj performing the evening prayer on the eve of his execution, and then whispering "a ruse, a ruse (*makr, makr*)," far into the night? What of the silence that followed, and then the cry, "Truth, truth (*haqq, haqq*)"? Here, at any rate, are a few lines of the prayer that followed:

> We are your witnesses (*shawahid*) . . . . It is You who manifest as You wish the likeness of Your manifestation in Your decree, as "the most beautiful form" (i.e., Adam), the form in which is the Spirit speaking by science and explanation, power and proof. You have intimated Your essence, of which the quality is "He is," to Your witness (*shahid*, i.e., Hallaj), whose quality is "I am." What of You, then, when You have likened Yourself in my essence, at the end of my transformations, and You have

called my essence "My Essence." You have shown the realities of my sciences and my miracles, by rising in My ascents to the celestial canopies of My eternities, in the speaking (of *shathiyat*) by My creatures . . .[148]

This powerful utterance is closely related to the previously mentioned themes. Immediately there is the tension between "He" and "I," the tension of selfhood. Then comes the doctrine of the apotheosis of humanity, "he is He." This leads at last to a consummation of the theory of the witness, as the divinized man experiences the proofs of divinity as divine acts in his soul, acts whose overwhelming Agency completely annihilates the limited role of the separate observer. The transformation is developed with great subtlety. The activities ordinarily considered merely human—"science and explanation, power and proof"—are modes by which the Spirit speaks. Yet when God calls the human essence His, then, as the progression from the human "my" to the divine "My" attempts to show, the human speaks with the authority of God.

This "theory of the witness" was extremely suspicious in the eyes of many, so much so that all the received texts of *Akhbar al-Hallaj* have been altered to remove the offending phrases. It is only by indirect tradition that the authentic version survives. It is probably for this reason that the first two sentences quoted, about the "witnesses," are not found in our text of Ruzbihan's version. A glance at his version of the text and his commentary, however, reveals an amazing instance of the principle of *shath* in Ruzbihan's experience. Where the Arabic of his own *Mantiq al-Asrar* retains the first person of the original in the account of the prayer ("*my* transformations," "*my* essence"), somehow in beginning the account in his Persian translation (which differs in other ways as well), Ruzbihan has slipped it into the second person:

> How do you see Us? If they make an example of *you* at the end of *your* punishments, they will call *you* "*Your* essence" in *your* essence. Then *I* will show the realities of my sciences and miracles. I will rise in My ascensions to the heights of My eternities with speech from the creatures who make Me present."[149]

Since he lacked the opening of the prayer, which contains the sentences on the witness, Ruzbihan's reading of the text, his translation and commentary, obviously must develop in a slightly different direction. The amazing thing is that in making his translation he has been so imbued with the spirit of *shath* that he has, as it were, entered into the text, addressing Hallaj with foreboding of his fate, and speaking, apparently, with the voice of God. In the same way, when amplifying on the end of the prayer, where the original has, "I will be killed, I will be hung on the gibbet," Ruzbihan comments, "I will kill you with signs, I will burn you with powers, I will pour your dust in the Tigris."[150] This transposition of I and Thou indicates the form in which the transforming power of *shath* manifests itself.

Finally, let us turn to a text, the longest single fragment from Bayazid, that brings the process of witnessing to an agonizing level of tension, without actually using the word *shahid*. This remarkable passage, of which only the first tenth is preserved by Ruzbihan, seems not to have attracted much attention from scholars; Massignon seems not to have noticed that the phrase *ana al-haqq*, "I am the Truth," is here part of God's dialogue with Bayazid, decades before Hallaj could have said it. Arberry seems to be the first to have recognized the importance of this text, which he has translated in full. Ruzbihan's truncated text, besides having a few scribal errors, contains a significant inversion of persons, similar to the case of Hallaj's last prayer.[151] Ruzbihan's version also includes several interpolations, the most interesting of which is the concluding phrase, "and I knew that all is He (*hamah ust*)," possibly the earliest occurrence of this phrase, which later became the motto of the school of Ibn `Arabi.

The original account is too long to reproduce here, but a brief summary will be helpful. This is an encounter between Bayazid and God, described in terms of visions, conversations, and actions. Bayazid looks upon God with various supernormal faculties and attributes. God, speaking in the absolute first person, endows Bayazid with divine selfhood by fiat, and Bayazid begs God not to deceive him or lead him astray. Bayazid undergoes several annihilations, first in terms of his sensory consciousness, then of his human attributes, and finally of his very existence. God purifies him, endows him with knowledge, illuminates him, crowns and adorns him, calls him by His name, resurrects him, destroys him, and manifests His essence in his place. The account gives the impression of an ascending spiral of spiritual experiences; each time that an overwhelming event takes place, it is surpassed by another even greater. The description is not systematic, for it preserves the rough contours of raw experience. The descriptions of the different stages carry conviction and evoke a response in the reader, although the precise details of the different phases are not clearly distinguished. It is interesting to notice that, while Ruzbihan has at his disposal only a small part of this text, the inversion of persons brings about in this short compass a sense of progressive self-annihilation quite similar to that in the complete version, although it is not as richly evocative. Thus, in spite of the compression and alteration of the text, Ruzbihan correctly observes, "Abu Yazid, at the beginning, was himself, but at the end, he spoke from God."[152] The tradition has managed to safeguard the true intention of this document, despite textual corruption.

The following section of the Arabic recension is extremely significant for our understanding of *shath*:

He (God) said: "What you said is true (*haqq*), what you heard is true, what you saw is true, what you verified is true." I said, "Yes! You are the Truth (*anta al-haqq*), and the Truth sees by the Truth; You are the Truth, and the Truth verifies by the Truth. The Truth hears the Truth by the Truth. You are the Hearer and You are the One who makes hear, You are the Truth and You are the one who makes true, there is no god but You." He said, "What are you, if not the Truth? You speak by the Truth." So I said, "No! You are the Truth, and Your speech is true, and the Truth is true by You. You are You, there is no god but You." Then He said to me, "Who are you?" I said to Him, "Who are You?" He said, "I am the Truth (*ana al-haqq*)." Then I said, "I am through You." He said, "If you exist through Me, then I am you and you are I." Then I said, "Don't beguile me by Yourself from Yourself. Yes! You are You, there is no god but You."[153]

Here Bayazid has ascribed the phrase *ana al-haqq* to God, during this strange conversation that records his own successive annihilations. One can see how Bayazid has prepared the way for Hallaj's utterance of this phrase with his own voice. Although God here confirmed to Bayazid the authenticity of his experience and speech ("you speak by the Truth"), Bayazid did not explicitly announce it as Hallaj did. The conclusion of Bayazid's narrative seems to indicate, however, that Bayazid finally will reach a position very similar to that of Hallaj. He said, "Then my attributes became the Attributes of divine Lordship, and my tongue the Tongue of attestation of unity (*tawhid*), and my attributes were He; truly, 'he is He (*huwa huwa*),' there is no god but He."[154] Here, where *shath* is the attestation of unity by the voice of God within man, Hallaj is of the same mind: "If one says 'God is God,' then God is God, for the same is the same; and 'he is He;' that is, the attestation of unity is itself the Essence (*al-tawhid huwa al-dhat*)."[155] Bayazid incipiently described an experience structurally identical to the witnessing that Hallaj, with his greater theoretical acuity, brought to fuller articulation.

Although the main structure of *shath* as testimony seems to be present in both Bayazid and Hallaj, there is an important difference in their expression of testimony. Bayazid was less inclined to reach the public; like many early Sufis, he associated with a few like-minded companions, and sought personal communion with God rather than a wide diffusion of ideas. On one occasion, when an enthusiastic follower had been repeating Bayazid's sayings indiscriminately, and some negative reactions had occurred, Bayazid told him that if he could not control himself, he should go to the desert and speak to the camels instead.[156] This privacy was not an attempt to escape controversy, but was a policy founded on his own vision of the nature of salvation. When asked why he did not preach, Bayazid replied, "How could Bayazid release anyone whom God has bound? For forty years I turned to the people and called them to God, but none followed my call. Then I turned away from them. But when I came to the court of God, I saw that they all had come there already."[157] Bayazid did not want to be an intermediary who might act as a veil for others. Once Bayazid was being followed by a large crowd of people who sought his company. He said to God, "O Lord! I pray that you do not veil the people from Yourself by Yourself, but you are veiling them from Yourself by me!" Then, after leading the people in the morning prayer, he turned to them and said, "I am I, there is no god but I; therefore worship me!" Hearing this, the people said, "Abu Yazid has gone mad," and departed.[158] What Ritter called Bayazid's longing "to eliminate himself from in between" took a much more public form in Hallaj.[159] As Hallaj told a disciple, "God Most High is the very one who Himself affirms His unity by the tongue of whatever of His creatures he wishes. If He Himself affirms His unity by my tongue, it is He and His affair. Otherwise, brother, I have nothing to do with affirming God's unity."[160] Yet God's unity was continually attested through Hallaj. He travelled to far-away countries, calling people to the Truth, and he felt that his testimony could only be fully given in martyrdom. Thus it was that he broke the customary discipline of secrecy. His last words on the gibbet were these: "It is enough for the ecstatic that the One be single in Himself," implying his recognition of the necessity of his death, as an expiation for separateness, and as a testimony to "essential union."[161] Hallaj became the example of public testimony in Sufism, and he showed how severe the fullest demands of this path could be.

C.

Conclusions

In this exposition, I have tried to bring out a wide range of symbolic and experiential associations, to clarify the basic structure of *shath*. Theoretically, it would be possible to refine this analysis by distinguishing between the experiences of the different Sufis in their *shathiyat*. Such a study would have to examine each Sufi's ecstatic sayings in the light of all other sayings and writings attributed to that person. Having established the apparent meanings of these sayings by lexical comparison, it would then be necessary to evaluate all these sayings in terms of relevant and appropriate Sufi works describing the varieties of ecstatic experience. Although such an exhaustive cataloging of mystical expressions and experiences is beyond the scope of this study, it is possible to establish here some general lines for interpreting *shathiyat*.

The interpretations of *shath* made by such scholars as Massignon and Ritter are good, but incomplete. They stressed the momentary transposition of subject and object, the temporary replacement of the human "I" by the divine "I."[162] This needs to be tested further, though, in the context of certain descriptions of the highest degree of ecstasy as a continuous experience.[163] In addition, one has to account for the possibility of deception in apparently inspired ecstasies; this danger was certainly well-known to the early Sufis.[164] It was with this idea of deception in mind that Massignon maintained that Hallaj had accused Bayazid of confusing his ego with God.[165] Such psychologizing should not be pushed too far, however; it seems more likely that Hallaj's criticism is itself a *shath*, in the same vein as Wasiti's and Shibli's caustic comments on Bayazid. Thus while it is important to try to distinguish the different states alluded to in *shath*, this task is made difficult by the formulaic tendencies and literary conventions of *shath*. How much can we deduce about the spiritual state indicated by a comment made in the manner of the boasting-match? There are structural continuities in the various forms of expressing *shath*, but the attempt to discern the underlying states can only, I think, be carried out in a general way, within the framework provided by the Sufi tradition.

Yet can there be an adequate interpretation of *shathiyat*? Are these strange utterances at all susceptible to rational analysis by a non-mystic? Massignon has summed up the problem in a provocative way:

> The goal of the commentary of Baqli on Hallajian texts is to elucidate the method that Hallaj follows in giving testimony to God by a language of paradoxical appearance, by means of expressions that are from an ecstatic intoxication only in appearance, for they are perfectly composed and measured, denoting an author who has mastered his mental state of mysticism (*malik halihi*). This is the problem of the philosophical and theological value of the Hallajian *shath*.[166]

This represents something of the authentic attitude of the early Sufis toward *shathiyat*. It must be remembered that the commentators Sarraj and Ruzbihan placed a great emphasis on the knowledge (`*ilm*) necessary to understand *shath*, knowledge partly viewed as a form of learning, but considered mainly as a gnosis, a participation through grace in the divine knowledge. But is this ecstatic knowledge accessible, or is it a form of intoxication that has nothing to do with the mind? This is a serious question. Massignon has teasingly suggested that *shathiyat* are ecstatic and intoxicated only in appearance, while in reality they are produced in a state of self-possession, at least in the case of Hallaj. Although a few *shathiyat* have to do with complete unconsciousness of the outer world, the majority are admittedly answers to questions, written replies to letters, or actions taken in response to some need. The forms of these expressions are strange, yet they do not presuppose complete intoxication. The technical vocabulary of states and stages was developed so that the Sufis could converse among themselves about their experiences. *Shathiyat* also serve this purpose. They are utterances in the service of the spirit. These may be experimental in character and deliberately unconventional, and they refer to a wide range of experiences, although the ultimate states serve as the orientation around which the rest are constellated. The highest form of *shath* is that in which the speaker is God, testifying to His own unity on the tongue of His lover. *Shath* in general is an expression of a spiritual state, and it stands in a relation of more or less immediacy to the original experience, but this immediacy does not on principle exclude a certain amount of analysis and reflection.

The very problem of sobriety versus intoxication is to some extent an artificial one that has been introduced into Sufism for polemical purposes. It is true that these two terms were used very early to signify one kind of polarity of spiritual experience. Abu Sa'id ibn al-A'rabi (d. 341/952) wrote in his *Kitab al-Wajd* ("Book of Ecstasy") that there is no reason to prefer the settled ecstatic (*sakin*) over the agitated soul (*mutaharrak*), for to each has been revealed something different, not comparable with any other in terms of simple superiority.[167] In a similar fashion, Ruzbihan, commenting on the wrangling of Hallaj with 'Ali ibn Sahl, points out that intoxication and sobriety, self-possession (*tamkin*) and rapture (*talwin*), are two complementary aspects of ascending revelation rather than mutually exclusive opposites. He further observes that "Sobriety and intoxication are one, for the lover dives into the oceans of Greatness and Might, and there the intoxicated is not distinguished from the sober."[168] I think that Massignon's remark could be improved by saying that ecstasy does not necessarily imply obscurity and unintelligibility; there can as well be an ecstatic apprehension characterized by total clarity. This, at least, has been the assumption of Ruzbihan. This is not to say that he always "finds" the expected esoteric meaning in every innocent or ambiguous phrase, although he does have a consistent mystical theology. His exegesis rests on genuine insight, but he is not afraid to say, "but God knows best," after an especially enigmatic saying. His position has not always been shared by others, however.

The problem has been that *shathiyat* have in general been ill-received by jurists. Opponents of ecstatic expression have been willing to settle for a compromise in which *shath* is ascribed to intoxication, because that neutralizes the expression and makes it the equivalent of a madman's ravings. Then, as a frequently quoted phrase announces, "it is neither to be accepted nor rejected." If there is any suggestion that ecstatic expressions are made deliberately, then they are immediately seen as dangerous. "Anyone," says the philosopher and historian Ibn Khaldun (d.808/1406), "who says such things while conscious and in his senses, while not mastered by a spiritual state, is therefore to be blamed also. It was for this reason that the jurists and the leading Sufis decided on the death of al-Hallaj, because he spoke consciously, having mastered his state (*malik li-halihi*)."[169] Voicing a similar feeling, the moderate Sufi master 'Abd al-Qadir al-Jilani (d. 561/1167) said, "If ecstatic expressions come forth from the Sufi in the state of sobriety, one must assume they come from Satan."[170] It was felt that a literal understanding of ecstatic expressions would lead to heresy, and therefore the terms "intoxication (*sukr*)" and "sobriety (*sahw*)" took on a polemical character, due to heresiographical concerns.

This heresiographical tendency is first evident among the Sufis in the *Kashf al-Mahjub* of Hujwiri, whose artificial system of "sects" in Sufism is discussed in part III. Hujwiri described the "sober" school of Junayd as opposed to the "intoxicated" school of Bayazid, assuming that the two masters taught radically differing "doctrines." Hujwiri refused to consider the sayings of Hallaj as meaningful, saying that Hallaj was merely a novice overcome by ecstasy, lacking the settledness required for authoritative statements. Hujwiri was theoretically opposed, in any event, to the attempt to analyze one's own spiritual states at all, because of the possibility that people would be led astray by unusual "uncontrolled" expressions. As he put it, "Expression of the meaning of reality is futile. If the meaning exists it is not lost by expression, and if it is nonexistent it is not created by expression. Expression only produces an unreal notion and leads the student mortally astray . . ."[171] This protective statement is made in spite of the extensive commentary on spiritual states in Hujwiri's treatise. Much later, in Ottoman Baghdad, Ahmad ibn Muhammad al-Kilani (d. 970/1561) continued a long tradition of polemics against Hallaj in the Rifa`iyah Sufi order, by ridiculing Ruzbihan's commentary and calling *shath* a disease of the soul.[172] The point, again, is that only a sane person's statements are worth analyzing.

If Hujwiri's report is to be believed, Hallaj broke with Junayd precisely on the subject of sobriety and intoxication. Junayd maintained that they were pre-ordained qualities, and that sobriety denoted soundness while intoxication implied excess. Hallaj said that the two were correlative human attributes on the path, both of which must be transcended to reach the goal.[173] Useful although intoxication may be for heresiography, the term does not encompass the phenomenon of *shath*. Hujwiri quotes Shibli as saying, "I and Hallaj are of one mind, but my madness saved me, and his intellect destroyed him."[174] Against Hujwiri's agnosticism regarding the description of states of ecstasy, is the fact, of capital importance, that Junayd was the first to comment on the *shathiyat* of Bayazid; this is hardly the act of one who only allows significance to apparently "self-controlled" utterances. It further reveals the artificiality of separating the "schools" of Junayd (sobriety) and Bayazid (intoxication). In spite of the agnostic tendencies of Hujwiri, the very commentaries on *shathiyat* by Junayd, Sarraj, and Ruzbihan are decisive proof of a tradition of exegesis. The spiritual riches of *shath* are, on principle, potentially accessible to those who wish to find them, as much, indeed, as any profound religious statements are accessible to sympathetic investigators.

Aside from the defective nature of the texts, it seems to me that the only significant objection to the validity of the commentaries on *shathiyat* would be directed at a certain tendentiousness, due to the apologetic orientation of the commentaries. Sarraj points out that Junayd was not an apologist, however: "In this commentary of Junayd, he only described the spiritual state of which Abu Yazid spoke, and he explained the position to which he (Abu Yazid) alluded (in these sayings).

He did not encounter the stubborn and obstinate person who would verbally condemn anyone saying something of this sort without explaining it."[175] Yet it is just this sort of stubborn person to whom Sarraj is speaking, one such as the theologian Ibn Salim, whose incredulity toward the sayings of Bayazid he frequently mentions. It must be admitted that this apologetic tendency vitiates Sarraj's interpretations. Sometimes his explanations are so forced that one must suppose it is deliberate protective dissimulation.

It is not clear exactly when the apologetic trend set in. Some of the explanations attributed to Junayd suggest that Sarraj may have underestimated the amount of controversy about ecstatic expressions during the time of Junayd. Junayd is presented as explaining a daring statement by Bayazid, "I am my highest Lord," as a mere quotation from God. Yet in another place, Junayd explains a similar saying by a comparison to the story of the lovers Layla and Majnun; Majnun so loved Layla that he could say, "I am Layla."[176] Sarraj must have known of Junayd's favorable commentary on this saying, but he deliberately suppressed it in his conversations with Ibn Salim, who was under the impression that Bayazid, unlike Pharoah, had at least not said that he was the Lord.[177] Bayazid's descendents in Bistam, as Sarraj took pains to point out, denied that their ancestor could have said, "Glory be to Me!"[178] Ritter has well described the mechanism of these apologetics: "This tendency brings it about that the expressions of the early Sufis are subjected to a severe censorship, which only permits that which is tolerable by appropriate interpretation."[179] For our purposes, though, the apologetic tendency is not a fatal flaw, except where it leads to alteration and suppression of *shathiyat*. Moreover, Sarraj is the only principal commentator who is really concerned to sanitize the sayings of Bayazid, and even so, his annotations are more often helpful than not; besides, he is the only writer who has preserved Junayd's commentaries besides Sahlaji. Ruzbihan's commentary is of tremendous value, primarily because of his profound understanding of spiritual states, but also because of his supple mystical theology. He admits to an apologetic purpose, but because he explains the sayings in terms of both *shari`at* and *haqiqat*, he largely retains the essential meanings without suppressing anything. If one is sufficiently aware of the existence of this apologetic tendency, the commentaries on *shathiyat* will lose none of their usefulness.

Finally, I should like to point out the validity of Ruzbihan's linkage of *shath* with the Qur'an and *hadith*. He uses favorite texts from the Qur'an and certain suggestive *hadith* reports to illustrate and explain the sayings in his *Sharh-i Shathiyat*, and he uses *shath* as a method of exegesis in his great Qur'an commentary, `*Ara'is al-Bayan*. The results of this approach are generally illuminating, and always evoke the essential experiences that are at the source of his inspiration. Until the Sufi Qur'an commentaries, especially the `*Ara'is*, are edited and indexed, our understanding of early Sufism will have a serious lacuna. The researches of Massignon, Nwyia, and Boewering have shown what rich materials can be found in the scriptual exegesis of Sufism. Corbin's excellent edition of the *Sharh-i Shathiyat*, with its large index of terms and motifs, is a model of the kind of presentation that this material deserves. Yet he apologized for not giving a complete inventory of Qur'an and *hadith* citations, saying, "The *hadith* alone would demand a separate study. They are cited sometimes in Arabic, sometimes in Persian; sometimes fully, sometimes recalled by a few words comprising an image, or even a single allusive word that resounds like a *leitmotiv*, orchestrated by each context."[180] It is to be hoped that a complete study of Ruzhiban's spiritual exegesis will be undertaken, using not only his collection of *shathiyat* but also his compilation of Qur'anic interpretations, with a complete collation of sayings as found in early Arabic sources. Studies of this type will help to bring to the fore one of the most significant and characteristic aspects of Islamic mysticism.

Part II

ECSTATIC EXPRESSIONS ON FAITH AND INFIDELITY IN SUFISM

Faith (*iman*) and infidelity (*kufr*) are terms that express the fundamental religious distinction between acceptance and rejection of God and His revelation. "But God has made *iman* loveable for you, and has adorned it in your hearts, but He has made hateful *kufr* and iniquity and rebelliousness" (Qur. 49.7). Throughout Islamic history, these terms have been of great importance for determining membership in the community of the faithful as well as ultimate salvation. This chapter will investigate the ecstatic sayings on faith and infidelity as a special topic for *shathiyat*. This group of sayings, and related discussions of faith and infidelity, constitute a self-reflection on the fundamental problems of *shathiyat*. They not only summarize the deepest intuitions regarding mystical experience, but also reveal the limitations of language in expressing that experience. Although this topic may appear opaque and hermetic at times, it deserves separate treatment as a self-interpretation of the ambiguous position that mystical speech necessarily has.

To give a survey of this topic, it is necessary first to establish the ordinary meanings of faith and infidelity, not only as they were used in Qur'an and *hadith*, but also as used in theological contexts. The scriptural and theological meanings of such terms are basic for the development of the Sufi vocabulary. After reconstructing the primary meanings of faith and infidelity in Sufism, it will then be possible to analyze the ecstatic expressions of faith and infidelity as a particular type of *shath*, using the categories developed in the previous chapter. Our analysis will focus on three authors: Hallaj, `Ayn al-Qudat, and Ruzbihan. Although there are other figures who deal with this topic in significant ways, these three present the fullest and most original interpretations of faith and infidelity through the medium of *shath*. Since this analysis is exploratory, it will take the form of a running commentary on the main presentations and discussions of the *shathiyat* on faith and infidelity, rather than a systematic exposition of topics. Our final interpretations of these sayings will be reserved for the conclusion of this study.

A.

Faith and Infidelity
in Early Islam,
and the Sufi Concept of Faith

In the Qur'an and *hadith*, faith and infidelity are frequently mentioned in terms of acceptance or rejection of the Qur'anic revelation. The following verse, addressed to Muhammad, closely links faith with the Qur'an itself, and metaphorically describes both as the light of divine guidance: "You did not know what the Book was, nor *iman*, but We made of it a light by which We guide whomever We wish among Our servants" (Qur. 42.5). Another impressive verse describes the descent of the spirit of peace (*sakinah*, Hebrew *shekhinah*): "He it is who made the spirit of peace descend into the hearts of the faithful, that they might increase in *iman* upon *iman*" (Qur. 48.4). The basic import of these verses is that faith is a quality of openness toward the divine, by which the heart receives revelation. Those who witnessed the revelation of the Qur'an to Muhammad were affected so strongly by it that this was frequently the occasion for their conversion. One of the Prophet's companions, ʿUthman ibn Marwan, saw Muhammad while he was experiencing a revelation from Gabriel. This was so impressive to him that, as he later stated, "That was the moment when faith settled in my heart and I loved Muhammad."[1] Here is a personal testimony to the point made in the Qur'an itself, that the guidance of faith comes through the Qur'an, i.e., through the word of God. In Sufism there was a tremendous devotion to the Qur'an, characterized by assiduous study and prayerful repetition of Qur'anic verses as a supererogatory form of worship. Qur'anic devotion in Sufism was a pietistic development of one of the basic qualities of faith, in terms of openness to the divine word. The closed state of mind represented by *kufr* rejects the divine word. "Infidelity and hypocrisy

55

(belong to) him who does not answer when he hears God's crier calling to prayer, inviting (him) to salvation."[2] *Kufr* means literally "to cover up," with the specific implication of the covering over of the bounties of God, in a mean and ungrateful fashion. The stony-hearted infidel (*kafir*) rejects the divine revelation, though he may know it to be true.

Faith begins in the heart, but it needs to find an extension through action; if action does not truly reflect the condition of the heart, the result is hypocrisy. Faith is itself described as an action (`amal*): "The Messenger of God was asked which action is best. He said, 'Faith in God and His Messenger.'"[3] Thus it is that the *hadith* literature frequently identifies faith with the performance of certain rituals, such as ablutions, prayer, and funerals.[4] Infidelity, on the other hand, is hypocritical, and does not act out the true feelings of the heart. Of the hypocrites, it is said, "They were on that day nearer to *kufr* than to *iman*. They say with their mouths what is not in their hearts, but God knows what they conceal" (Qur. 3.167). They form a secret opposition within the community. "O Prophet! Struggle against the infidels and the hypocrites! . . . They swear by God that they said nothing, but they said the word of *kufr* and were infidel after their submission" (Qur. 9.73–4). The radical disconnection between the heart and the outward act nullifies the value of external actions. This is of great consequence for the Judgment, since the deeds of a hypocrite, who acts only in order to give the appearance of faith, are worthless in the afterlife.

The distinction between faith and infidelity as openness and hypocrisy obviously had important social consequences. Sometimes *iman* and *islam* were even used to signify the religious community as a whole. In a similar way, other religious groups, such as Christians and Jews, were considered infidels (*kuffar*) for rejecting the prophetic message of Muhammad. Generally, however, the Sufis preferred to emphasize the idea of faith as an internal act, as distinct from the more formal *islam*, "submission to God." There was definitely a precedent for this. "The Prophet said, 'Submission is public and faith is in the heart.' Then he pointed to his breast three times and said, 'Fear of God (*taqwa*) is here, fear of God is here!'"[5] Thus the pietistic attitude towards faith and infidelity stressed the internal aspects of these qualities, which were viewed in terms of salvation and damnation, true worship and idolatry, the heart open to the light of faith and the closed and stony heart. There were other tendencies, though, which emphasized the social and communal aspects of these terms. Since hypocrisy cuts at the very root of the moral foundation of society, infidelity in its extreme form was regarded as the equivalent of apostasy. Infidelity, along with adultery and murder, was one of the three crimes for which a Muslim could be put to death. The popular imagination therefore seized upon the semantic breadth and religious importance of *iman* and *kufr*. In *hadith*, one finds such unusual metaphors as the following: "Faith resorts to Medina as a snake resorts to its lair."[6] A remarkable image of *kufr* appears in an apocalyptic *hadith* prophesying the antichrist: "There is no prophet who has not warned his community of the one-eyed *kafir*. Behold! He is one-eyed, and your Lord is not one-eyed! Between his eyes (*sic*) is written K-F-R."[7] Here *kufr* has become personified in the arch-tempter and ultimate enemy of mankind. Such expressions show that faith and infidelity were all-encompassing terms surrounded by powerful evaluative auras. So it was that faith was the general term for all that is beneficial for the religious life, while infidelity denoted all that is opposed to it.

With the rise of factionalism, faith and infidelity began to take on polemical and theoretical overtones. The movement of the Kharijis, arising out of the struggle over the leadership of the community, was characterized by its definition of faith in terms of action. Anyone who committed a grave sin was no longer of the faithful, and was considered an infidel deserving only death. The practical consequences of this view were so repugnant to the majority that the earliest Sunni creeds explicitly repudiated the Khariji view of faith. Already in the *hadith* literature, the verbal appropriation of *iman* was a way of legitimizing and gaining approval for one's own party while at the same time attacking one's opponents.[8] The theological enterprise was also stimulated by a natural desire to attain precision in the descriptions of the objects of faith, i.e., God, the prophets, the revealed books, the angels, and predestination.[9] Theology, however, has a tendency to become formalized into dogmatic propositions, and in the various Islamic schools this tendency had the unfortunate but inevitable side-effect of producing doctrinal rivalry. The polemical form that this took was the anathematization of opponents by the process of *takfir*, "calling someone a *kafir*." The result of this trend was that certain theologians began to anathematize all Muslims who did not belong to their school. Such a step effectively restricted salvation to professional theologians adhering to the one correct doctrine. The unbridled use of theological anathemas threatened to go out of control and create a vicious factionalism based on purely theoretical grounds. Recognizing this danger, the theologian al-Ash`ari on his deathbed begged his disciples not to charge their opponents with *kufr* over a difference of opinion, although he himself was not so merciful during his own lifetime.[10]

The solution to this problem of theological orthodoxy was discovered by Abu Hamid al-Ghazali, who removed the question of infidelity from the realm of doctrine altogether. He observed that

he is a downright fool who, when asked to give his definition of *kufr*, answers: "*kufr* is anything that is opposed to the Ash`arite theory, or the Mu`tazilite theory, or the Hanbalite theory or indeed any other theory, (as the case may be)." Such a man is more blind than a blind man, an uncritical follower of authority.[11]

Ghazali makes the important point that determination of *kufr* should not be made in terms of reason or doctrine, since it is essentially a matter of juridical status. The basic legal principle suggested by Ghazali is that *kufr* means calling the Prophet a liar in any respect. He insists that there should be no anathema of those who pray toward Mecca and make the confession of faith, unless there is clear proof against them, and further, that there should be no anathema in non-essentials. Like Ghazali, Sufis in general eschewed the rationalistic approach to faith and infidelity characteristic of some theologians. Regarding the practice of anathema, Ruzbihan observed, "There was no heresy, infidelity, innovation, or insolence in the sure religion before theological discussion (*kalam*), disputation, quarreling, and conceit (entered in)."[12] Sufis preferred to treat faith and infidelity in personal terms. They used the term "infidelity" in a searching psychological analysis, which identified any hidden hypocrisy or self-adulation as infidelity. This kind of spiritual *takfir* was particularly appropriate for expression in *shathiyat*, as the next few sections will show.

Nonetheless, despite their generally anti-dogmatic approach, Sufis inevitably discussed subjects such as *iman* in terms of the standard theological definitions found in the credal statements of the various schools. Although we can only indicate very briefly the relationship of Sufi positions to the main theological views on the nature of faith, it will be instructive for us to examine some of the principal mystical formulation of this central religious topic. Kalabadhi (d. 380/990) specified that faith is "a speech, an action, and an intention (*qawl wa `amal wa niyah*)," and he quoted with approval the *hadith* that states, "faith is confession by the tongue, confirmation in the heart, and action with the limbs."[13] This formulation is closer to the position of the Hanbali school than to any other, in its insistence on the involvement of the whole person. The Ash`ari school and the Hanafi-Maturidi position inclined to a more intellectualist explanation of faith, while other schools stressed the verbal element (e.g., the Karramiyah) or outward actions (the Khawarij).[14] The Sufi Ibn al-Khafif (d. 371/980) presented the formula of Kalabadhi, and also supported the Hanbali view that faith increases and decreases.[15] For major dogmatic positions, Ibn al-Khafif and Kalabadhi both relied heavily on the *Fiqh Akbar II* attributed to the jurist Abu Hanifah. Yet Sufism added an experiential stress to the juristic formulation. In this spirit Ibn al-Khafif said, "faith is the hearts' confirmation of the truth (*tasdiq*) of the hidden things that God has brought about (in them)."[16]

Faith is not something to be claimed lightly, either; Sufis generally preferred the conditional formula, "I am faithful, if God will (*in sha' allah*)" to the Hanafi creed, "I am really faithful (*haqqan*)." Regarding the latter, Wasiti commented, "'Reality (*haqiqah*)' implies command, acquaintance, and comprehension; one who lacks these makes his claim in vain." Qushayri also objected, saving, "that which the Sunni theologians say, 'I am the really faithful one (*al-mu'min al-haqiqi*),' refers to one who is destined to go to Paradise, but he who does not know that from the mystery of God's wisdom wrongly claims that he is 'really faithful.'"[17] Part of the reason for this was the recognition that no one could be absolutely sure of his faith under ordinary circumstances. al-Hakim al-Tirmidhi said, "How many an infidel far from God is granted faith and dies in bliss, and how many a believer close to God is forsaken by his Lord and dies in misery!"[18] Indeed, this problem of the mystery of how one's life will end (*khawatim*) greatly impressed mystics such as Muhasibi (d. 243/857), who pointed out that ʿUmar himself converted only late in life, and that many followers of the Prophet Muhammad apostatized in the Riddah rebellion after his death.[19]

In describing the qualities of faith, the Sufis drew freely on the imagery of light and vision, which was already prominent in the descriptions of faith in Qur'an and *hadith*. Ibn al-Khafif said, "It (faith) is a light that is cast into the heart, although (it is) not the light of the Essence."[20] As Kalabadhi said, "Faith in God is the witnessing of divinity (*mushahadat al-uluhiyah*)."[21] This imagery is further complemented by a discussion of the interior (*batin*) and exterior (*zahir*) aspects of faith. "Faith is in the exterior and the interior, and the interior is a single thing, which is the heart, while the exterior is different things."[22] Here Kalabadhi distinguishes between the internal conviction and the outward acts. Ibn al-Khafif gives a more overtly mystical distinction, saying, "in faith, and *tawhid*, and knowledge, there is an external (*zahir*) and a reality (*haqiqah*) . . . He who is exalted calls humanity toward the exterior of these (three), but He guides whom He wishes to their reality."[23] Here one has a sense of levels of faith, one that is general, and one that is reserved for the elect. Considered as an inner quality, faith is distinguished from outward submission to God (*islam*). Kalabadhi says, "submission is outer, faith is inner," and, "faith is realization (*tahqiq*) and adherence (*iʿtiqad*), submission is subjection (*khuduʿ*) and compliance (*inqiyad*)."[24] Submission is a prerequisite for faith, yet as Ibn al-Khafif points out, "every faithful one (*mu'min*) is a submitter (*muslim*), but not every submitter is a faithful one."[25] Muhasibi went so far as to say, "*islam* is (only) a name; it means the confessional religion (*millah*). Faith is (only) a name; it means confirmation of the truth and real action in accordance with prescribed duties."[26] There appears to be a realization here that the term *islam* has become somewhat externalized in the course of time, as shown by its identification with the community as a whole. In making this distinction, Sufis part company with the Hanbalis.[27]

The ultimate horizons of faith are to be found in the precreational colloquy between humanity and God, and in the final degrees of knowledge, certainty, and love. One of God's names in the Qur'an is "the Faithful (*al-mu'min*)," and God's faith is considered to be the existentiating power of His assent by which He confirmed the existence of His Attributes. This thesis of God's eternal faith was affirmed by Hallaj, the Hanbalis, and the Salimis.[28] When God addressed the souls of humanity in pre-eternity, he apportioned a particle of this uncreated faith to those whom He foreknew to be faithful. As Kalabadhi said, "It is allowable that faith is from God, the Great and Mighty, Who apportioned it to the servant in His foreknowledge; it does not exceed the time (decreed) for its manifestation, nor does it fall short of that which God knew of the devotee and apportioned to him."[29] Sahl al-Tustari (d. 283/896) connected this event with the verse, "(God) inscribed faith on their hearts" (Qur. 58.22), and he made this comment: "The writing in the heart is the gift of faith that He gave them before their creation, in their loins and wombs. Then He displayed a burst of light in the heart, and tore the veil off of it (the heart), to make them see by His blessing the hidden writing and the light of faith."[30] If the souls of the faithful possess a particle of this divine faith, then it is clear that the potentiality of faith goes far beyond its dogmatic formulation. Sufis have generally called this higher dimension of faith certainty (yaqin), although they also referred to it as knowledge in the sense of gnosis (ma`rifah). Again to quote Sahl, "Certainty is an addition to faith, and is a realization of it. . . . Certainty is a part of faith that is beyond confirmation."[31] When the Sufis say that faith increases (i.e., beyond minimal assent), it is by one's inherent power (quwwah) and by certainty that it does so.[32]

What does this certainty consist of, to make it so different from ordinary faith? It is the knowledge that one is a recipient of divine mercy; in effect, it is assurance of salvation. In distinguishing this gnosis of salvation from discursive theological knowledge, Ibn al-Khafif said, "knowledge of the attributes (ma`rifat al-sifat) is an acquisition, but the gnosis of election (ma`rifat al-takhsis) is a gift; and the origin of faith is a gift, though its conditions are acquired."[33] The momentousness of this experience of certainty may be judged from the fact that it makes faith necessary, but not sufficient, for salvation.[34] According to Massignon, Sahl al-Tustari found certainty when, "in the moment when God dictated certain inspired words by the tongue of the ecstatic, He made him taste an ineffable 'certitude' in his heart, an uncreated yaqin."[35] This certainty, which indicates the possibility of union with God, is here expressed in terms of the phenomenon of shath, in which God speaks by the tongue of man. "The realities of faith," says Kalabadhi, "are four: tawhid without limit, recollection of God without end, a mystical state of no (single) description, and an ecstasy without time."[36]

In summary, it can be seen that the Sufi position on faith was consciously opposed to the more intellectualist and literalist views, and it took an approach, closely akin to that of the Hanbalis, based on a deepened experience of the Qur'anic revelation. This deepening process not only led to an expansion of the understanding of faith as a personal act, but also led to the elaboration of higher forms of faith, which assumed separate positions (*yaqin, ma`rifah*). By thus making faith something at once more important and less ultimate than it was usually considered, the Sufis made the concept of faith much more flexible and all-inclusive. It can mean everything from blind imitative faith (*iman mu- qallad*) to the general form of human participation in divine reality. This very flexibility now would lend itself to paradoxical use in the form of *shathiyat*. The earliest example of this that I have found is a saying of Bayazid's: "The infidelity of those endowed with spiritual ambition is closer to *islam* than the faith of those endowed with grace."[37] This deliberately provocative statement, evidently aimed at those who passively await grace rather than strive for union, sets the stage for the radical and disturbing sayings of Hallaj, who is the real formulator of the mystical *topos* of faith and infidelity.

B.

Hallaj

Hallaj's understanding of faith was thoroughly in consonance with the Sufi position just outlined. For Hallaj, *iman* was the first step on a ladder leading to overwhelming love of God (*walah*) and astonishment; in addition, when fear of God (*taqwa*) combined with perfect gnosis, the state of total surrender (*istinyat*) to the Qur'an became possible, "and this is the reward of the stations of faith."[38] Yet Hallaj also spoke of faith as only a beginning, for "he who looks for God by the light of faith is like him who seeks the sun by the light of the stars.'[39] Although ordinary faith is inferior to gnosis, faith in a more general sense includes all relationships to divinity: "No one can claim God in any way except by faith, for in reality, there is no claim (to having attained God)."[40] Nonetheless, insofar as faith is identified with "speech, action and intention," it is occupied with intermediaries (*wasa'it*), with something other than God.[41] According to Hallaj's doctrine of "the eclipse of intermediaries (*isqat al-wasa'it*)," at the dawning of the experience of the realities (*haqa'iq*) of faith, these outward expressions of faith are obliterated from consciousness, and remain only in form (*rasm*).[42] Although this view is not precisely antinomian, it is certainly a significant relativization of the law. The *shari`ah* is still obligatory, but it has receded in importance before the overwhelming meeting with the Master of the *shari`ah*.

Hallaj's strange utterances on faith and infidelity need to be understood in terms of the characteristics of *shath*, as discussed in part I; we shall note in particular the relevance of the topics of knowledge and unknowing, transcendence of duality, and audacity in the special form of blame. The characteristics of the highest form of *shath*, that is, *shath* as the divine word, *shath* as testimony, and the nature of selfhood, are not very prominently involved in Hallaj's statements on faith and infidelity. The implication here is that the ecstatic sayings on faith and infidelity refer to the experience of the nothingness of creation (*fana'*), not that of deification (*baqa'*).

There are two sayings of Hallaj that present faith and infidelity in close dependence upon the topics of knowledge and unknowing and the transcendence of duality. The first, preserved only in an ambiguous Persian recension, is as follows:

> The knower (*'arif*) looks upon his initial mystical states and realizes that he does not have faith except after he becomes infidel. . . . In the beginning the poor man takes a position with respect to something. Then his position becomes advanced with respect to that thing. In the end he becomes infidel. Don't you see that if he goes back on that (*agar baz-i an gardid*), he has been infidel?[43]

Although the terminology of this saying is terribly vague, I interpret this to mean that initial faith, the creature's acceptance and recognition of the creator, is a partial kind of knowledge, which, from the viewpoint of the real knower, nonetheless appears to be ignorance and unconscious rejection of the truth. When the real knower looks back on his first attainments, he realizes intensely the dualistic limitations of that first intimation called faith. And just as unknowing is prerequisite to real knowledge, so a realization of the limitations of one's initial faith is necessary in order to transcend its intrinsic duality. "In the end he becomes infidel" because he now realizes his nothingness, and can call himself "infidel" to signify that he knows that his faith is no faith at all. Like the impotence, blindness, and astonishment of unknowing, becoming infidel is a descent into the dark night of the soul.

Hallaj further explains the relationship between infidelity, knowledge, and duality, in a famous letter addressed to one of his disciples.

> In the name of God, the Merciful, the Compassionate, who manifests Himself (*tajalla*) through everything to whomsoever He wishes. Peace be unto you, my son. May God veil you from the exterior of the religious law, and may He reveal to you the reality of infidelity (*haqiqat al-kufr*). For the exterior of the religious law is a hidden idolatry, while the reality of infidelity is a manifest gnosis (*ma'rifah jaliyah*). Thus, praise belongs to the God who manifests Himself on the head of a pin to whom He wishes, and who conceals Himself in the heavens and the earths from whom He wishes, so that one testifies that He is not, and another testifies that there is none other than He. But the witness in negation of Him is not rejected, and the witness in affirmation of Him is not praised. And the purpose of this letter

is that I charge you not to be deceived by God, and not to despair of Him; not to covet His love, and not to be satisfied with not being His lover; not to utter affirmation of Him, and not to incline towards negation of Him. And beware of affirming the divine unity! Peace.[44]

In this important passage Hallaj has indicated the purpose of his strange venture into self-proclaimed heresy. His "reality of infidelity" is "a manifest gnosis," that is, a form of the essential gnosis that can only be bestowed by theophany or divine manifestation (*tajalli*). It is the kind of gnosis that sees the absolute nothingness of creaturehood and realizes that separate existence constitutes infidelity. The outward, literal aspect of the law he calls "a hidden idolatry (*shirk khafi*)," just because in itself it is inextricably bound up with duality and opposition. As long as one is preoccupied with the details of the law, one will be unable to focus exclusively on God. Here Hallaj hovers on the threshold of divine grace without expectation or despair, in a renunciation of the dualistic attributes of createdness.

The convergence of unknowing and transcendence of duality is shown in the doctrine of the coincidence of opposites in God. Hallaj enunciated this principle clearly in saying, "in none but Him can two (opposite) attributes mingle at once, but He is not thereby in contradiction."[45] One such example has already been quoted, "Knowledge is concealed within ignorance." Now it is applied to *iman* and *kufr*: "Infidelity and faith differ in name, but in reality there is no difference between them."[46] This *coincidentia oppositorum* is a transcendence of duality that only takes place on the level of the divine Essence in itself, the *haqiqah* or transcendent reality.

When transcendence of duality is considered as the process of transcending, it applies to the level of creation, and implies a radical rejection of any hidden idolatry; this is a necessary implication of the concept of *tawhid*, literally "making one." Junayd's definition of *tawhid* thus applies to both the state and the process of transcendence: "*Tawhid* is the isolation of the eternal from the temporal." In addition to meaning the isolation of the divine reality in itself, "transcending duality" means the rejection of the idolatry and infidelity of considering any temporal and partial creature as self-sufficient. When Shibli was asked to explain *tawhid*, he said, "He who answers a question about *tawhid* is a heretic, he who knows *tawhid* is a polytheist, he who does not know it is an infidel, he who points to it is an idol worshipper, and he who asks about it is ignorant."[47] Every one of Shibli's phrases denounces the attempt to confine the eternal in temporal relations.

The negative aspect of *tawhid* may be called *takfir*, i.e., "calling something *kufr*," "accusing of infidelity." *Takfir* as practised by Sufis is quite different from the anathemas hurled at each other by rival theologians; spiritual *takfir* is a process of purification that aims at the elimination of duality and hidden idolatry in oneself. It was in this sense that Shibli said, "Sufism is idolatry, since it is the safeguarding of the heart from the vision of that which is other (than God), and there is no other."[48] All such denunciations can be considered as spiritual *takfir*. A fine example of this kind of *takfir* is the lofty credal statement of Hallaj:

> He who thinks that the divine mixes with the human, or the human mixes with the divine, is unfaithful *(fa-qad kafara)*. For God has isolated Himself in His Essence and His Attributes from the essences and attributes of creatures. He does not resemble them in any respect, nor do they resemble Him in anything. How could there be any resemblance between the eternal *(al-qadim)* and the temporal *(al-muhdath)*? He who claims that the Creator is in a place or on a place or is connected to a place, or can be conceived of in the mind or imagined in thought, or is included under attribute and quality, is idolatrous *(fa-qad ashraka)*.[49]

The reliance of this *takfir* on Junayd's *tawhid* is striking. Perhaps the most remarkable *takfir* made by Hallaj is the anecdote told by his friend Ibn Fatik, who came to visit while Hallaj was reciting the Qur'an at full length. When Hallaj had finished, he turned to Ibn Fatik, laughing, and said, "Don't you see that I pray to try to please Him? But he who thinks that he has pleased Him has put a price on His pleasure." Then he laughed again and recited these verses:

> When a youth's ardent love reaches perfection,
>   and ecstasy makes him to forego union,
> Then he attests in truth what love attests to him —
>   the prayer of lovers is just infidelity.[50]

Absorption in ritual prayer is attachment to intermediaries that obscure the realities of the spirit; Hallaj here blames himself for placing too much importance on the effect of prayer, as the youth in the poem became too involved in the thought of his own love—all deviation from the way to the Beloved is infidelity.

Another important aspect of Hallaj's use of "infidelity" and "faith" is his desire to be blamed as an infidel and killed as a martyr. His longing for martyrdom is presented in a series of texts so striking and so dramatic that I propose to translate them in full, because of their intrinsic interest. Here is another episode narrated by Ibn Fatik, in which Hallaj shows the earnestness of his desire for self-sacrifice.

> One day I called on Hallaj at a house belonging to him at a moment when he was distracted. I saw him standing on his head, saying, "You who make me near in my mind by Your Presence, and who set me at a distance by Your absence as far as is eternity from time—You manifest Yourself to me so that I think of You as the All, and You withdraw Yourself from

me so that I deny Your existence. But Your Absence does not continue, Your Presence does not suffice, war with You does not succeed, and peace with You is not secure." And when he sensed that I was there, he sat upright and said, "Come in, don't be afraid!" So I came in and sat before him, and his eyes were like two burning flames. Then he said, "My son, some people testify against my infidelity (*kufr*) and some of them testify to my saintliness (*wilayah*). And those who testify against my infidelity are dearer to me and to God than those who affirm my saintliness." Then I said, "Master, why is that?" he said, "Those who testify to my saintliness do so from their good opinion of me, while those who testify against my infidelity do so from zealous defense of their religion (*ta'assuban li-dinihim*), and he who zealously defends his religion is dearer to God than him who has a good opinion of anyone." Then he said, "Ibrahim, what will you do when you see me crucified and killed and burnt? For that will be the happiest day of all the days of my life!"[51]

In this passage, there is a delineation of the decisive effects of God's absence and presence on human hearts, just as in the letter on "the reality of infidelity." In this case, Hallaj is making it clear to Ibn Fatik that he wants to be labelled an infidel and die.

In another extraordinary episode, which took place at the tomb of the great jurist Ibn Hanbal, Hallaj again expressed this desire, but in a moment of intense personal prayer, after which he cautioned an eavesdropper not to mention the incident. Here is the account as transmitted by the prominent judge Ibn al-Haddad al-Misri:

I went out one moonlit night to the tomb of Ahmad ibn Hanbal (God have mercy on him!), and I saw there from far off a man who was standing, facing in the direction of prayer. I got closer to him without him knowing, and it was al-Husayn ibn Mansur, who was weeping and saying, "You who made me drunk with Your love, and who astounded me on the plains of Your nearness, You are the One isolated in eternity, the One who alone is established on the throne of truth. Your support is through justice, not through levelling; Your distance is from isolation, not from separation; Your presence is through knowledge, not by transit; and Your absence is from veiling, not from departure. There is nothing above You to overshadow You, nothing below You to lessen You, nothing behind You to overtake You, nothing beyond You to comprehend You. I beseech You, by this hallowed dust and these sought degrees, that You do not reject me except after ravishing me from myself, and that You do not make me see my soul again after veiling it from me; and multiply my enemies in Your land, and those intent on killing me." But when he sensed me, he turned and laughed in my face, and came back and said to me, "Abu al-Hasan, this state in which I find myself is the first stage of aspirants." In amazement I said, "Master! If this is the first stage of aspirants, what is the stage of him who is beyond it?" He replied, "I lied! This is the first stage of the submitters to God, nay, I lied again! This is the first stage of the infidels." Then he

cried out three times and fell, and blood streamed from his throat. And he
motioned with his hand that I should go, so I went and left him. When I
saw him the next morning at the Mansur mosque, he took my hand and led
me to a corner, and said, "By God! You must not tell anyone what you saw
me do yesterday!"[52]

Once again the fervent prayer begs the omnipotent God to bring about
the lover's doom. In this orison, Hallaj also calls upon God to annihilate
his limited selfhood and not allow it to exist again. The quest for ravishment of self, which is one of the main characteristics of *shath*, is here
linked with the desire for martyrdom. Hallaj's final words to the
eavesdropper, Abu al-Hasan, show by their spontaneity the profundity
of the experience that led Hallaj to call himself an infidel. Full of the
feeling of dust and ashes, he calls himself the lowest of the *muslimun*,
then the lowest of the *kafirun*.

Hallaj's desire for martyrdom is further expressed in another
episode, which contains the famous poem on ravishment of selfhood
discussed in the section on selfhood in part I, above.

I saw al-Hallaj enter into the Mansur mosque and say, "People, listen to
one word from me!" Many people gathered around him, some being his
supporters and some his detractors. He said, "Know that God most high
has made my blood licit for you; so kill me!" Some of the people wept.
Then I stepped out from the crowd and said, "Master! How shall we kill a
man who prays and fasts and recites the Qur'an?" He replied, "Master, the
reason for which blood should be spared is beyond prayer, fasting and
reciting the Qur'an; so kill me! You will have your reward, and I will be
happy. You will be fighters for the faith, and I will be a martyr." Then the
crowd wept, and they followed him to his house when he left. I said,
"Master, what does this mean?" He said, "There is no duty in the world
more important for Muslims than killing me." Then I asked, "Of what sort
is the path to God?" He replied, "The path to God lies between 'two,' but
'there is no one else with Me.'" Then I said, "Explain!" He answered, "He
who does not understand our allusions will not be guided by our expressions," and he recited,

"Is it you or I? . . .
    so take away by Your grace,
    my 'I am' from in between."

Then I said, "Will you comment on these verses?" He answered, "Their
meaning is not consigned to anyone except the Messenger of God, by actual
experience, and me, in emulation of him."[53]

Here Hallaj has begun to reveal publicly his desire for martyrdom and
for ravishment of his selfhood, but he is still enigmatically refusing to
reveal his purpose in so doing. Is it only because of his private unease

that he formed this purpose, in a pathological urge to self-destruction? What is the "reward" that he hinted at, which will accrue to the Muslim community if he is killed as an infidel? Will his death accomplish the ravishment for which he longs?

Louis Massignon, in an astonishing and brilliant reconstruction, has presented a compelling interpretation of Hallaj's desire for martyrdom as a blood-sacrifice designed to bring about a vicarious atonement on behalf of all Muslims. Standing with the pilgrims on Mount `Arafat, on his last pilgrimage in the apocalyptic year 290/903, "Hallaj, like the saints who preceded him, must express the victimal desire to become absolutely poor, transparent, annihilated, that God expose him under the appearance of weakness (`ajz), of death, of condemnation, of guilt, signifying thereby the approach of His Hour, that of the Judgment."[54] In this view, Hallaj sought to make himself totally empty, lost in the bewilderment of unknowing, and hence to be rejected by all: "Guide of the bewildered, increase me in bewilderment; if I am infidel, increase me in infidelity!"[55] What was Hallaj trying to accomplish here, at the high point of the *hajj*, on the ninth of Dhu al-Hijjah, when Muslims address God in penitential prayer? In one verse, he explains,

> You who blame my longing for Him, how long can you blame? If you knew what I meant, you would not blame me. The people have their pilgrimage, but I have a pilgrimage to my Love. They lead animals to slaughter, but I lead my own heart's blood. There are some who circle the Ka`bah without the use of limbs; they circled God, and He made them free of the sanctuary.[56]

In his spiritualization of the *hajj*, which ultimately cost him his life, Hallaj evidently saw himself as a sacrificial victim, the replacement for the sheep and the goats that were to be slaughtered the following day on `Id al-Adha. Whether Massignon can be followed completely in his view of Hallaj's sacrifice is open to debate; some have felt that Massignon read Christian doctrines of atonement into the "passion" of Hallaj. Of course, Hallaj did say, "My death will be in the religion of the cross," and he told his surprised interlocutor, "you should kill this accursed one," pointing to himself.[57] There is no question of "Christianizing" in Hallaj, however; if he used the language of "Christianity," it was in order to shock his listeners.[58] Hallaj's whole effort to get himself condemned as a *kafir* is summed up in this verse: "I became infidel to God's religion, and infidelity is my duty, because it is detestable to Muslims."[59] We may take a phrase from another branch of Sufism to describe this particular motive in Hallaj: it is *malamah*, "self-blame," a practice designed to draw the censure of the community by outwardly disgraceful behavior, while inwardly and secretly performing all religious duties with the utmost sincerity and devotion. While Hallaj was not part of the *Malamati*

Sufi group that originated in Nishapur in the third/ninth century,this term aptly characterizes his wish to be considered an infidel. His desire for martyrdom, to suffer under the law, takes *malamah* to its extreme. It is not accidental that Hallaj has been called *Sultan al-Malamatiyin*, "King of the Self-blamers."[60]

Hallaj's self-blame in terms of infidelity was not merely antinomian, however. As one who invoked the piety of people like Ahmad ibn Hanbal and Hasan al-Basri, Hallaj sought to invest the *shari`ah* with the utmost meaning, and he consciously sought out and practised the most difficult devotions recommended by each school. This is how he explained it to one of his attendants:

Abu Ishaq Ibrahim ibn `Abd al-Karim al-Hulwani said: I attended upon al-Hallaj for ten years, and I was one of the people closest to him. And from all that I heard from people who slandered him, and who said that he was a heretic, I began to have doubts in myself, and so I put him to the test. One day I said to him, "Master, I want to learn something of the esoteric teaching." He replied, "The false esoteric or the true esoteric?" As I stopped to reflect, he said, "Indeed, the exterior aspect of the esoteric Truth is the law (*al-shari`ah*), and he who fully realizes the exterior of the law will have its interior aspect revealed to him, and this interior aspect is the knowledge of God. But the false esoteric has an interior more hateful than its exterior, and its exterior is more repugnant than its interior, so have nothing to do with it. My son, I shall mention something to you from my experience of the exterior of the law. I have not adopted the teaching of any of the religious leaders; I have only taken from every sect the hardest and most difficult part of it, and I now follow that. I have performed no obligatory prayer without washing myself first and performing ablution. Now I am seventy years old, and in fifty years I have performed the prayers of two thousand years, and every prayer is the fulfillment (*qada`*) of a previous one."[61]

Hallaj's servant evidently had heard the gossip that accused Hallaj of being an agent of the Qarmati insurgents, who were feared and hated as enemies of the caliphate and opponents of the externalist legalism of the Sunni majority. al-Hulwani's question was an attempt to see if Hallaj was really an esoteric (*batini*), a follower of the Isma`ili heretics. This suspicion was thoroughly dispelled by Hallaj's stern and uncompromising reply. Hallaj's insistence on the law is in fact a necessary preliminary to his demand for martyrdom, as shown by his praise of his attackers who "zealously defend their religion."

Nonetheless, as we have seen, there is a strand in the thought of Hallaj that redirects attention away from ritual to the sole object and goal of that ritual. He states the principle of "the eclipse of intermediaries" here: "He who considers actions is veiled from the Object of action, and he who considers the Object of action is veiled from the vision of the actions."[62] In a letter to one of his disciples, Hallaj put it in greater detail thus:

> Know that man remains standing on the carpet of the *shari`ah* as long as he has not reached the outposts of *tawhid*. But when he attains it, the *shari`ah* is eclipsed from his vision, and he occupies himself with the glimmerings that dawn from the mine of sincerity. And when the glimmerings come upon him continuously, and the dawnings pursue him uninterruptedly, affirmation of unity (*tawhid*) becomes a dualistic heresy (*zandaqah*) for him, and the sacred law a folly. Then he remains without identity or trace. If he observes the law, he observes it only in form, and if he utters the affirmation of divine unity, he only utters it by force and compulsion.[63]

Familiar themes are alluded to here. Moving from the safe enclosures of the *shari`ah* to the desert wilderness of true *tawhid* is an entry into unknowing and astonishment. With the onset of the luminous experiences of reality, the *shari`ah* is cast in to the shade (not abolished). At this point, spiritual *takfir* condemns the outward affirmation of the divine unity and the outward obedience to the letter of the law as wholly inadequate, as "heresy" and "folly." The one who has reached this point may perform the outward requirements to the letter, but without attachment. It is this rejection of the ultimate importance of the external religious practices that has always alarmed the upholders of tradition, who see in it an encouragement to neglect basic religious duties. But again, Hallaj was not insensitive to this problem, and he insisted on full application of legal discrimination on the social level; anyone who follows the path taken by Hallaj must himself be prepared to accept the legal consequences. "He who distinguishes between infidelity and faith has committed infidelity, but he who does not distinguish between the infidel and the faithful has committed infidelity."[64] In other words, spiritual *takfir* is to be applied against anyone who tries to distingush between the opposites that are unified in the divine *haqiqah*, but legal *takfir* must be levelled against anyone who fails to distinguish between obedience and rebellion on the level of the *shari`ah*. Fine talk about mysticism is no excuse for neglecting to distinguish good from evil.

This, at least, is the structure of the phenomenon of Hallajian infidelity: self-annihilation through unknowing, realization of the *coincidentia oppositorum* in God, self-blame and desire for martyrdom, and fulfillment of the law (though it be ambivalent). As Kraus and Massignon put it, in the path of the elect, "deification is not realized except under the appearance of a denial of the law (*kufr, zandaqah*), an anathema incurred by love, a momentary ravishment of the intellect."[65] The precise degree to which this remarkable ideal was realized in action cannot be known. After the prayer at `Arafat, Hallaj spent some years in hiding from the police, under a false name, and at the trial that sentenced him to death, he protested his innocence vehemently. In the great prayer the night before the execution, he seemed to give way to despair, as he murmured over and over, "a ruse, a ruse (*makr, makr*)," but at last he arose, shouting, "Truth, truth (*haqq, haqq*)!" After reaching the height of the reality of infidelity, he said that same night, ". . . and I have hope in You, for I am faithful. . . ."[66]

C.

`Ayn al-Qudat Hamadani

Abu al-Ma`ali `Abd Allah ibn Muhammad al-Miyanji al-Hamadani (d. 525/1131), better known as `Ayn al-Qudat, was one of the most brilliant figures of early Sufism. Well-trained in Arabic literary culture, religious sciences, theology, and philosophy, he turned at the age of twenty-one to the encyclopedic religious treatise of Abu Hamid al-Ghazali, *Ihya' `Ulum al-Din*, which occupied him completely for four years. `Ayn al-Qudat then had the good fortune to spend twenty days in seclusion with Abu Hamid's younger brother Ahmad, a pivotal figure in early Sufi lineages. Those days were the most significant of his life, and confirmed his predilection for Sufism. His works include the Arabic metaphysical treatise *Zubdat al-Haqa'iq*, a large collection of Persian letters written to his disciples, and the defense he wrote in prison just before his death. His various Persian writings, originally addressed to his close disciples, attained a vast popularity because of their direct and powerful style. Of him Jami remarked that "few others have had the power he showed of revealing realities and explaining subtleties."[67] The events that led to his execution for heresy at the untimely age of thirty-three will be discussed in part III.

Here we shall not attempt an analysis of his entire teaching on faith and infidelity; instead, in order to provide the reader with a typical example of the Hallajian interpretation of faith and infidelity in sixth/twelfth century Sufism, we shall consider two long passages from his classic Persian treatise on mysticism, the *Tamhidat*. Our remarks will be in the nature of a running commentary on these texts. `Ayn al-Qudat's thoughts on this subject are not systematic; they are couched in poetic reflections that illuminate these concepts from a variety of angles. In these two passages, `Ayn al-Qudat develops a multi-levelled interpretation of faith and infidelity as experiences based on different visions of the luminous face of God. All this he presents in the imagery of Persian love poetry, seeing the faith-inspiring Muhammad as the cheek and mole of the Beloved's face, and Iblis (Satan) as the black tress of the Beloved and the source of infidelity. The concept of infidelity here takes on an ambiguous character, implying simultaneously both the idolatry of dualistic existence and the systematic transcendence of all limitations.

The first passage to be onsidered is a long digression on faith and infidelity that occurs in the sixth chapter, on love. It is not accidental that true infidelity is mentioned in connection with the perfect love that is the union of the witness and the witnessed. He defends this as the authentic teaching of the mystics and rejects charges of "incarnationism (hulul)." The essence of this unitive love is total forgetfulness of self in the divine beloved.

> This is not incarnation; it is the perfection of union and oneness. In the sect of the realizers of truth, there is no other teaching. Have you not heard these verses?

> > He whose (whole) life is not that beautiful idol
> > is no striver or devotee in the sect of infidelity.
> > Infidelity means that you yourself
> > become the Beauty; since infidelity
> > is such, no one is the One.[68]

The teaching of infidelity is the separate individual's quest for union with God, yet `Ayn al-Qudat concludes that no one attains this. Perhaps this is because union between two separate beings cannot, strictly speaking, be conceived of. Like the Platonic eros, infidelity is a longing that can never be fulfilled without ceasing to exist. `Ayn al-Qudat elsewhere says that the lover and beloved (the witness and the witnessed) are one in the divine reality, but separate on the level of discursive thought.[69] The use of the term "infidelity" to describe this longing for perfect union with God is jarring, but deliberate.

`Ayn al-Qudat here embarks on a critique of religion, not in the manner of an enlightenment critique that denies the possibility of religious meaning, but in a critique that sees externalization of the religious life as a fatal error. He calls externalized religion "tradition-worship (`adat-parasti)," which is no better than idolatry. Building on Hallaj's saying, "I am in the sect (madhhab) of my Lord," `Ayn al-Qudat says that the lovers of God have nothing to do with the sect or teaching of Abu Hanifah or al-Shafi`i or any other jurist, for "they are in the sect of love (madhhab-i `ishq) and the sect of God . . . When they see God, the meeting with God is their religion (*din*) and sect (*madhhab*). When they see Muhammad, the meeting with Muhammad is their faith, and when they see Iblis (Satan), seeing that station is for them infidelity." `Ayn al-Qudat's concept of the religious life is based on direct experience and vision, not creed or ritual.

It may be noted in passing that just as the standard religious schools are subject to harsh criticism in these terms, the historical non-Muslim traditions come in for criticism as well. Why should this be the case? This would seem to be incongruous, since elsewhere `Ayn al-Qudat comes close to suggesting that all religions are simply different names for the same reality.[70] The reason for his critique of non-Islamic religions is that these other religions are no closer to true infidelity than is externalist Islam, even though they are usually thought of as "infidel." Furthermore, by this time Sufi poetry had become saturated with the blameworthy imagery of winedrinking, idolatry, Christianity, and Zoroastrianism. The Sufis used the profane themes developed by the Arabic poets of the `Abbasi period, who had frequently extolled the Christian monasteries where they obtained wine normally forbidden to Muslims. The extra-Islamic religions were symbolic, to the Sufis, of the internal spiritual life invoked by the blameworthy name of infidelity.[71] Despite the positive value of these symbols, `Ayn al-Qudat wishes to point out that Magians, Christians, and idolaters are not, after all, "real" infidels. Although they are outside the limits of the Islamic community, their infidelity only exists on the literal level of rejecting the revelation given through Muhammad. They may be symbolic of the self-blame that Hallaj and others courted, but `Ayn al-Qudat makes it clear that only metaphorically do they figure as spiritual guides (e.g., the Magian master, or the Christian boy, who dispense the wine of inspiration in innumerable Persian poems). In reality these figures receive only a reflected lustre from the truly transcendent mystical infidelity.

> O infidelity! The Magians have a certain glory
>   from you, and from your traceless beauty
>   they have a certain perfection.
> But they are not infidels; infidelity is a far
>   path. Alas! how can they imagine what
>   infidelity is?[72]

To learn what true infidelity is, we shall have to move beyond such poetic commonplaces.

`Ayn al-Qudat's stress on visionary experience as the source of faith and infidelity allows him to elaborate a theory of theophany expressed wholly through images of the face of the divine Beloved. It is summarized in these verses:

> Our religion is the face, and the beauty, and
>   the royal countenance; our infidelity is that
>   dark tress and darkling brow.
> Our intellect is maddened by the beauty of His
>   cheek and mole, and from the wine of His love,
>   both worlds have become taverns.
> Our spirit is that idol itself, our heart the idol
>   temple; whoever's religion is not this is no
>   friend of ours.[73]

This is a poetic version of the philosophical concept of "the face of God (*wajh allah*)," which `Ayn al-Qudat developed in his Arabic philosophical treatise *Zubdat al-Haqa'iq*. As Izutsu explains, "All things are sustained in existence by being directly exposed to the existence-providing light which emanates from God's face."[74] There is a strong resemblance between the text just quoted and Hallaj's dialectic of divine absence and presence; both emphasize that one's religious state depends completely on the degree of theophany that has been experienced, on the extent to which God has manifested Himself in the soul. Yet where Hallaj focussed on the mysterious appearance and disappearance of the divine Essence itself, `Ayn al-Qudat spoke of a dualistic manifestation of opposing divine Attributes, which the Islamic tradition typically identified as grace (*lutf*) and wrath (*qahr*). His awareness of divine transcendence is perhaps stronger, or more formalized, than Hallaj's, since he finds it necessary to describe these Attributes in poetic form as the vehicles of manifestation, as intermediaries between the soul and God.

　　`Ayn al-Qudat describes for his reader the luminous appearance of the face of God, whose different features, personified as Muhammad and Iblis, exert an overwhelming influence over all who experience their theophanies. "What do you know, my dear, of the effect of the beloved's cheek and mole and tress on the lover? You won't know until you get there!" Then he makes explicit the identification of the positive aspect of God's countenance: "The cheek and the mole of the Beloved are nothing but the light of Muhammad the Messenger of God. . . . the light of Ahmad (Muhammad) became the cheek and mole on the beauty of the light of the One (*ahad*)." Here Muhammad is seen as part of the self-manifestation of God as light, following the traditional Sufi concept of Muhammad as the primordial light.[75] `Ayn al-Qudat here has also alluded to the celebrated *hadith qudsi* in which God states, "I am Ahmad without the 'M.'" Ahmad is another name for Muhammad, and to remove the "M" from Ahmad gives *ahad*, "the One." Thus the letter "M" is the human nature that is the only thing standing between God and Muhammad.[76] To have a vision of Muhammad is undoubtedly a lofty experience, but it is still "the cheek and mole," that is, the human nature of the prophet, which both reveals and conceals the divine nature of God.

> If, my dear, you arrive at this station, sell your soul to be an infidel; what other benefit is there in seeing the Beloved's cheek and mole, besides infidelity and the infidel's belt? Wait until you arrive and see! Then you will forgive this helpless one for saying these words. Have you never seen an infidel Muslim? From the beauty and fairness of Muhammad the Messenger of God, all of the faithful became infidel, and none knew it! Until you find these infidelities, you will not reach the faith of idol-worship, and when you reach the extreme end of faith and see idol-worship, then "there is no god but God, Muhammad is His Messenger" has been written in the royal court, and your faith has become perfect.[77]

The vision of the light of Muhammad is still within the realm of duality, and is not the unmediated experience of God. Therefore even this exalted vision is a form of infidelity, but an ambiguous one, since recognition of the Prophet is part of the confession of faith.

The attribute opposite to the light of Muhammad is the light of Iblis; the first is symbolized by the cheek and the mole, while the second is symbolized by the tress and eyebrow, which in a particularly bold metaphor is called "the black light."

> You have heard of the cheek and mole of this Beauty, but do you know what this Beauty's tress and eye and eyebrow are? Alas, doubtless they have not not shown you the black light, high above the canopy! That is the light of Iblis, which they symbolize by that tress of this Beauty, and which, in relation to the divine light, they call darkness; but in any other (comparison), it is light. Alas, doubtless Abu al-Hasan Busti has never said to you, and you have never heard from him, these verses:
>
> We saw the hidden world, and the people
>   of both spheres,and we easily passed
>   beyond accident and reproach.
> Know that the black light is higher than the
>   unpointed word; even this we passed by.
>   Neither this (world) nor the
>   other remained.[78]

The black light is higher than the word with no points, *la* ("no"), the negation that announces the nothingness of all save God: *la ilaha illa allah*, there is no god but God. The imagery of the black tress and eyebrow expresses this negative power, and Iblis (Satan) is the one who wields it. `Ayn al-Qudat now reveals Iblis as an honoured servant of God; infidelity is his robe of honour, and he works through the power of God:

Do you know what the black light is? "And he was of the infidels" (Qur. 2.34) has become his robe of honour. He drew the sword of "Truly will I lead them all astray by Thy power" (Qur. 38.82). Unwillingly he has committed his excesses in the darknesses (called) "in the darknesses of land and sea" (Qur. 6.97). He has become the watchman of Power. He has become the doorkeeper of the majesty of "I seek refuge from the accursed Satan." Alas, who has it within his power to see the Beloved, with such a cheek and mole and tress and brow, and not say, like Husayn, "I am the Truth"? . . .
He whose life is not that heart and heart's thief,
    and is not that mole and cheek, that sugar lip —
When tress and brow ravage his heart and soul,
    he'll be no idolater, or even infidel, in these
    two worlds.
You don't believe in going from infidelity to infidelity,
    because none is worthy of Him, save Him.[79]

Here `Ayn al-Qudat is developing a synthesis of many symbolic expressions: the tress, the black light, Iblis as the instrument of divine negation. The reference to Hallaj is also appropriate; it was Hallaj who seemingly rehabilitated Iblis in the *Kitab al-Tawasin*, where Iblis claims to be the only real lover of God. Despite the dualistic tendencies of this passage, which may have old roots in Zoroastrian and extremist Shi`i views, it is overwhelmingly oriented toward a loving union with God.[80] Infidelity occurs as a major component of the process of negation that is entrusted to Iblis, and it also figures as a part of every theophany, whether of the divine light through Muhammad or the black light through Iblis. There is also a curious ambiguity about this infidelity, since, on the one hand, it represents an inspiration through the divine Attributes, but on the other hand, it still implies the separate, and hence infidel, existence of the soul witnessing the theophany.

`Ayn al-Qudat's other long passage on this subject is in the ninth chapter of the *Tamhidat*, appropriately entitled "The Elucidation of the Reality of Faith and Infidelity." Here he begins by amplifying on the critique of religion already discussed. Most of those called "the faithful" or "the believers," he tells us, are in reality idolaters. Then in an analogy with the bonds and shackles with which madmen were laden in medieval Iran, `Ayn al-Qudat says, "the master of the religious law knows, by the light of prophecy, that madmen must be put in chains; the religious law has been made the chain" of these maddened wayfarers of reality. "Those burned up by love are melancholy, and melancholy is related to madness, and madness is on the road to infidelity . . ."

In the legal sect, infidelity is infamous
    because madness is from melancholy love.

Everyone who sees by the infidelity of love
    becomes single by the beautiful idol's
    power.[81]

As one might suspect, having a taste for infidelity is a matter of temperament or innate disposition. Still, despite his critique of the limitations of
the religious law, `Ayn al-Qudat enthusiastically surrenders his melan-
choly temperament, prone to love, madness, and infidelity, to its destined
punishment under the law. This is quite in the spirit of Hallaj's insistence
on the law's fulfillment. Happy resignation to the chains of the law is
perhaps inevitable, once one realizes that all separative existence is tinged
by *kufr* and *shirk*. Then, whether sober from the vision of religion or intoxicated from the vision of infidelity, the sincere seeker will
acknowledge his infidelity by publicly donning the belt worn by infidels
(the Zoroastrian sacred thread, or Christian monk's belt).

> The wayfarers of the divine presence have come to the religious sciences and
> their discrepancy. Some had a vision of religion (*din*), and they became
> aware of themselves and the reality of the matter; they saw that they wore
> an infidel belt (*zunnar*). Then they wanted to have their exterior in confor-
> mity with their interior, so they also tied an infidel belt on externally.[82]

This consciousness of inward idolatry is symbolized by the Zoroastrian
thread or infidel's belt, which in this account is worn by those who rightly
follow the path of religion, who have experienced the positive theophany
of the cheek and mole. These are the sober wayfarers who ruthlessly examine their souls for idolatry.

> Another group became intoxicated, and they also tied on the infidel's belt,
> and began to speak intoxicated words. Some of them were killed and others
> were subjected to the affliction of His jealousy, just as will happen with this
> helpless one. I don't know when it will happen; it is still far off. . .[83]

`Ayn al-Qudat classes himself with the intoxicated wearers of the *zunnar*,
and he knew well that he would suffer the fate decreed by the law for infidels. "Alas, the people do not know the intent of infidelity and the *zunnar*! . . . Their infidelity and *zunnar* are from the path of God."[84] `Ayn
al-Qudat is able to reconcile himself to the infidel's fate, however, since
death of the body merely means fewer obstacles in the path to the Beloved.

Next `Ayn al-Qudat takes up the subject of infidelity in itself, and tells
us that it is time to enumerate its divisions, many of which have been
alluded to already. Infidelity is not just one thing, as is commonly
thought. The sober wayfarers who follow the conditions of the *shari`at*

will one day, if patient, reach their goal, and then they will learn the meaning of wearing the *zunnar*, idol-worship, and fire-worship. The divisions of infidelity can be summarized as follows:

1. Outward infidelity (*kufr-i zahir*). This is the infidelity that the common people know. It consists of rejection (*radd*) or denial of the truth (*takdhib*) of some part of the religious law (*shar*`). Anyone who commits such an action is an external infidel.

2. Infidelity of the lower self (*kufr-i nafs*). Since, as the *hadith* has it, "the *nafs* is the greatest idol," this is the infidelity that worships one's selfish desire as if it were a god. "We are all, ourselves, prisoners of this infidelity," inasmuch as we are all still in the dualistic realm of time and space. In addition, this infidelity includes the egotism of those wayfarers who have reached a stage where they think they have attained the Creator Himself. Every day there are a hundred thousand such who halt in this infidelity. *Kufr-i nafs* is therefore the special province of Iblis, who deludes the wayfarers, for, as Hasan al-Basri said, "if he (Iblis) manifested his light to creation, he would be worshipped as a god." This is in fact of the same order as worshipping one's own ego.

3. Muhammadan infidelity (*kufr-i muhammadi*). As Abu Sa`id said, "Whoever saw his (Muhammad's) beauty at once became an infidel." Those who experience the light of Muhammad (which is to Iblis's light as the sun is to the moon) immediately prostrate themselves in adoration. Is there not a *hadith* in which Muhammad said, "He who has seen me has seen God"? This is a sublime truth, but it is still infidelity and idolatry.

4. Real infidelity (*kufr-i haqiqi*). "If one passes beyond all the other stages, one sees the Lord, and one becomes ashamed. Here, *tawhid* and faith begin."[85]

This four-fold classification of infidelity was very popular among later Sufis, especially in India. As one can see from the second and third divisions of infidelity, infidelity is existentially inescapable, even in the higher ranges of spiritual existence. The solar light of Muhammad and the lunar light of Iblis are the sources of all light in the world. But all worldly existence, including light, is tinged with duality; thus even Muhammad prayed, "I take refuge with You from hidden idolatry." To recognize and admit idolatry and infidelity of this order is extremely difficult. `Ayn al-Qudat illustrates this further with the story of Bayazid's recantation on the day of his death, when he apparently repudiated his most famous ecstatic saying: "God, if I said one day, 'Glory be to Me, how great is My dignity,' then today I am only a Magian infidel. (Now) I cut the *zunnar*, and I say: 'I testify that there is no god but God, and I testify that Muhammad is the Messenger of God.'"[86]

Although infidelity is thus all-pervasive, the process of spiritual
takfir, i.e., the recognition of *kufr* in oneself and the consequent self-
accusation, has an inherent momentum toward transcendence, a longing
for completion analogous to Platonic *eros* or Aristotelian *orexis*.

> Attend to the divine infidelity, my dear. Gaze until you see by the first in-
> fidelity, then travel the path until faith takes you by the hand. Then give
> your life, so that you see the second and third infidelities. Then uproot
> your soul, so that after these you find the path through the fourth infidelity.
> After this you become faithful. . .[87]

Thus the path of infidelity is the path of progressive self-annihilation. By
an ingenious juxtaposition of *hadith*, `Ayn al-Qudat reveals the connec-
tion between *kufr* and the spiritual poverty of *fana' fi allah*, annihilation
in God. He begins by quoting Abraham's renunciation of the worship of
the sun (Qur. 6.79, here seen as equivalent to renunciation of *kufr-i
muhammadi*):

> "I turned my face (to the Creator of the heavens and earth, as a true wor-
> shipper of God, and I am not one of the idolaters)" — God gives His splen-
> dor to you, He casts your selfhood into His selfhood, so that you become
> "all He" (*hamah u*). Then poverty shows itself when poverty becomes
> perfect, for "when poverty becomes perfect it is God." That is, all of you is
> He; what would you say, is this infidelity or not? This is "Poverty is nearly
> infidelity." Here is *tawhid*, and oneness. Perhaps Hallaj spoke of this place
> (when he said,) "I became infidel to God's religion, and infidelity is my duty,
> since it is detestable to Muslims." . . . See this great man; how will he
> ask forgiveness for this? Would that I had the infidelity that is his religion![88]

`Ayn al-Qudat clearly understands the path of infidelity in terms of an-
nihilation of selfhood, a major theme of *shath* (although `Ayn al-Qudat
does not use the term *shath* here). This is another instance of the way in
which the early Sufi tradition (particularly Hallaj) has retained its essential qualities in `Ayn al-Qudat's understanding of infidelity.

In the final pages of the *Tamhidat*, `Ayn al-Qudat introduced a let-
ter on the subject of "real infidelity," supposed to have been written by
the philosopher Ibn Sina (Avicenna, d. 428/1037) to the Iranian Sufi
Abu Sa`id ibn Abi al-Khayr (d. 440/1049). Although the letter is pro-
bably not authentic, it is still a very interesting document attesting the
importance of infidelity as a symbol for the transcendence of limited in-
dividuality. `Ayn al-Qudat describes the letter as follows:

> Shaykh Abu Sa`id wrote to Shaykh Abu `Ali (ibn Sina), "Guide me to the
> proof (of God)," and in his answer he wrote, "(It is) entry into real infideli-
> ty and departure from metaphorical Islam, and that you do not turn your
> face towards (anything) except that which is beyond the three in-

dividualities, so that you become a submitter (*muslim*) and an infidel. For
if you are beyond these, you are neither faithful nor infidel, and if you are
below these, you are a Muslim idolater. If you are ignorant of all this, then
you are worthless, so do not count yourself as a part of the totality of beings." Shaykh Abu Sa`id said in the *Masabih*, "I derived from these words
that which I would have derived from a hundred thousand years of devo-
tions."[89]

The bold phrasing of this letter deliberately recalls Hallaj's letter on "the
reality of infidelity," which is a criticism of the "hidden idolatry" of
legalism. The main thrust of Ibn Sina's letter seems to be the
transcendence of the three "individualities (*shukhus*)," probably meaning
the three "persons" of grammar, and hence, all multiplicity; acceptance
of these distinctions is equivalent to dualistic idolatry. Despite the
vagueness of the terms used in the letter, it became a favorite text for
many later Sufis.

`Ayn al-Qudat's formulation of the mystical theory of infidelity was an
influential synthesis of current Sufi speculation. The basic categories that
he used — the coincidence of opposites in God, self-annihilation, assertion of God's unity and the duality of all else, and the acceptance of
blame and martyrdom — had been developed by Hallaj and others, but
`Ayn al-Qudat interpreted them in original ways. He also drew in threads
from Ibn Sina, Ahmad al-Ghazali, and the Sufis of eastern Iran (it is
likely that Ahmad al-Ghazali's influence on this topic was greater
than we have indicated, but this cannot be ascertained until the corpus of
his writings are edited). The wide circulation of `Ayn al-Qudat's writings
in Iran and India helped to establish the Hallajian *topos* of faith and infidelity as a standard element in Persian poetry. Though his formulation
became in this sense typical, he was criticized by some Sufis, such as the
conservative Indian Sufi Gisu Daraz (d. 822/1422), who concluded his
commentary on the *Tamhidat* by complaining of `Ayn al-Qudat's im-
maturity and frivolity in advocating heretical theories like those of Ibn
`Arabi.[90] Others, such as Mas`ud Bakk, who was executed in Delhi in
790/1387, saw `Ayn al-Qudat as a spiritual guide and model, to be im-
itated both as author and as martyr. In any case, the passages discussed
above were widely read by medieval Sufis.

`Ayn al-Qudat's distinct contribution to this topic was to illuminate
the experiences of unity and duality, of annihilation and subsistence, that
underly the ambiguities of mystical infidelity. To take but one example:
his critique of religious externalism shows that the vision of oneness is in
a sense incompatible with the world's religion.

When the "Day of Religion (*ruz-i din*, Doomsday)" is mentioned (in the
Qur'an), it is not the religion of the world that He means; He speaks of a
religion of the next world, in which religion there is self-effacement (*kam-*

zani). Their religion *(din)* is the religious community *(millat)* of oneness, but in this world, this is (called) infidelity. Yet in the path of the wayfarers and in their religion, what is infidelity and what is faith? The two are one.[91]

The limited earthly religion, by a sort of reciprocity with spiritual *takfir*, cannot help but call the religion of oneness "infidelity." In another instance, `Ayn al-Qudat describes a dialectic of faith and infidelity that is ultimately an alternation between the experiences of annihilation *(fana')* and subsistence *(baqa').* It is precisely the transcendent implication of infidelity in `Ayn al-Qudat's writing that makes his *takfir* into a negative dialectic that spurns every successive approximation to the real union.

Alas, could it be that you were never a lover of God and His chosen one (Muhammad), and that in the midst of this Iblis never whispered his insinuations to you, and that you never heard these verses on his power?

We became helpless in the deception of your tress's tip;
  we became forlorn in the wrath of your wild eyes.
We consumed our hearts because of our nature's impurity;
  now by nature we also consume grief. . . .

Whoever is wounded and half-killed in the world of Iblis is healed in the world of Muhammad, because infidelity is a sign of annihilation *(fana'),* and faith is a sign of subsistence *(baqa').* Subsistence cannot be attained without annihilation. The greater the annihilation in this path, the more perfect the subsistence in this path. These verses explain something of annihilation and subsistence:

If your mole and cheek and eye were infidel,
  this heart and soul of mine were ever pilgrims there.
Make a condition, that if your tress becomes unfair,
  O idol, you will make your lip our judge![92]

One gets a sense here of progression on the path, by negation and affirmation, by *fana'* and *baqa'.* When the theophanic power of the tress (black light, Iblis, wrath) is exerted, one is overwhelmed, but one can take refuge in the theophany of the countenance (Muhammad, grace). Infidelity *(kufr)* is the negative half of the confession of faith, *la ilah,* "There is no God," which is the equivalent of annihilation *(fana').* It is then followed by the positive half, *illa allah,* "but God," which is the equivalent of subsistence *(baqa').* It is perhaps no accident that the word of negation, *la,* as written in Arabic script, can be likened to the twin tresses of the Beloved. So the negative force of the spiritual "accusation of infidelity" is directed both outwardly, against religious externalism, and inwardly, in a dialectic that ascends toward union. In both these emphases `Ayn al-Qudat has considerably refined the original formulations of Hallaj.

`Ayn al-Qudat frequently expressed the "science of opposites" and the *coincidentia oppositorum* through the symbolism of the theophanic countenance of Persian poetry. The dualistic flavor of this imagery is in contrast with the theory of Hallaj, in which the path of unknowing leads to a transcendence of duality in the recognition of the divine unity. Hallaj speaks of the *coincidentia oppositorium* in the Essence, but is not drawn to either of the opposed polarities. `Ayn al-Qudat's illuminism, in contrast, feels a strong magnetic power in these dualities, considered as manifestations of divine attributes. His focus on the divine attributes may be an acknowledgement of the *sifatiyah* or attributist strand of Sufi thought, which recognized only the possibility of attaining union with God's Attributes, and not with the absolute Essence. Yet despite the dualistic tendencies of this symbolism of cheek and tress, `Ayn al-Qudat ultimately appears to seek union with the Beloved in Essence.

> My dear, attend to what the great man said about these two stations: "Infidelity and faith are two stations from beyond the canopy, which are veils between God and the devotee." . . . A man ought to be neither infidel nor *musulman*. He who still exists with infidelity or faith is still within these two veils, but the wayfarer who has reached the goal exists with no veil but "God's Majesty and His Essence."[93]

His contributions show great originality, but `Ayn al-Qudat continues to see himself as following the path of Hallaj in search of union. "So when a maddened lover says that a drop in the ocean calls itself the ocean, he is just like that chivalrous youth who said 'I am the Truth.' He also is to be forgiven. He is a real infidel (*kafir-i haqiqi*)."[94]

D.

Ruzbihan al-Baqli

Ruzbihan's development of the Hallajian *topos* of faith and infidelity is a complex one, made difficult by his elliptical style and by his habit of scattering remarks on this subject throughout his various writings. His works were less commonly read than `Ayn al-Qudat's, because of their greater difficulty, but they were influential among learned Sufis. Ruzbihan, probably more than any other, made the mystical understanding of faith and infidelity an integral part of the technical terminology of the spiritual path. His approach is radically experiential; by examining the way in which he links faith and infidelity with different stages of spiritual development, we can hope to achieve an adequate representation of his viewpoint.

Ruzbihan's concept of faith begins with the familiar theological definitions, but advances to the typical Sufi understanding of faith as an initial stage on the path to union with God. From external faith one proceeds to the inner degrees of certainty and vision, then to mystical unknowing, and finally annihilation—all this as a prerequisite to the unveiling of divine subsistence in gnosis. Infidelity enters as the duality present at every stage, which begs to be condemned by spiritual *takfir*, so that infidelity ambiguously can also mean the longing for transcendence. Faith and infidelity are mutually related as opposites deriving from God's qualities of grace and wrath, and thus they are dialectically contained in one another. These metaphysical gymnastics, according to Ruzbihan, will not apply to the "infidelity" of non-Islamic religious traditions, which is not "real infidelity." Ruzbihan also wishes to remove infidelity from the path of self-blame, and this leads him to protest vigorously against the persecutors of the Sufis. All of this results from Ruzbihan's use of "infidelity" to represent the necessarily dualistic relationship between the creature and the creator. Here infidelity has taken on a truly cosmic status, describing even the highest spiritual realization.

Ruzbihan defines "exterior faith" as "external knowledge, or saying, 'There is no god but God,' or prayer with the limbs, or submission, or humility, or peace. Its root is the instinctive faith that is the root of nature (*fitrat*)."[95] This is the faith that every child is born with, which too often becomes merely imitative faith. Faith is externally defined by theological creeds, and is dependent on the scriptural resources of tradition. It is unfortunate that we do not possess Ruzbihan's *Kitab al-Haqa'iq fi al-`Aqa'id* ("The Book of the Realities in the Articles of Faith"), in which, according to his grandson, he describes

> the belief of the Sunnis (*mu`taqad ahl al-sunnah*) and the orthodox teaching (*madhhab al-salaf*), after which he introduces the reality of the belief of the gnostics (*haqiqat i`tiqad al-`arifin*) in their gnosis, through God, by way of existentiation (*sabil al-ijad*)."[96]

This work might have provided a detailed discussion of the relation between credal articles and the realities of Sufi experience. As it is, we have already seen that Ruzbihan stresses the qualitative difference between faith and gnosis when it is a question of understanding the symbolic statements (*mutashabihat*) of Qur'an and *hadith*. There is an esoteric knowledge that enables the elite to understand the true inner meaning; those who lack this knowledge approach the divine word by faith. Since, according to Ruzbihan, the inspiration of the saints through *shathiyat* is a continuation of the divine revelation, it is also necessary for the faithful to have faith in the saints, just as in the Qur'an and the Prophet. "For the pious man of faith it is necessary that he have faith in the symbolism of the Book and the *sunnah* and the court of the saints, so that he may find release from denial and the punishment of hellfire."[97] This is the mediate position of faith, which is the attitude of a finite creature towards the transcendent reality.

When defining the inner meaning (*ma`na*) of faith, Ruzbihan speaks as follows:

> The meaning of faith is the confirmation of the whole (*tasdiq al-kull*) by the vision (*ru'yah*) of the whole, (which is) gazing upon the secrets prior to (receiving) illuminations, acceptance of the outward by certainty (*yaqin*) of the inward, beginning in servitude after the revelation of Lordship, and beholding the hidden by the hidden.[98]

Terms such as "vision" and "certainty" indicate that this inner dimension is indeed the higher range of faith. As Hallaj pointed out, faith is comprised of the intermediaries through which one must pass to attain realities. Ruzbihan also equates faith with a perception through intermediaries, and uses it to justify seeing nature as the medium through which God reveals Himself to the faithful. "In love, the requirement of faith is to make one see the eternal by the intermediaries (*wasa'it*) of existence. Don't you see what 'the joy of the lovers' (i.e., Muhammad) — on whom be peace — asked of the slave girl? He said, 'Where is He (God)?' She pointed to the sky, and he said, 'Free her, for she is faithful,'"[99] Ruzbihan alludes here to a *hadith* report, in which a man who was troubled because he had beaten his heedless slave girl had gone to the Prophet for advice. Muhammad asked to speak to her. In response to his questions about her knowledge of religion, she replied that God is in the sky, and that Muhammad is God's messenger. Deeming this sufficient, Muhammad turned to the man and told him to free her from slavery, since she was one of the faithful.[100] This *hadith*, which legitimizes the faith of untutored and simple believers in spite of any crude misconceptions that they may have, allows Ruzbihan to underscore God's universal theophany in nature. The girl was right, because God *does* manifest Himself in the sky; approaching God through this theophany is a matter of faith, seeking the hidden by the manifest.

Yet faith is a transcending movement that is never absolute. Proceeding by the path of unknowing, it hovers on the threshold that only gnosis can cross, after annihilation in unknowing.

How does the temporal resemble the eternal? The faith of humanity is confirmation of the (divine) promise, establishing Him by the hidden and not by the visible. If they become witnesses to Him, faith will become gnosis. But since they have stood in faith outside the door, from impotence they are in the mansions of unknowings. How does one enter into the astonishment of the impotent? Since impotence is His veil, how shall temporal beings find the eternal by faith?. . . Faith is from Him, to Him. He knows Himself. The saying of (Abu Bakr al-) Siddiq, "the inability to attain comprehension is (true) comprehension," describes the annihilation (*fana'*) of the creature in God.[101]

Faith is a stage in the approach to God, but it must be continually transcended. A deeper faith realizes that God is the source of faith; the creature realizes its utter helplessness and impotence, and in unknowing finds annihilation.

Like `Ayn al-Qudat, Ruzbihan links infidelity with progressive annihilations and unknowings, which are absolutely essential for the advent of subsistence, real knowledge, and selfhood. To identify this transcending infidelity by its proper motive force, Ruzbihan calls it the "infidel of love" and the "infidel heart."

If every day one does not become an infidel of love a thousand times, one will never become a unitarian in *tawhid*. If one looks into the soul with the garb of unknowing, one will see the soul vanishing on the earth of annihilation. One will not find *tawhid* from it, nor faith. One then looks into the soul with the quality of gnosis, and sees the soul in the eternity of eternities, full of the qualities of unity.[102]

The constant restlessness of this transcending infidelity is again identified with the power of love:

This infidel heart is not satiated with seeking the unknown beauty . . . I have lost my heart, for I am in the scent of that rose that grows not in clay; pain does not enter into me, nor does my heart's seeking submit to this nothingness. Who could think that my infidel heart has had enough of that eye, and those two brows, of my Beloved?[103]

This is a truly remarkable conclusion, that the motive power of the universal ascription of infidelity is love. *Takfir* is the mirror image of *tawhid*. The way from the temporal to the eternal is concentraton the one (*tawhid*) and rejection of the many (*takfir*). This two-fold movement of transcendence, which Ruzbihan calls love, could also be compared to the two-fold movement of the soul in Platonic *katharsis*, "purification." This consists, on the one hand, of attaining "likeness to God, as far as possible," and on the other, of "separating the soul from the body, as far as possible." Abdel-Kader has pointed to the Plotinian affinities of the thought of Junayd. Consider the last words of Hallaj: "It is enough for the ecstatic that One be isolated in Himself." May we not see here also a remarkable affinity with Plotinus, whose serene "flight of the alone to the Alone" is here achieved by the passion of a condemned lover? Mystical infidelity is a powerful symbol, which differs from more familiar terms in that it conceals the longing for transcendence behind a mask of blame.

Yet the divine unity is absolute, and admits of no compromise. If those who seek the divine unity come to rest in an inferior state, this is idolatry, to be attacked with spiritual *takfir*. Again and again Ruzbihan repeats this message: "Stopping (in one place) in eternity is infidelity"; "when the ship is sunk in the sea, grasp nothing save seawater, for to seek anything save ourself in ourself is infidelity."[104] Any intermediate state on the path can turn into a trap, and no one is completely secure from the possibility of self-delusion. "In his intoxication he lays claim to the I-ness that is the vain creature's attribute; thus he is veiled from the One-who-is-found (*al-mawjud*) by his own finding (*wajd*)."[105] As indicated by the verse, "Whoso rejects (*kafara*) faith, his deed is in vain" (Qur. 5.5), so the previous "deeds of gnosis (*a`mal al-ma`rifah*)" are nullified for the mystic who has rejected divine lordship by imagining himself to be the divine self. This delusion contradicts "the isolation of the eternal from the temporal."[106]

In speaking of faith and infidelity as opposites, Ruzbihan recognizes that they are unified in their source, in this recalling `Ayn al-Qudat's dualistic conception of the opposed Attributes of grace and wrath.

> Next to His glory, what difference is there between the faithful and the infidel? No faithful one adds to His kingdom, and no infidel detracts from His kingdom. When infidelity and faith exist in the essence of unity, there is one color in oneness. Its dual coloring is of the nature of relationships (*idafat*). "Whoso gives thanks gives thanks for his own soul, and whoso is ungrateful (*kafara*) — my Lord is surely wealthy, generous" (Qur.27.40). Infidelity and faith are the two purses of wrath and grace. Those who learn wisdom know this much, that those containers are nothing but (God's) command and prohibition; otherwise, how will non-entities take on different hues in eternity?[107]

God's dual aspects of wrath and grace are the means by which oppositions pass from His foreknowledge into actuality. Interestingly, despite his use of this dualistic framework, Ruzbihan, in contrast to `Ayn al-Qudat, avoids reference to the theophanies of cheek and tress; in his view, these have become confused with the reprehensible activity of "gazing at young men".[108] Ultimately, however, in oneness and in reality, the opposition of faith and infidelity does not exist.

Again, while opposites coincide in God without contradiction, in all creatures opposites define and contradict each other. In describing the overwhelming experience of illumination, Hallaj had said that for one who has reached this goal, "the affirmation of unity becomes a (dualistic) heresy."[109] This remark can be understood in two ways. The existence of a separate ego that proclaims God's unity is dualism, but from the point of view of the opposite qualities created by God, the two positions of proclaiming unity and dualistic heresy are simply opposite formulations that cancel each other out. Therefore Ruzbihan says, in a particularly dense passage,

> "Whoso likens God to anything is unfaithful." In this path, my soul, at first all infidelity is faith, and in the end all unity is idolatry.
>
> What is the faithful one's condition? To be an
>   infidel within himself.
> What is the infidel's condition? To desire
>   faith in infidelity.
>
> "Infidelity and religion both are following in
>   Your path,
> crying 'He alone, He has no partner!'"[110]

In this passage, Ruzbihan begins by observing that any description of God is infidelity, for it will always be dualistic. The corollary is that faith and infidelity are opposite finite qualities that contradict and qualify each other. They are inextricably connected in the dialectic of opposites. Finally, in the last verse, Ruzbihan has quoted the Sufi poet Sana'i on the dualistic qualities that God has created to proclaim His unity.[111]

Ruzbihan, like `Ayn al-Qudat, is quite emphatic about separating metaphysical infidelity from the infidelity of non-Muslim communities. This is illustrated in his commentary on a *shath* of Shibli, in which he reveals that true infidelity derives from God's deception of His lovers by means of the Attribute of wrath:

> Shibli said to Husri, "If I compare my baseness with the baseness of Jews and Christians, my baseness is more contemptible than their baseness." . . . Beloved! He (Shibli) saw the infidelity of imitation infidels (*kafiran-i taqlid*). Among their fathers they found no one who was really experienced (*mutahaqqiq*) in their infidelity, because the real experience of infidelity is in the webs (*shabakat*) of the eternal deception (*makr*), and in the vision of the primordial acts of wrath (*qahriyat-i azaliyat*). If it (imitation infidelity) fell into the original reality of infidelity, near the overwhelming unknowing, in the loss of the power of gnosis, when the wrath of the unknowing came into possession of its soul's existence, then the infidelity of all the (ordinary) infidels would find itself, in its unknowing, to be like a mustard seed in a desert.[112]

Again in his typical imagery of getting lost in the desert, Ruzbihan suggests the awful power of the negative expression of God's wrath in the mysterious reality of infidelity. This is so far removed from the "infidelity" of non-Islamic religious groups as to make comparison absurd.

The nature of mundane or non-Islamic infidelity appears a little more clearly in the following passage, which comments on the Qur'anic depiction of the Judgment, when hearts yield up the secrets they have suppressed.

> The people did not recognize the realities of infidelity in this world; if they had recognized it, they would have been affirmers of unity (*muwahhidin*). On the Day of Judgment the reality of infidelity will be manifest to them, but it will do them no good. . . . That station (the reality of the infidelity) is in the (inner) places of their breasts, but they have concealed it by following the outward form of infidelity and rebellious desire—involuntarily, because of their very slight knowledge of it.[113]

The reality of infidelity is a cosmic principle, the consuming divine wrath that eventually makes annihilation possible. We do find, however, that Ruzbihan is relatively indifferent to outward religious distinctions; one of the experiences that he records is the "revelation of the unknown knowledge, in which one sees all of creation in paradise, faithful and infidel and sinner."[114]

On the subject of martyrdom and the fulfillment of the law, Ruzbihan has developed a significantly different position from the previous Sufis in this tradition. Hallaj deliberately sought martyrdom, and he approved of the religious zeal that put him on trial to uphold the shari`ah. `Ayn al-Qudat also recognized the inevitability and necessity of his own approaching doom. With Ruzbihan, however, a note of protest is felt. He also sees the greatness and the inevitability of martyrdom, given the narrow understanding of the common people, but he cries out against the injustice of the persecution of the saints and the prophets. In a section entitled "The Persecution of the Folk," he begins his lengthy diatribe thus:

> These mannerless ones of the day saw one thing and heard another, and in their misguidedness they killed some and burned others to death. Aspirants came to them, and aspirants fled in fear, "Thereby He leads many astray, and thereby He guides many" (Qur. 2.24). The detainees of time were busy reproaching and injuring; they thought it was faith and did not know that it was oppression. Inevitably the trap of affliction fell on those ardent ones, so that they were reduced to dust. These insolent fools from envy sought the blood of the light-spirited ones, and gave those pure ones of God into the hands of the impure mobs, so that those rightly-guided kings were wounded by the multitude. From the beginning to the end, these heavy souls, worshippers of robe and turban, have enviously turned upon the prophets and the saints with a bloody hand.[115]

This lament, which in its vigorous protest recalls the tone of the Shi`i mourning over the martyred imams, introduces a description of sixteen prophets and a total of forty saints, and a detailed analysis of their persecutions, which will be discussed in the next chapter.

The reason why Ruzbihan protests against the persecutions of the saints is, I think, related to his renunciation of the path of blame (malamah). Blaming oneself, says Ruzbihan, is an act of idolatry, since it amounts to ascribing to oneself the responsibility for one's destiny.[116] The extremely subtle form of ego that is set up by courting blame is seen in the figure of Iblis in Hallaj's Kitab al-Tawasin. Ruzbihan comments, "that which Iblis said on top of Sinai was all deception, pretension, and fraud, although it might be said to resemble the state of the self-blamers (malamatiyan)."[117] Many Sufis (e.g., Hujwiri) realized that the conspicuous effrontery so natural to the practitioner of blame could easily become a perverse pre-occupation with one's (ill)-repute. By removing this incentive to blameworthy action, Ruzbihan has removed the main stimulus for the enthusiastic seeking-out of martyrdom. In other respects, Ruzbihan was a firm upholder of the law and the sunnah, and he was the author of several treatises on law, jurisprudence, and creeds, of which only a few fragments survive.[118] He sharply attacks the licentious "traitors to Sufism" who "do not know the *shari`at* of Muhammad," but fill their bellies and satisy their lusts while pretending to piety; according to the *shath* of Abu al-Khayr al-Tinati, most of the inhabitants of hell are pretenders of this type.[119] In Ruzbihan's view of martyrdom and the law, justice and propriety loom larger, now that the bizarre urge to self-blame has been disciplined. This defensive attitude regarding persecutions of the saints confirms, moreover, our earlier remarks about the apologetic aim of his commentary on *shathiyat*.

Ruzbihan summarizes the relationship between faith and infidelity in a complex passage that recapitulates the spiritual path outlined above, from faith to unknowing to gnosis. This takes the form of a commentary on Hallaj's saying on the gnostic (`arif`) who could not become faithful until he became an infidel:

> Faith is infidelity, in oneness (*wahdah*), since it is a sign of the temporal in the eternal. It (faith) is connected with external closeness, but it is far from reality. Infidelity is faith, in the reality of *tawhid*, because it is confession (*iqrar*) by unknowing, and unknowing is the real truth (*haqq-i haqq*) for created existence. . . . He (the gnostic) did not discern except after unknowing; he was not confounded in unknowing except after gnosis. Faith is the infidelity of infidelity, and infidelity is the infidelity of faith. This is the state of the temporal in the eternal, for ever and ever.[120]

This statement is framed in terms of Junayd's definition of *tawhid*, "the assertion of divine unity is isolation of the eternal from the temporal." The significance of this exposition, unsystematic though it may be, is that here faith and infidelity are always part of one another. This is the inevitable condition of the relation between the creature and the creator, and it persists up to the very highest level of existence. A further hint of this is found in one of Ruzbihan al-Baqli's most interesting works, a recently edited treatise called *Mashrab al-Arwah*, "The Spirits' Font,' which is devoted to a description of the one thousand one and stages (*maqamat*) of the spiritual path. Beginning with the pre-creational experiences of disembodied spirits, it pursues an odyssey through all the different classes of wayfaring until it culminates in the experience of divine lordship (*rabbaniyah*) and knowledge of the universal names of God. From the point of view of this study, it is extremely interesting to see that stage number 990, eleven stages short of the goal, is "the falling away of the traces of *kufr* and *islam* from the heart." This is explained as follows:

> When he falls in the sea of the realities of Lordship and he knows the paths of the unknowings of eternity, then by the quality of immersion in the

waves of essential union, the traces of infidelity and submission fall away
from his heart. He sees the onrush of the outflow of the eternal Will in
every atom. He sees the Doer and the deed as one, in reality. Saith the
gnostic: when he tastes the sweetness of union, the trace falls away from
him, and he knows that the two (infidelity and submission) have no effect
on the state of being God's chosen (al-istifa'iyah).[121]

This is clearly felt to be on the verge of union with God, a state of exaltation and near-ultimacy. Still, mystical infidelity, though it may lead to
the very threshold of union, is nonetheless only the attitude of a creature
in duality; infidelity is still a word of blame, as faith (or submission) is a
word of praise, and reality is beyond them both. When the creature looks
back on its own nature and antecedents, it realizes that all it ever was,
and all it ever saw, was nothing but infidelity.

Ruzbihan's insight into the infidel nature of all existence is expressed
in the form of a *shath* that occurs in the midst of his Qur'anic commentary:

"He is not pleased with *kufr* in His servants" (Qur. 39.7) . . . And on this
verse, by way of *shath*: God most high has made infidelity nothing, and has
explained that there is no infidelity for anyone between heaven and earth.
How could there be infidelity when God is not pleased with infidelity in
anyone? In this way, infidelity has departed from our midst, for pleasure is
His eternal Attribute; otherwise infidelity would have abided in eternity.
Infidelity will not ever exist. . . . The explanation of that is that the reality
of infidelity exists in His creation.[122]

Infidelity exists only on the level of the creation, not on the level of the
divine reality (though it is dependent on God as is all else). It does not exist in the absolute reality, but it is the ineradicable taint of all created existence.

Creation, in the beginning of the act of creating, was "approved
(*mustahsan*)" in (the state of) essential union (`ayn-i jam`). To become
other than that, (to fall) from its own place, in reality is infidelity, even
though it is (to enter) into the forms (decreed) by the command (of
God).[123]

Any falling away from that primordial unity acquires otherness,
and hence is infidelity; only complete self-annihilation can conquer it.

Finally we see infidelity as the last and most transparent veil between
the spirit and God. In a small treatise entitled *Sharh al-Hujub wa al-
Astar* ("Commentary on the Veils and Coverings"), Ruzbihan gives a
mystical explanation of the seventy veils between God and man, alluded
to in a well-known *hadith*. In the sixty-ninth of the seventy veils, we find

a curious twist on the whole subject of infidelity, that gives it the last push of self-transcendence.

> Then is the station of unification (*ittihad*), of which the beginning is annihilation (*fana'*), the middle subsistence (*baqa'*), and the end essential union (`*ayn al-jam*`). Annihilation is the veil of subsistence, and subsistence is the veil of annihilation, but essential union is pure unification. The appearance of God (*zuhur al-haqq*) from this (station) is by the quality of essential manifestation (*bi-na`t `ayn al-tajalli*), which, in the experience of *tawhid*, is the infidelity of reality. That is the greatest veil in gnosis, and the sixty-ninth veil.[124]

Here the technical terms for the highest spiritual experiences are all summarized as "the infidelity of reality." How far can the nuances of these terms be pushed? We cannot be too precise, but in these phenomena on the threshold of unity there is a sense of the surge of transcendence, an ever-living power in us that is invoked under the condemned name of infidelity.

Part III

THE SPIRIT AND THE LETTER

The nascent Sufi movement arose in a society of great complexity, in which religious and intellectual currents of widely divergent character mingled together. Aside from the many traditions of the ancient world, a wide variety of schools had developed within the Islamic fold. The political vicissitudes of the `Abbasi caliphate added to the uncertainty of the times, as one or another sect gained official approval. The caliphs al-Ma'mun, al-Mu`tasim, and al-Wathiq (218-234/833-848) established an inquisition in an attempt to enforce universal acceptance of the Mu`tazili dogma that the Qur'an is created and not co-eternal with God. This followed the precedent of the inquisition established fifty years previously against the *zindiq*s, a class which included dualistic ascetics, crypto-Manichaeans, and irreligious poets like Bashshar.[1] Victims of these purges received punishments ranging from banishment and imprisonment to execution. From a very early period, ascetics had been regarded with suspicion by the authorities (e.g., `Amir ibn `Abd al-Qays, banished to Syria by the caliph `Uthman), and in the tense doctrinal and political atmosphere of `Abbasi Baghdad, a number of Sufis were prosecuted by the state for religious reasons. In this chapter, our first task will be to examine the issues raised in the trials of three Sufis, Abu al-Husayn al-Nuri and Hallaj (both in `Abbasi Baghdad) and `Ayn al-Qudat Hamadani (under the Saljuq Turks in Western Iran). Our aim is to establish the precise charges involved, the political influences brought to bear on the cases, and the legality of the trials. The purpose of this investigation is to analyze the tension between the spirit and the letter in those cases of greatest apparent conflict, in which mystics were put on trial and sometimes executed by the state with juristic approval. This will provide more precise grounds than are usually available for questioning the assumption that mysticism is inevitably in deadly conflict with the law. Second, we shall discuss ecstatic sayings (in particular those involving faith and infidelity) from the viewpoint of the main legal interpretations, which typically found expression in the heresiographic terms "incarnationism" and "libertinism." Reflection on the process of dogmatization which these terms involved will permit an examination of the different types of interpretation pursued by the mystics and the jurists. Of special interest here is the chain of legal reasoning that can define ecstatic utterances as an offence punishable by death. Finally, some attention will be given to the Sufi interpretation of the continual persecutions of Sufis in Islamic society, and the rise of an historiography of martyrdom.

A.

Three Sufi Trials

1. ABU AL-HUSAYN AL-NURI

A Sufi of Iranian origin, Nuri (d. 295/907) was one of the most eminent mystics of Baghdad. He transmitted *hadith* from Sari al-Saqati and
knew both Kharraz and Junayd. Sarraj said, "he was one of the ecstatics,
one who makes subtle allusions; much that he says is difficult, and he has
written many poems which he has ladled out, as it were, from a great
ocean."[2] He was also quite fearless, and did not hesitate to put himself
into situations of great danger if his principles demanded it; to conquer
fear of lions, he lived in the jungles along the Tigris where lions roamed.[3]
He was one of those mystics who saw affliction as a sign of closeness to
God, and he seemed to seek it out as a special blessing. His testament to
his disciples, containing ten articles, shows his strict regard for the
shari`ah.[4]

Nuri was not the only one on trial; the charge of *zandaqah* had been
levelled at several of the Baghdadian Sufis. The charge was raised against
them by one Ghulam Khalil (d. 275/888), a strict Hanbali who would not
permit the slightest variation from the usage of the Prophet and the companions. He rejected any attempt at introducing new terminology for
theological discussion, and refused to consider any description of God
that was not given in the Qur'an. Thus when he heard that Nuri had said,
"I love God and He loves me," Ghulam Kahlil was enraged, for he considered those who speak of "desire" and "love" to be no better than
adulterers.[5] He convinced the regent al-Muwaffaq (who ruled for his

brother, the titular caliph al-Mu`tamid) that Nuri and his companions were *zindiq*s and must be killed. Apparently the sentence was decided immediately, without trial, since the executioner was summoned to behead the Sufis. Nuri stepped in front of his friends and asked the executioner to kill him first. When the amazed headsman asked why, Nuri replied that his rule was to give preference (*ithar*) to his friends' lives over his own, even to the extent of these few moments. The headsman stopped the proceedings and al-Muwaffaq cancelled his orders, belatedly summoning a jurist to examine the Sufis. This jurist was the Maliki scholar Isma`il ibn Ishaq al-Jahdami (d. 282/895), qadi of Baghdad.[6] He examined them on matters of ritual purity and prayer, which were answered quite properly, but then Nuri began to speak to him of the devotees "who see by God and hear by God." Hearing this, the qadi wept, and reported back to the caliph that "if these people are *zindiq*s, there is no monotheist on earth!"[7] The Sufis were spared, but Nuri was exiled to Raqqa, several hundred miles up the Euphrates in Syria whence he returned some years later, much deteriorated physically.[8] That is the kernel of the story of Nuri's trial, which took place probably in 266/878.[9]

There are several loose ends to the story, however. Our sources inform us of other conversations said to have taken place with the caliph. According to Sulami, the sultan (*sic*) asked Nuri and the others whence their food came, perhaps wondering if they were vegetarians (Manichaeans) or ate unlawful meat. Nuri answered, "We know no (mediate) causes by which sustenance is provided; we are a people guided (by God."[10] Here Nuri affirms the Sufi practice of trust in God (*tawakkul*). Sarraj adds much more detail. He says that when Nuri was called on to explain his saying, "I love (*a`shuqu*) God and He loves me (*ya`shuquni*)," he replied, "I have heard God—His remembrance is exalted—say, 'He loves them and they love Him (*yuhibbuhum wa yuhibbunahu*, Qur. 5.59),' and passionate love (`*ishq*) is not greater than serene love (*mahabbah*), except that the passionate lover (`*ashiq*) is kept away, while the serene lover (*muhibb*) enjoys his love."[11] In other words, Nuri is using a non-Quranic term to describe his own experience of a stage of love and yearning for God, which does not yet approach to the ideal of closeness that he sees in the Qur'an.[12]

In addition, Sarraj relates another incident that was brought up in the trial (*shahidu `alayhi*). Nuri once heard a *mu'adhdhin* give the call to prayer, and replied, "A curse, and deadly poison!" But when he heard a dog bark, he said, "Here am I! Blessings to You!"[13] In the trial, Nuri explained that he had acted this way because of jealousy. The *mu'adhdhin* was only reciting the name of God for his pittance of a salary, unaware that by his chanting he was laying up treasure in heaven. Nuri's jealousy was then the divine jealousy that does not tolerate adoration of any save God. Nuri had regarded the dog's bark as a suitable invocation of God, since "there is nothing that does not glorify Him with His praise, but you do not understand their glorification" (Qur. 17.46). Unlike the *mu'adhdhin*, God's creatures praise him without hypocrisy and seek no recompense, and hence are more worthy of praise. Sarraj then gives another story which is not confirmed by other sources. "On another occasion, Nuri was brought to the caliph, and they testified against him that he had said, 'Last night I was in my house with God.'" Nuri admitted this, and explained that he was now with God, as were they all, in this world and the next, for "We are closer to him (man) than the jugular vein" (Qur. 50.15). The caliph extended the hand of protection to Nuri and told him to say what he liked; Nuri then said things that had never been heard before, and the caliph and all those present wept and praised Nuri.[14] This account may be a doublet of the original trial scene (with lavish praise for the Sufi by the court), so it may have to be rejected as unauthentic.

There are, however, two other stories about Nuri and the later caliph, al-Mu'tadid. Nuri one day saw a man bringing sealed jars into the palace, and when he learned that they contained wine for the royal table, he smashed the jars to bits. The enraged Mu'tadid summoned Nuri, and demanded to know who had made Nuri *muhtasib* (censor of morals). Nuri fearlessly told him, "He who appointed you to be imam appointed me to be censor!" This remark shocked the caliph sufficiently to awaken his conscience. Now subdued, he asked Nuri what he desired. Nuri requested exile. When about to smash the last jar of wine, he had started to think about his own importance instead of God's will, so he asked the caliph for this punishment. This incident probably took place around 283/896.[15] In another anecdote, Sarraj mentioned that the wazir of al-Mu'tadid gave Nuri a large sum of money, "in order to cut him off from the Sufis." This may have been connected with the incident of the wine, if the wazir hoped by bribing Nuri to avoid a public protest by piety-minded elements. Nuri distributed the money to all comers, and then lectured those who accepted it on the non-spiritual nature of money.[16]

Finally, the story has it that Ghulam Khalil was said to have been inspired to bring charges against the Sufis by a woman who had fallen in love with the Sufi Sumnun al-Muhibb, but had been repulsed by him. Knowing of Ghulam Khalil's antipathy to the Sufis, she went to him and informed against the Sufis, claiming that she had participated in orgies with them.[17] Although the scorned woman's accusation is a stock element in popular stories, such an incident might explain the warning of Ghulam Khalil, "Beware lest you sit with anyone who claims desire (*shawq*) or love (*mahabbah*) and who goes off alone with women. . . ."[18]

How valid were the charges against Nuri? The first, *zandaqah*, was clearly a catch-all term for heresy deemed dangerous by the state. Nuri was not a Manichaean or a crypto-Shi'i, nor was he lax in ritual. One specific crime that Ghulam Khalil seems to have had in mind was innovation (*bid'ah*) in speaking of God, which in itself is not a capital crime.

This particular innovation, however, ascribed passionate love to God, and the suspicion had been planted that Nuri and Sumnun were illicitly involved with women. In this case *zandaqah* could refer to the pre-Islamic heresy of Mazdak, who preached (according to his enemies) common ownership of property and women; this movement had been ruthlessly suppressed in 528 A.D. and was still a by-word in Islamic times.[19] Although Nuri's saying on loving God has been traced back to the respected ascetic al-Hasan al-Basri,[20] there is evidence that some of the early Sufis had been classed as *zindiq*s for similar ideas. al-Khushaysh al-Nisa'i (d. 253/867), a Hanbali scholar, wrote one of the earliest heresiographies delineating the traditional number of seventy-two erring sects, and in this he enumerated five subsects of the *zanadiqah* whom he called "spirituals" (*ruhaniyah*). The second of these subsects is of particular interest:

> Among them is a group of spirituals who claim that the love (*hubb*) of God overpowers their hearts, their desires, and their will, so that love of Him becomes the most powerful thing for them. When their situation is thus, in this position they receive friendship (*khullah*) with God. He allows them to commit theft, adultery, wine-drinking, and fornication in the spirit of the friendship which exists between them and God. Not that these things are lawful — it is in the spirit of friendship, as a friend is allowed to take from his friend's belongings without permission. Among them are Rabah and Kulayb, both of whom affirm this and urge it.[21]

Rabah al-Qaysi (d. 195/810) was one of the Sufis of Basra, a contemporary of Rabi'ah. Regardless of the accuracy of Khushaysh's report, it is interesting to notice that some early Sufis were accused of licentiousness in connection with their affirmation of the love of God. The description of the "spirituals," and the name itself, are remarkably similar to the reports of the Brethren of the Free Spirit in medieval Europe.

The other charge against Nuri mentioned by Sarraj was that he said, "A curse, and deadly poison!" to the *mu'adhdhin* who was giving the call to prayer, and then said, "Here am I (*labbayk*)!" to a barking dog. Ruzbihan recorded several similar incidents, in which someone experienced the presence of God in some living creature. Abu Hamzah shouted *labbayk* to the bleating goat that Muhasibi was about to kill for their dinner, and once while preaching, Abu Hamzah heard a raven caw, and to it also he replied, "*labbayk!*"[22] One Sufi saw God's presence in a brook running over a lawn.[23] This type of behavior has been termed *hulul*, "indwelling," by the heresiographers, who saw it as equivalent to the Christian term "incarnation" (Greek *enoikesis*). We shall return to this topic in detail later, but for now it should be pointed out that the incidents referred to are not part of a systematic doctrine of indwelling divinity borrowed from Christianity, but the expression of a sudden and intimate experience of God, as Nuri eloquently explained. The preponderance of the evidence indicates that Nuri and his companions were arrested on trumped-up charges of licence (*ibahah*) and incarnationism (*hulul*) based on suspicion and hearsay.

The tense political situation in Baghdad doubtless contributed to an atmosphere in which the government acted on accusations of heresy without delay. During these years the Saffari governors of Iran revolted and later tried to conquer Iraq. The Turkish garrisons had brought about anarchy in the caliphate a few years previously, so that four different caliphs ruled in the space of ten years (247/861-256/870). Then for over a decade, the rebellion of the black slaves (the Zanj) in Basra created further turmoil. Outlying sources of revenue were unreliable, and the authority of the caliph was in question. Under such circumstances it is perhaps natural that strange religious expressions should be suspected of having revolutionary content. The conduct of the trial, moreover, was so summary as to lack procedure entirely. The initiation of the trial and the decision were made strictly on an *ad hoc* basis, in which personal considerations were uppermost. Thus Ghulam Khalil impetuously raised the charge of *zandaqah* on the word of one informer, and he was able to interest al-Muwaffaq through his close relationship with the regent's mother, Ashar.[24] The executioner was the one who halted the proceedings when he saw the generous sacrifice of Nuri for his brethren, and only after Nuri's act had been reported to al-Muwaffaq did a qualified jurist enter on the scene. The reason for the ensuing sentence of exile for Nuri is not clear; was it the caliph who banished Nuri, as an example to all non-conformists? This was evidently not an ordinary *shar`i* law court, and there is every indication that the institution of the extraordinary court (*nazar al-mazalim*) was quite disorganized at this time.[25] It was normally supervised by the wazir, but in this case, the wazir, Isma`il ibn Bulbul, was not involved. On the accession of the next caliph, al-Mu`tadid, in 278/891, the wazir was immediately put to death himself on the charge of *zandaqah* (in reality for having offended al-Mu`tadid some years previously).[26] Heresy trials could be very political indeed. In Nuri's case the legal process depended entirely on the whims of the ruler and those who had his ear.

Let us note, finally, that Nuri's manner of death was completely in accord with his life-long ideal of love. Hearing some verses on love, he became completely absorbed in his Beloved, and wandered through the countryside. He cut his feet badly on a reed-bed, and died from the wounds a few days later.[27]

2. HALLAJ

The case of Hallaj is somewhat more complicated than Nuri's, for religious, political, and personal reasons, and there is a far more abundant documentation for Hallaj as well. The sources have been analyzed with great care by Massignon, who presented his conclusions in two lengthy chapters of *La Passion de Hallaj*.[28] We will summarize here the remarkable researches of Massignon, at the same time taking care to consult the primary evidence.

Hallaj had been a disciple of Nuri for a time, before Nuri's trial, and the example of Nuri was surely a prominent one for the young Hallaj. Hallaj's first encounter with the authorities was in some ways a repetition of Nuri's first trial. The charge against him evidently concerned his view that there could be love between man and God. Sometime after Hallaj's return from a two-year stay in Mecca, in 292/904, the Maliki qadi of Baghdad, Abu 'Umar, consulted Ibn Da'ud, son of the founder of the Zahiri rite, for his opinion of Hallaj. The latter delivered the following decision (*fatwa*): "If that which God revealed to His Prophet is true, and that which he brought is true, then that which al-Hallaj says is false."[29] Ibn Da'ud was vehement in this assertion, and he further stated that it was lawful to put Hallaj to death.[30] The *fatwa* tersely accused Hallaj of giving the lie to God and the Prophet, without stating the precise grounds, but it is most likely that Ibn Da'ud criticized Hallaj for publicly preaching that one could love God.[31]

Ibn Da'ud considered himself a great authority on love, having written the *Kitab al-Zahrah* as a poetic anthology expounding the theory of "chaste love (*hubb 'udhri*)" based on a "platonic" conception of Arabic love poetry. In his view, love is a fatal disease closely related to melancholy, which a noble nature will endure without yielding to it. Ibn Da'ud specifically reproaches the Sufis for daring to aim their love at God.[32] In the absence of any stronger evidence, the suggestion that divine love was the issue should be accepted. We do not know precisely what Hallaj was saying publicly about love, but we do know that he was publicly calling the people to God, and we have his long description of divine love "in the language of *shath*" and a list of ascending stations (*maqamat*) concluding in "mad love (*walah*)," which claims to attain to God.[33] Ibn Da'ud also made a list of the eight stages of love, culminating in the same term, *walah*, which for him serves to indicate the incurable delirium wrought by love.[34] Clearly the two men held opposite points of view. For the Zahiri school, to attribute love to God was sheer anthropomorphism (*tashbih*), hence Ibn Da'ud's *fatwa*.

This decision was not the final word for Hallaj, however; the qadi Abu 'Umar also consulted the Shafi'i jurist Ibn Surayj, whose school recognized the need for interpretation, unlike the literalist Zahiris. Ibn

Surayj's reply was brief: "He is a man whose spiritual state is hidden from me. Therefore I will say nothing concerning him."[35] Not willing to rule out all changes from traditional vocabulary, Ibn Surayj accepted the possibility of a legitimate spiritual state (*hal*), but disqualified himself from judging Hallaj because of his inability to grasp the source of his words. Later Sufi tradition expanded this laconic opinion, as in this version ascribed to Wasiti:

> I said to Ibn Surayj, "What do you say about Hallaj?" He said, "When I see that he knows the Qur'an by heart and is learned in it, is skillful in jurisprudence, learned in *hadith*, sayings and prophetic examples, is one who fasts continually, and stands in the night preaching and weeping and saying words that I do not understand, then I cannot judge that he is an infidel."[36]

Here Hallaj's piety and learning are considered to be sufficient to exonerate him from any charge of infidelity. While this account, to judge from the admiring detail, was probably retouched by Hallaj's followers, it is curious to note that in one of the two manuscripts, Ibn Surayj seems to be privately admitting to Wasiti that he understands and approves of Hallaj's language: "saying words that I *do* understand . . ."[37] This variant indicates the importance that Sufis assigned to Ibn Surayj's *fatwa*. Ruzbihan also quotes the *fatwa* in this form, and adds, "thus it is with a learned man whose soul is informed of the hidden secrets; he knows that (Husayn) is a lover in His court, and that his words are beyond the beyond."[38] Although the evidence does not allow us to see Ibn Surayj as a partisan of Hallaj, his abstention was a highly significant action in the determination of legal jurisdiction over Sufism, as will be seen below. With such a statement from an eminent jurist, the proceedings against Hallaj collapsed at this time, and lay in abeyance for several years. This was more of a judicial skirmish than an actual trial.

The first real trial began around 298/911, when four of Hallaj's disciples were arrested in Baghdad, on the charge of following one who claimed divine lordship (*rububiyah*).[39] Although the charge named Ibn Bishr (himself a disciple of Hallaj) as the ringleader, there was evidently a hunt for Hallaj in progress, for the Shi`i wazir Ibn al-Furat appointed his secretary to run Hallaj to ground. Another Hallajian, Dabbas, was imprisoned, but was granted freedom on the condition that he turn police spy and help track Hallaj. Meanwhile Hallaj was in hiding in Ahwaz with friends, where he was discoveed in 301/913 by a caliphal post agent. He was accused by the governor, Rasibi, of "claiming divine lordship and preaching incarnationism (*hulul*)." Interestingly, it was the Shi`i financiers of Ahwaz who urged Rasibi to take this course of action.[40] The governor of Wasit, Hamid (who as wazir would later preside over

Hallaj's last trial) came to meet the prisoner and conduct him to Wasit. Either at Wasit, or possibly in both Wasit and Ahwaz, he interrogated Hallaj and concluded that Hallaj was a "Mahdi," a claimant to the role of the Messiah. Finally Hallaj was brought to Baghdad tied onto a camel, while a crier announced, "behold the apostle of the Qarmatis." He was then examined by the pious and cultured wazir `Ali ibn `Isa. Certain suspicious-looking documents on Chinese paper had been found in his possession, but the wazir apparently found them to be nonsensical, as he told Hallaj to remedy his deficiencies in religious and literary culture: "Learn your legal duties, and purification, which will be of more use to you than treatises in which you say things you know nothing of. How often have you written to the people — woe unto you! — 'Blessed be the Master of the resplendant light in resplendance'? This shows that you have need of some education."[41] The phrase "resplendent light" (*nur sha`sha`ani*) does not occur in Hallaj's writings in precisely this form, but it is a characteristic term in the Qarmati gnostic vocabulary, which Hallaj introduced into Sufism in a modified form. The fact that the wazir was so lenient in his criticism means that he respected the verdict of Ibn Surayj, who was his own spiritual adviser. Thus he refrained from ordering a heresy trial, but he went along with the caliphal police, and ordered that Hallaj undergo a minor punishment. Hallaj was pilloried publicly for four days, while again a crier announced, "Behold the apostle of the Qarmatis!" Afterward, Hallaj was imprisoned, and there he remained until his final trial began seven years later. It is worth noting that this entire process took place without the presence of any religious jurists; the officials of the secular arm had complete charge, in an atmosphere where Shi`i sympathies played a dominant though covert role.

In the following years Hallaj remained imprisoned, mostly in the palace, where his supporters included the chamberlain Nasr al-Qushuri, the queen-mother Shaghab, and the Sunni secretary al-Hamd al-Qunna'i; presumably it was due to this support that he was not prosecuted again when Ibn al-Furat regained the wazirate in 304/916-306/918. The reason for this imprisonment is not clear — perhaps to keep a charismatic figure under control, perhaps to protect him from Shi`i enemies. For a time he wore heavy chains, but at other times he lived in comfort. The officials were divided in their attitudes toward Hallaj. During this time a financier and one-time Sufi named `Awariji wrote a book on "The Miracles of Hallaj and their Fakery," attempting to prove that certain miraculous events attributed to him had been cunningly staged. Part of the charge that Hallaj claimed divinity was based on the belief that he had performed the miracles of giving life and death.[42] Yet it was not until 309/922 that a decisive action was taken. Hallaj had been active during this time, writing some of the material later assembled as the *Tawasin*. Somehow a Qur'anic commentary (*tafsir*) in his handwriting was shown to Ibn Mujahid, head of the Qur'an-reciters' guild. Having noticed several suspicious phrases mentioning "gods (*alihah*)" and "lords (*arbab*)," Ibn Mujahid (now spiritual adviser to `Ali ibn `Isa since the death of Ibn Surayj) turned the book over to `Ali ibn `Isa. The latter, now vice-wazir under Hamid, was also shocked at the contents of this work, and had Hallaj's books seized. Several of his disciples were also arrested, and other writings were discovered, among them a book on "The Secret of the God (*sirr al-ilah*)," which contained "more impiety, corporealism, and heresy than the tongues of the faithful could tell."[43] At this point the caliph, al-Muqtadir, intervened personally, and over the objections of the chamberlain Nasr turned Hallaj over to the chief wazir Hamid, who had brought Hallaj to trial in 301/913. Since neither the complete Qur'an commentary nor the other book have survived, it is difficult to tell what theses were under attack. In one of his prayers Hallaj used the phrases "God of gods (*ilah al-alihah*)" and "Lord of lords (*rabb al-arbab*)," which reportedly had been used already by Ibrahim ibn Adham (d. ca. 160/776); Hallaj employed these phrases in the most direct kind of *shath*.[44] Probably Massignon is right in saying that Hallaj was accused because of the "theory of the witness," according to which the divinized human becomes the earthly witness of divinity, speaking with the voice of God. Now under Hamid, the final trial began.

The main task of the investigators was to find some evidence in Hallaj's papers that would justify sentencing. Having assembled the judges and jurists, Hamid said to them, "what do you say about klling him, although he was uttered both confessions of faith?" When they replied that this was not possible without a proof acknowledged by Hallaj, Hamid authorized a thorough examination of Hallaj's papers. The historical sources tell of a number of pieces supposedly found among these papers, of a missionary Shi`i, even Qarmati, character. Calligraphic designs in honor of `Ali, instructions on the gradual initiation of neophytes, praise of the Fatimi dynasty, as well as letters full of the most exaggerated epithets addressed to Hallaj—all these were said to be among these papers.[45] This material, although it excited the suspicions of Hamid greatly, was not enough to convict Hallaj; he had made the confession of faith, and thus had to be regarded as a good Muslim until proven otherwise. The decision of Ibn Surayj was still effective.

Meanwhile, Hallaj's friend and fellow-Sufi Ibn `Ata' had roused the common people, who were ever ready to respond to the leaders of Hanbali pietism, and they took to the streets, praying against the persecutors of Hallaj.[46] For four days the processions continued, so that Hamid and the chief of police feared that the mob would break in and free the prisoner. Yet the wazir was able to summon Ibn `Ata' to the trial as a witness, to comment on two other pieces of evidence found in Hallaj's papers. First was a letter, written by Hallaj and beginning "From the Merciful, the Compassionate, to so-and-so." Under interrogation, Hallaj had acknowledged that the letter was his. To this, the questioner responded, "You were claiming to be a prophet, but now you claim divine lordship!" Hallaj replied, "I do not claim divine lordship; rather, this is 'essential union' in our terms. Can the writer be other than God? I and my hand are but tools in this." When asked if any others supported him, Hallaj mentioned three Sufis, Shibli, Jurayri, and Ibn `Ata'. When summoned, the first two failed to approve the statement. Jurayri, a disciple of Junayd, said, "this man is an infidel, who should be killed along with whoever agrees with him." Shibli, less firm, said, "he who says this should be stopped." Ibn `Ata', however, expressed his approval. At some point in the process Hallaj had been asked to write out a creed (*i`tiqad*), which had been judged unacceptable, and this too was given to Ibn `Ata' to read. He said, "this creed is correct, and I believe in this creed. He who does not believe in this creed has no creed." When the outraged wazir read this opinion, he challenged Ibn `Ata'. With incredible boldness, the Sufi replied, "what have you to do with this? Worry about the seizure of people's property with which you involved, and oppressing them, and killing them! What have you to do with the sayings of these noble ones?" Hamid then ordered his guards to punish Ibn `Ata', and they beat him to death with his own shoes.[47]

For Hamid, who had complete control over the trial, it was a predetermined case. When he first saw Hallaj, he told him, "Don't you know me? I took you prisoner at Dur al-Rasibi and brought you to Wasit. You told me once that you were the *mahdi*, and you told me another time that you were a pious man. You claim to worship God and enjoin what is approved, so how is it that after seing me, you are pretending to divinity?"[48] But at last something appeared which provided Hamid with the evidence that he was looking for. A passage was found in which Hallaj advocated that those unable to make the pilgrimage to Mecca should build a replica of the Ka`bah in a special room, circumambulate it on the appropriate days, and conclude by giving a feast for orphans and clothing them. This would then be a substitute for the pilgrimage. The passage was read out loud, and we have the following account from Ibn Zanji, son of the wazir's secretary, describing the investigators' reactions.

And when my father read this section, the judge Abu `Umar (who had requested the verdict of Ibn Da'ud against Hallaj) turned to al-Hallaj and said to him, "Where did you get this?" He said, "From *The Book of Sincerity* by al-Hasan al-Basri." Then Abu `Umar said to him, "You lied! Your blood may be shed! We heard *The Book of Sincerity* by al-Hasan al-Basri at Mecca, and there is nothing in it of what you said!" And when Abu `Umar said, "You lied! Your blood may be shed," Hamid said to him, "Write this down!" But Abu `Umar was busy addressing Hallaj, while Hamid started asking him to write down what he had said, but he resisted him and kept busy (with Hallaj). Then Hamid put the inkpot right in front

of Abu 'Umar and asked for paper (for him), which he nevertheless handed
back. But Hamid urged his request for a written verdict with an insistence
that would not be denied, and so he wrote down that his (Hallaj's) blood
could be lawfully shed, and after that (he wrote down) who who was present at the session. . . .[49]

Massignon questioned the veracity of Ibn Zanji's version, saying that according to the two other accounts, the whole thing was staged in advance. On this assumption, the judges would already have seen and
discussed this piece of evidence, although Abu 'Umar pretended to be
outraged on hearing Hallaj's theory, ostensibly for the first time.[50] A
hereditary judge and a man "of doubtful integrity" according to
Dominique Sourdel, Abu 'Umar here played his part well, just as he continued to adjust his opinions in later years for whomever was in power.[51]
Hallaj protested his innocence vigorously but uselessly. Hamid sent the
signed *fatwa*s to the caliph, requesting an immediate confirmation so
that the execution could take place. There was, however, a delay of two
days. The queen-mother tried to influence the caliph to block the execution, but he finally approved it. Hamid had told him, "Commander of the
faithful, if he is not put to death, he will change the religious law, and
everyone will apostatize because of him. This would mean the destruction of the state. Allow me to have him killed, and, if any evil conse-
quence befall you, put me to death."[52] The result is well-known. The
sentence was carried out two days later, when they gave Hallaj a thousand
lashes (twice the number usually considered fatal), cut off his hands and
feet, exposed him on the gibbet, burned his body, and cast his ashes into
the Tigris.

In glancing over the charges against Hallaj, one notices a considerable diversity in their composition, with a curious prominence given
to "proofs" of crypto-Shi'ism. From the first accusation by Ibn Da'ud,
where love of God was the issue, to the first and second trials, the range
of accusations is very wide: divine lordship (*rububiyah*), incarnationism
(*hulul*), divinity (*ilahiyah*), prophecy (*nubuwwah*), all are supposed to
have been claimed by Hallaj. The strangest charges of all are those that
make Hallaj into a Shi'i missionary, preferably of the Qarmati variety. It
is true that Hallaj used terms from the Isma'ili-Qarmati vocabulary, but
this was probably necessary in order to communicate with the Arab
population of Iraq, since most of the agricultural laborers around
Baghdad were Qarmatis.[53] Far from being Shi'is, Hallaj and his
followers were known for their devotion to Abu Bakr, whom extremist
Shi'is curse for having usurped the caliphate from 'Ali. More importantly,
Hallaj's teaching of personal unmediated contact with divinity was totally
at odds with the hierarchical authority structure of the extremist Shi'i
groups. In fact, the prominence of Shi'is among Hallaj's persecutors is
quite evident; the financiers of Ahwaz, the wazir Ibn al-Furat, and the

prominent Shi`i scribes of the Baghdad administration all fit into this category. The bizarre part played by these sectarians seems to have been the attempt to discredit Hallaj by accusing him of their own Shi`i convictions. Families such as the Banu Nawbakht and Banu Furat had entrenched themselves politically in a government the legitimacy of which they secretly denied. Their real allegiance was to the hidden Imam, or, in the extremist groups, to the incarnate deity. For them, Hallaj was repugnant both as a political usurper and as a spiritual leveller who would do away with the exclusive possession of saintship by the descendants of `Ali. One example will suffice: the refined courtier, chess-player, and literary dilettante Suli ascribed to Hallaj a saying which is derived from the Nusayri litany in praise of the divinized `Ali, "I am the drowner of the people of Noah, and the destroyer of `Ad and Thamud."[54] Suli goes on to describe, ironically, how the chamberlain Nasr tried to save Hallaj, a Sunni, from "the Shi`i (rafidah) scribes who want to kill him." Nasr only consented to the prosecution by Hamid when it was pointed out to him that the wazir Hamid was a Sunni.[55] Suli knew quite well that Hamid consulted closely with Muhassin (son of Ibn al-Furat) and Shalmaghani, two heresiarchs of the most extreme Shi`i sect, the Mukhammisah. The accusations of Shi`ism and Qarmati propaganda made against Hallaj were fabrications designed to excite prejudice against Hallaj and pave the way for his execution. In addition, there was a powerful faction covertly mobilizing itself against Hallaj as part of a court power-struggle.

This brings us to the political situation. According to the historian Hamzah ibn Hasan al-Isfahani, the situation was critical. "For 177 years, the empire of the `Abbasis kept itself up . . . until the thirteenth year of the reign of Muqtadir . . . This was at the end of the year 308. At that time fighting and riots began in the capital, and the army and the citizens lost all respect for their rulers. The treasury was empty, and precious ancestral treasures were plundered. These disorders continued for twenty-five years in the capital of their empire."[56] An Iranian Shi`i, Hamzah saw the salvation of the ruined `Abbasi caliphate in the coup d'état of the Shi`i Buwayhi dynasty in 334/945. The combination of bread riots due to artificial shortages, the peasant uprisings of the Daylamis in Iran, and the constant threat of the Qarmati groups in Arabia and Iraq were combining to create an enormous crisis. Within the administration there were two factions. One consisted of Sunni loyalists of the military and the administration. The other was made up of Iranian Shi`i financiers and certain Arab tribes. Hallaj, who was closest in spirit to Sunni pietism, recognized the legitimacy of the `Abbasi caliphate, and was therefore supported by the loyalists, who had already attempted a reform of the government in the tragic one-day caliphate (296/908) of Ibn al-Mu`tazz, with Hanbali support. Hallaj's political involvement is shown also by the fact that he wrote treatises for the guidance of the wazir and on political theory for `Ali ibn `Isa and Nasr.[57] Although he was protected by the caliphal faction during his imprisonment in the palace, Hallaj's support was eroded when his theory of the replacement of the *hajj* was represented to the caliph as, again, a Qarmati-inspired plot to abolish the pilgrimage rite.[58] The situation was further exacerbated by the mutual enmity of the different wazirs who served al-Muqtadir (eleven wazirs were appointed during his twenty-five year reign). When one gained power, it was customary among the less scrupulous to ask the caliph for permission to torture the previous wazir into yielding up his illegally acquired wealth. The caliph usually acquiesced, on condition that he receive a substantial cut. In taking over the second trial of Hallaj in 309/922, Hamid saw a chance to ruin the vice-wazir `Ali ibn Isa, who had allowed only a mock-punishment for Hallaj in the earlier trial.[59] A tangled web of personal vendetta, subversion of the state, and party factionalism overlay the affair of Hallaj.

In terms of legal procedure, it should first of all be noted that Hallaj was evidently tried in an extraordinary court, the *nazar al-mazalim*. This was presided over by the wazir, with the assistance of military, financial, and secretarial officers, clerks, professional witnesses, and jurists. The secular officials were naturally selected by the wazir. The jurists in attendance at this particular trial, and the majority of the witnesses, were mainly of the Maliki school, since the Hanbalis boycotted the trial due to the murder of Ibn `Ata', and the Shafi`is were not involved because of the suspended verdict of Ibn Surayj. Since the chief qadi of Baghdad, the Hanafi jurist Ibn Buhlul, ultimately refused to endorse the death warrant, the trial ended under Maliki supervision. The principal judge for this investigation was, as we have seen, the Maliki qadi Abu `Umar. The Shafi`is viewed him as incompetent in his knowledge of Maliki jurisprudence, while the third *wakil* of the Twelver Shi`ah, Ibn Rawh al-Nawbakhti, said of him, "I have never seen a man who, when utterly refuted, shrugs away the proof with such hypocrisy as he does."[60] The contemporary historian al-Tabari described Abu `Umar's treachery in luring a prince to his execution under a false safe-conduct.[61] In short, there were reasons for doubting this judge's impartiality. Because of the abstention of the Hanbalis, Shafi`is, and (to a certain extent) the Hanafis, the professional witnesses (*shuhud*) who signed the death-warrant were mainly of the Maliki school, along with some Zahiris and Mu`tazilis. The number of the signatories is supposed to have been eighty-four, out of a pool of probably five hundred qualified, caliphally-appointed witnesses.[62] From Hamid's point of view, it was advantageous to have a court composed largely of adherents of the Maliki school, since in their view the apostate (*murtadd*) or heretic (*zindiq*) should be executed immediately, whereas the other schools generally allow a grace period of three days for recantation.[63] The organization of the court, then, facilitated the production of a death-sentence without delay. The second point about the procedure of the trial is that the judgment itself was reached by a certain amount of chicanery. Hallaj's proposition, again, was not a general abolition of the *hajj* rites, but a substitution for those who were unable to perform pilgrimage otherwise. In view of such practices as vicarious pilgrimage (whereby one could perform *hajj* on behalf of an incapacitated person), and the model of the Ka`bah erected at Samarra by an earlier caliph for his Turkish troops, Hallaj's recommendation was not as far-fetched as it might seem. Since in this ritual dispensation Hallaj altered the location of the rite while retaining all the required actions, this is probably best viewed as an innovation (*bid`ah*) in legal terms, as a late Imami writer pointed out.[64]

The spiritualization of the ritual, the emphasis on intention, was admittedly of a revolutionary character, but Hallaj's teaching of the "eclipse of the intermediaries" was not designed to abrogate the outward performance of religious ritual. Many others had made similar suggestions about the *hajj*, but Hallaj's remarks were, in the words of Henri Laoust, "politically inopportune" because of the self-proclaimed plan of the Qarmatis to destroy the pilgrimage.[65] Thus Abu `Umar's *fatwa* read: "This proposition is *zandaqah*, which necessarily calls for capital punishment, for one need not invite the *zindiq* to recant." On the other hand, the chief qadi Ibn Buhlul said there were no grounds for execution, since even in terms of procedure, it had only been determined that the proposition was recorded in one of Hallaj's books, and his adherence to this idea had not yet been established.[66] In other words, the legal requirement that Hallaj acknowledge the condemned view as his own had not been fulfilled. These reservations of the chief qadi of Baghdad, in addition to the support of Hallaj by Ibn `Ata', himself an eminent religious scholar, reveal that Hallaj's execution could scarcely be considered as a decision by the consensus (*ijma`*) of all jurists. Thus, both the classification of the proposition as heresy and the determination of guilt were reached hastily, under considerable political pressure. The charge simply does not do justice to the real challenge posed to the community by Hallaj; the deeper reasons underlying his trial will be examined at the end of part III. Finally, a note on the barbaric manner of execution: the ordinary legal penalty for apostasy is execution by the sword, since most authorities agree that burning the apostate (as `Ali is reported to have done) is a usurpation of God's punishment of the damned by fire in the next world, and "torture and cruel methods of execution are forbidden."[67] Medieval rulers usually ignored this legality.

3. `AYN AL-QUDAT

The last of the cases we have to consider is that of `Ayn al-Qudat Hamadani, executed two centuries after Hallaj in 525/1131. In his case we lack the eye-witness accounts that are available for Hallaj. The relevant historical data on this case have been collected by the Iranian scholar Rahim Farmanish in his monograph on `Ayn al-Qudat. This study, along with `Ayn al-Qudat's apologia, written in prison while he awaited execution, are our main sources of information.[68]

Already in his *Tamhidat*, written in 521/1127, `Ayn al-Qudat reveals that his activities have led to charges of pretension to divinity. The source of these accusations was an event, which he himself relates, in which he apparently wielded the power of life and death.

> I know you will have heard this story. One night I and my father and a group of the leaders of our town were present in the house of the Sufi master's representative (*muqaddam*). Then we began to dance, and Abu Sa`id Tirmidhi spoke a few verses. My father looked on, and then said, "I have seen the master Imam Ahmad Ghazali when he used to dance with us, and his clothes were like thus and so," and he showed them how, in an inspired manner. Abu Sa`id said, "I cannot bear it!" Then he said, "I long to die!" I spoke: "Die, Abu Sa`id!" At that moment he became unconscious and died. Know that the *mufti* (juriconsult) of the time was present, and he said, "Since you make the living dead, bring the dead to life!" I said, "Who is dead?" He replied, "Faqih Mahmud (= Abu Sa`id Tirmidhi?)." I said, "Lord! Bring Faqih Mahmud to life!" At that moment he came to life.[69]

This incident at an ecstatic seance (which may have been just a case of fainting) evidently led to reports that `Ayn al-Qudat claimed divinity. One of `Ayn al-Qudat's close disciples was Kamil al-Dawlah, a government official who lived in Baghdad. He wrote to his master that "in the city people say that `Ayn al-Qudat is claiming divinity." to this `Ayn al-Qudat adds, "and they are giving a judicial decree (*fatwa*) for my execution."[70] People also called him a magician on account of his miracles, but he regarded these phenomena as deeds done by God through him, just as in the Qur'anic accounts of Jesus' miracles.[71] Nonetheless, it appears that nothing was done about this charge at the time, since it would be another four years until his imprisonment. It is interesting that Hallaj was supposed to have performed the same miracle, and for just this reason was thought to have claimed divinity. Also in the *Tamhidat*, `Ayn al-Qudat reveals that his opponents had accused him of "incarnationism (*hulul*)," a charge for which he has little respect, as he ironically twists it around to suit himself: "Alas for the power of the highwaymen of the day, the scholars full of ignorance, and the immature children, who reckon me as of the style and price of incarnationism! I would sacrifice my life for such an incarnationism!"[72] His opponents' use of the term *hulul* may be just a theological categorization of the claim to divinity, but it obviously carried an *odium theologicum*.

Another charge made against `Ayn al-Qudat was the innovation of speaking of God in the language of the philosophers. One Badi`

Mutakallim wrote to him that it was improper to use the Avicennian term "necessary existent" for God, because all the names of God are fixed by the Qur'an. Although this theologian is described as an opponent of `Ayn al-Qudat, their discussion had not reached the level of public accusation, but was still being conducted privately, through correspondence. `Ayn al-Qudat replied, saying, "He is my Beloved, and I call him by whatever name I wish," and appended the following quatrain:

> Sometimes I all you upright cypress, or full moon;
>   or I call you musk-deer, fallen in the trap.
> Tell me, which of these three shall I call you?
>   It is from jealousy that I do not want to say
>   your name (lest others hear it)!

It is said that the same Badi` Mutakallim was later involved in bringing about `Ayn al-Qudat's death, although this suggestion may be only a speculation based on the correspondence.[73]

While these charges were made unofficially by 521/1127, the actual trial of `Ayn al-Qudat that took place four years later used more specific accusations based on passages extracted from the philosophically oriented *Zubdat al-Haqa'iq* that he had written around 515/1121. These accusations fall into three categories: statements regarding prophecy, the assertion that one must follow a master (*shaykh*) for spiritual advancement, and philosophical and mystical statements on the nature of God. In the first category, `Ayn al-Qudat had argued against the philosophers that the state of prophecy should not be considered as the highest state of reason, but as a state beyond reason. Sainthood implies an intuition that transcends reason. Since the state of the prophet is higher than that of the saint, the state of prophecy must transcend reason even more. Apparently the objection to this sophisticated argument is that it will confuse the common people, since they are used to thinking that reason proves the truth of prophecy (as in *kalam* theology). Thus the statement that prophecy is beyond reason may lead some people to lose faith in the message of the prophet.[74] The second category is the assertion of the necessity of the master. `Ayn al-Qudat cited with approval the saying of Bayazid, "He who has no *shaykh* has Satan for an imam," but his enemies interpreted this as a piece of Shi`i propaganda. "The opponent has treated it as a teaching of those who speak of 'instruction (*ta`lim*),' and he understands by that the theory of the infallible imam. . . ."[75] `Ayn al-Qudat goes on to give proof of his innocence. Here we can recognize the same phenomenon that obtained in the case of Hallaj. Crypto-Shi`ism was a favorite way of discrediting one's enemies. The third category, the philosophical and mystical descriptions of God, was interpreted by some adversaries as an inclination to the Aristotelian theory of the eternity of the world, supposedly implied by calling God

"the origin and source of all being." 'Ayn al-Qudat repudiates this interpretation, pointing out that he had refuted the Aristotelians in a long section of the *Zubdat al-Haqa'iq*.[76]

Beyond these theologically phrased objections, 'Ayn al-Qudat
records an accusation that is based on his free utterance of ecstatic sayings. "They have imputed to me the claim to prophecy also, on account
of words from the technical vocabulary of the Sufis, such as the words
'becoming nothing' and 'annihilation.'"[77] He records several of his sayings, such as, "The power of primordial majesty dawned, and the pen remained, but the writer vanished," "The eternal He-ness overcame me,
and my temporal he-ness was wholly absorbed," "If an atom of what
passes between them manifested, the canopy and the throne would turn
to nothingness." His enemies claimed that such sayings were "infidelity,
heresy, and claiming prophethood."[78] These sayings are nothing but
shathiyat.

We have scarcely any other information on the trial itself. Propositions were assembled by jurists, at the instance of the Saljuq wazir Abu
al-Qasim Darguzini, whose enmity toward 'Ayn al-Qudat will be discussed below. Unfortunately the only detail available about the juristic conduct of the trial is the attack on philosophic terminology by Badi'
Mutakallim. The principle upon which this trial was based was Abu
Hamid al-Ghazali's decree that upholders of the philosophic thesis of the
eternity of the world were liable to execution. The weakness of this
charge has already been indicated by 'Ayn al-Qudat's own refutation of
the philosophic thesis. He also insists that everything in his writings is
perfectly in accord with the view of al-Ghazali, whose brother Ahmad
was his spiritual guide. The other charges are doubtless as 'Ayn al-Qudat
described them (the nature of prophecy, the need for a master, and
philosophical descriptions of God). The wazir had 'Ayn al-Qudat bound
and sent to Baghdad, where he was imprisoned for several months, long
enough to write his apologia, the *Shakwa al-Gharib*. The trial took place
in Baghdad, and after the death-warrant was arranged, 'Ayn al-Qudat
was sent back to Hamadan for execution. The sources all agree that he
was gibbeted, probably meaning that he was hanged. The later
biographical works add bizarre and poignant details, saying that he was
flayed alive and hanged in front of his own lecture hall.[79]

The execution of 'Ayn al-Qudat is inexplicable without an
understanding of the political context. To be sure, the motive of envy
which he and his biographers impute to his enemies among the scholars is
a believable and all-too-human characteristic. 'Ayn al-Qudat was a
brillant young scholar (thirty three years old at his death), whose writings
are of a profundity and delicacy seldom matched. His popularity was
tremendous, and it is entirely reasonable to assume that less gifted and
less successful religious scholars should have envied him. The power of
execution was not, however, in the hands of the `ulama'. As in the two

previous cases, here also no one could have initiated a trial without the backing of a high government official. In this case it was Abu al-Qasim Darguzini. Son of a peasant, he had entered the Saljuq bureaucracy and been promoted by `Ayn al-Qudat's friend and supporter, `Abd al-`Aziz al-Mustawfi ("the fiscal officer"), who had actually saved Darguzini from execution in 515/1121. Thinking that he could safely manipulate Darguzini, `Abd al-`Aziz had then urged Sultan Mahmud to appoint him wazir. The unscrupulous Darguzini soon established his own power, however, and he and `Abd al-`Aziz entered into a fatal power struggle. According to Carla Klausner, Darguzini "once again embarked upon a course of murder and bloodshed, attempting to exterminate the important and prominent men in the state, including qadis and members of the religious classes. . . . Darguzini's primary goal was to dispose of `Abd al-`Aziz who alone seemed to stand in the way of his assuming complete control."[80] Taking advantage of the established practice of bribery, Darguzini gave the Sultan 300,000 dinars in order to get `Abd al-`Aziz imprisoned; this money he then recouped by confiscating the property of `Abd al-`Aziz's relatives. It was after the imprisonment of `Abd al-`Aziz that `Ayn al-Qudat's trial commenced. Darguzini evidently feared that the popular `Ayn al-Qudat would rouse the public to free his former protector `Abd al-`Aziz, and perhaps oust Darguzini from office. A religious trial was the easiest way to get rid of `Ayn al-Qudat, so Darguzini sought out figures from the learned classes who would support his action.[81]

The final condition that created the atmosphere necessary for the execution of `Ayn al-Qudat was the extremely troubled religious situation. This was the time when the Nizari Isma`ilis—the so-called Assassins—were at the height of their power, and had created an international terrorism, while at the same time the Crusaders were invading Syria and Palestine. Sectarian fighting had broken out between adherents of the Shafi`i and Hanafi legal schools in Isfahan, and riots had occurred in Baghdad, as in 521/1127 when a mob attacked an Ash`ari preacher.[82] The mood of the times can be judged from the remark of Abu Sa`id al-Sam`ani, on hearing of Ahmad al-Ghazali's unconventional teaching about Satan: "This is pure infidelity, which requires the shedding of blood and the destruction of souls, but none of the eminent people of that time approached God for the blood of this sinner."[83] As Farmanish comments, this shows how common it was for people to think of religious executions as a solution, even though in this case the issue never went to trial. "The existence of the rebellion of the Isma`ilis throughout the Islamic countries and the deaths of eminent people at their hands, as well as a religious factionalism of ever-increasing violence in Iraq, were the reasons why the externalist `ulama' showed extreme fanaticism based on protection of the externals of religion."[84] It is possible that Darguzini was guilty of the same sort of duplicity that some of Hallaj's opponents exhibited, when he raised a charge of crypto-Shi`ism against `Ayn al-Qudat. al-Katib al-Isfahani accuses Darguzini of being a secret Batini himself, and says that he prevented the Turkish general Shirgir (also a friend of `Ayn al-Qudat) from capturing the Isma`ili fortress of Alamut in 511/1118 by recalling him on a pretext, and then having him put to death. It should be remembered, however, that al-Katib's father and brother were the relatives of `Abd al-`Aziz whom Darguzini ruined. He was also an ardent admirer of `Ayn al-Qudat, whom he refers to as the *qutb* or spiritual axis of the world.[85]

Sufism in general was not the object of widespread persecution at this time. The Saljuq Sultans and officials all patronized Sufis by providing hospices and other subsidies, as part of the official policy of promoting a Sunni revival among the people and combatting Isma`ili propaganda.[86] Darguzini, tyrant though he was, received a number of panegyric poems and letters from the great Sufi poet Sana'i.[87] So although the tense religious situation contributed to the opposition against `Ayn al-Qudat, it was not because of an anti-mystical trend, but because of a personal vendetta in Saljuq politics, that he received the full impact of the fears and frustrations of the `*ulama*'. The sensibility expressed in his apologia has a nobility that permitted him to rise above the fear and envy of those around him. He described the attacks on him with biting eloquence, and while protesting his innocence died in the full consciousness of being a martyr.

B.

Sufism, the Law, and the
Question of Heresy

The preceding analysis has shown that although the trials of the Sufis
had religious aspects and involved some jurists, they were essentially
political, and would not have occurred without the stimulus of political
crisis. A similar pattern occurred in other persecutions in which Sufis
were involved. Dhu al-Nun was persecuted during the Mu'tazili inquisition for upholding the uncreatedness of the Qu'ran, which placed him on
the side of Ahmad ibn Hanbal. A few years after, though, Ibn Hanbal
attacked the Sufi Harith al-Muhasibi for adopting innovative terminology from the Mu'tazilis. Two centuries later, the Sufi writer al-
Qushayri suffered when the Ash'ari school was persecuted in Khurasan
between 440/1048 and 455/1063. None of those attacks involved issues
specifically related to Sufism. These were purely theological persecutions.

In the legal literature one can find criticisms of Sufism from the
point of view of the legal critic, without the deformations caused by
political pressure or purely theological debates. Foremost among these
critics is Ibn al-Jawzi (d. 592/1200), a strict Hanbali jurist and litterateur
who also belonged to a moderate Sufi order.[88] The Hanbali school,
closest to Sufism of all the legal schools, has produced the most cogent
critiques of Sufism. The Hanafi literature on "sayings of infidelity
(*kalimat al-kufr*)" has practically nothing to say about Sufism, but was
standardized in Transoxania in the fifth/eleventh century to combat
blasphemy and denigration of religion by the common people.[89] Other
cogent critiques can be found in the works of al-Ghazali, Sarraj, and Hu-

jwiri; this shows that there was also intense concern in the Sufi orders about the necessity of maintaining moral uprightness and legal rigor.

Ibn al-Jawzi's criticisms primarily condemn the lack of religious knowledge (`ilm`) that permitted the Devil slowly to ensnare the Sufis. This is the basic theme of his book *Talbis Iblis*, "The Devil's Deception," which also describes the errors of other groups, such as the philosophers. By `ilm` Ibn al-Jawzi means the knowledge of the exemplary deeds (*sunan*) of the Prophet, which implies sound knowledge of *hadith*. The possessors of this `ilm` look back to the Prophet and his companions for their religious ideal, and they scorn those Sufis who use "weak" *hadith* to support their own strange views and practices. In the final analysis, Ibn al-Jawzi's position insists on the absolute primacy of `ilm` in religious life. It is the only guaranteed access to the prophetic revelation, since its accuracy is ensured by chains of unimpeachable transmitters. If the Sufis in any way give priority to things of their own invention, this is innovation (*bid`ah*), which substitutes for the true revelation.[90]

1. LIBERTINISM AND INCARNATIONISM IN HERESIOGRAPHY

Ibn al-Jawzi criticizes many innovations among the Sufis, such as the practice of listening to music (*sama`*), but these practices are outside the scope of this study. More relevant here are his criticisms of tendencies in Sufism that he describes in terms of libertinism (*ibahah*) and incarnationism (*hulul*). "Some of them are impelled by hunger to corrupt fantasies, and claim passionate love of God (`ishq al-haqq`), and rapture (*hayaman*) in Him, just as if they imagined a person with a beautiful form and fell into rapture because of him. They are between infidelity and innovation. They split up into different groups, among which are the *tariqah*s, and their beliefs were corrupted. Some of them speak of incarnationism (*hulul*), and some speak of union (*ittihad*)."[91]

These criticisms are sometimes confusing, because the two terms are frequently applied to the same phenomena, but we can still distinguish *ibahah* from *hulul* to a certain extent. First, libertinism is defined as finding some pretext for indulging in forbidden things such as wine, fornication, etc. The Hanbali heresiographer Khushaysh ascribed this position to the early Basran Sufi Rabah. Ibn al-Jawzi continues in this vein in his description of Muhammad ibn Tahir al-Maqdisi (d. 507/1113), a scholar of *hadith* and author of a no longer extant work on Sufism. Of him Ibn al-Jawzi records,

Ibn Tahir belonged to the school of libertinism. He wrote a book on the permissibility of gazing on young men, in which he narrates the story of

Yahya ibn Ma`in, who said, "I saw a beautiful slave-girl in Egypt, God's blessings upon her!" (N.B.: this is the blessing reserved for the Prophet Muhammad.) Someone asked him, "Do you call blessings on her?" He said, "God's blessings on her and on every beautiful man!"[92]

There is an element of sexual innuendo here, and also the suggestion that the beautiful objects of this immoderate love are almost worshipped, since the formula of prophetic blessing, *salla allahu `alayhi* (*ha*), is applied to them. This was blasphemy in Ibn al-Jawzi's view, but he cooly classifies it as a school (*madhhab*) in the manner of heresiographers. In a later section, Ibn al-Jawzi outlines six main types of libertinism. These consist of those who hold the following:

1) Since all of our acts are predetermined, we need perform no religious duty.

2) God does not need our prayers, and therefore we need not perform them.

3) Whatever we do, God is generous and will forgive.

4) Since the law does not eliminate human weakness, it is worthless as a means of spiritual advancement.

5) Contemplatives who see heavenly visions and hear celestial voices have reached the goal, and need not perform prayer.

6) Sanctity and the state beyond the law are proved by the performance of miracles.[93]

This list is nearly identical to the analysis of libertinism that Abu Hamid al-Ghazali (d. 505/1111) made in his treatise against the libertines, which he wrote in an archaic Persian vernacular. Ibn al-Jawzi has condensed and slightly rearranged the contents of Ghazali's epistle.[94]

Elsewhere Ghazali has given a succinct description of the nature of libertinism, in his treatise distinguishing faith from heresy (*zandaqah*):

Of the same type is that which is claimed by one of the pretenders to Sufism, that he has reached a state (*halah*) in relation to God, in which prayer is abrogated. Then it is lawful for him to drink wine, (to commit) acts of disobedience, and to partake of the sustenance of kings. There can be no doubt about the necessity of killing this man, although it is an open question whether he will suffer hellfire eternally. The execution of a man like this is better than the execution of a hundred infidels, for the harm done to religion is greater. With him is opened a door to licence that cannot be closed. This man is more harmful than one who advocates libertinism for all. No one would be able to favor that, because his infidelity would then be obvious. This man tears down the law with the law, for he claims that he has not sinned except in that which is specifically for the general public, and the specifics for the generality are the duties of those who have not attained his degree in religion. Frequently he pretends that he has commerce with the world and commits sins only externally, while internally he is untouched by them. He issues this call until every evil-doer claims an equal state, and thus is the bond of religion undone.[95]

From Ghazali's remarks, it is evident that this is a false manifestation of Sufism, and certainly not a school, as Ibn al-Jawzi suggests; it is the perverse reasoning of an individual, but a kind that unfortunately is all too likely to be rediscovered time and again. The habits of long scholastic debate have led Ibn al-Jawzi to classify these libertines as a sect or school in Sufism. The fact that Ghazali initially presented his treatise on libertines in the vernacular would also seem to indicate the popular and unscholarly nature of this aberration. Yet the terminology used has an echo of genuine mystical terminology. When Ghazali says that prayer is abrogated, the verb used (*saqatat*) is the same as that employed by Hallaj to indicate "the eclipse (*isqat*) of intermediaries." Hujwiri sees a connection between the libertines (*ibahatiyan*) and the misguided followers of Hallaj (*hallajiyan*), but he also thinks of them as a school.[96]

In my view, "libertinism" is a phenomenon that is at least partly imaginary. Heresiographers from Khushaysh onwards have been ready to believe that Sufis preach a doctrine of systematic immorality. The case of Nuri and his companions is a clear example of this tendency; no one familiar with the scrupulousness of Nuri would ever credit the rumors of orgies, but Ghulam Khalil did. There may have been individuals who used mystical terms to cloak their own immorality, but there is very little historical evidence available on them. It is conceivable that whatever antinomian strands existed in Sufism were influenced by Isma'ili extremists, for whom the law was ended by the appearance of the imam of the seventh era. Certainly the heresiographers' description of "libertinism" in Sufism is in accord with the kind of accusation usually made against the Isma'ilis.[97] We shall reconsider this hypothesis in the conclusion.

The second category of heresy applied to Sufism is incarnationism (*hulul*), which at first sight seems more abstract than libertinism, but the two have a tendency to become confused. For instance, Nuri's trial seems to have been based on charges of libertinism and use of the term "passionate love" (*'ishq*) of God, but the fifth/eleventh century Hanbali jurist Abu Ya'la says, "The incarnationists (*al-hululiyah*) have gone to the point of saying that God the Almighty exeriences passionate love!"[98] Who were the *hululi*s? One of the people most frequently mentioned in this connection was Abu Hamzah al-Khurasani (d. 289/902), also charged in Nuri's trial, whose strange behavior in calling out "Here am I, Lord!" on hearing a crow has already been mentioned. The conclusion of that event is worth narrating. "They accused him of heresy (*zandaqah*) and called him an incarnationist and a heretic. They testified against him and

banished him. His horse was sold, and a crier announced at the gate of
the mosque, 'This is the horse of the heretic!'"[99] Likewise, when Abu
Hamzah burst into the same response on hearing the bleating of
Muhasibi's sacrificial goat, Muhasibi threatened to kill him. Ruzbihan
records both these incidents as *shathiyat*, saying, "When Abu Hamzah
heard the voice of the wind, or a bird, or animals, or the movements of
the earth, ecstasy would come upon him, and he would say, 'Here am I,
Lord! Here am I!'"[100] The same type of experience was recorded of
another Sufi, Abu al-Gharib al-Isfahani, who "laughed sweetly from
love's ebullition" when he heard water trickling over a lawn. He also was
called a *hululi*.[101] As in the incident in which Nuri cried out *labbayk* to a
barking dog, these actions are responses to a perception of the divine
presence as revealed in nature, not a semi-Christian dogma of incarnation.

A suspicious element did, however, intrude itself in the definition of
hulul, and this was the focus on the beautiful human form as the locus of
divine manifestation. This divine beauty was usually contemplated in the
masculine form, in a society where women were more or less secluded.
Thus we find the phenomenon of "gazing upon youths (*al-nazar ila al-
murd*)" as one of the implications of *hulul*. Abu Hamzah was known for
his penchant in this direction, although Nuri was very strict about
avoiding it.[102] Obviously the latent threat of libertinism and homosex-
uality accentuated the controversial nature of *hulul*. Hellmut Ritter has
collected and commented on a series of remarkable texts on incarnationism, which is mentioned in a variety of exotic instances. The
theologian al-Ash'ari (d. 324/936) mentions those who

> hold that it is possible for God to take up an abode in bodies. And if the
> *hululi*s see a man whom they find beautiful, then they do not know whether
> their God may be in him or not. . . . And among the Sufi ascetics there are
> people who maintain and assert that the Creator takes up an abode in in-
> dividuals and that He can take up an abode in men, wild animals, and other
> individuals. . . . They tend to cast aside the sacred laws, and assert that
> when man attains to God, then no religious duty is binding on him any
> longer, and he need perform no further devotional exercises.[103]

The first part of this account reads exactly like a description of Abu
Hamzah's *hulul*, but the second part goes back to libertinism. The two
terms of reproach, *hulul* and *ibahah*, seem to coalesce. The same view is
taken by the heresiographer 'Abd al-Qahir al-Baghdadi (d. 429/1038),
who describes ten subdivisions of *hulul* (including Christian and extreme
Shi'i views). The one that pertains to Sufism he ascribes to one Abu
Hulman al-Farisi, a Sufi who lived in Damascus around the late
third/ninth century. Again, al-Baghdadi accuses him of teaching *hulul*,
the admixture of the human and the divine (*imtizaj*), transmigration,

and, of course, licentiousness. Sarraj tells the story that Abu Hulman fainted in the street on hearing the cry of a wild rue vendor, whose words reminded him of his divine beloved. This teaching now becomes the subsect of the Hulmaniyah, which is further connected with the theological school of the Salimiyah as upholders of the doctrine that the spirit in man is uncreated.[104] The same view of Abu Hulman is repeated by Hujwiri, who follows the heresiographer's division by "sects" even in Sufism, while he complains that "gazing upon youths" is a legacy of the *hululis*.[105]

The process of dogmatization here is an interesting one. *Hulul* as a technical term is used not only in grammar and law, but also in philosophy, where it means "inhesion of an accident in an object" or "the substantial union of soul and body," and various technical discussions of it can be found in the handbooks. In theology, a considerable amount of time is spent demonstrating that God cannot dwell in a creature because this would mean that 1) God is not a necessary existence; 2) there would be two eternal beings; 3) division would be created in God by his infusion into a divisible object.[106] The discrepancy between this level of discourse and that of the condemned *hululi* is enormous. After filling three pages with densely written definitions of philosophical and theological *hulul*, the Indian savant al-Thanawi (fl. 1158/1745) concludes with this brief notice of the *hululiyah*: "A sect of vain pretenders to Sufism who say that it is permitted to gaze on young men and women. In that state they dance and listen to music and say, 'This is one of the divine Attributes that has descended among us, which is permitted and lawful!' This is pure infidelity."[107] Is it possible that these revellers have arrived at their present state by studying incorrect theories about "infusion" and "substance"? The connection seems rather far-fetched. We even find the term *hululi* applied to the Volga Bulghars, the Ghuzz Turks, and the Khazar tribes, who according to travellers' reports prostrate themselves before beautiful youths.[108] Hellmut Ritter is certainly right when he says, "by the term *hululiyah* no particular, historically palpable sect is meant. . . . The sect as such is surely an invention of doxographers."[109]

There are steps, however adventitious, leading from the early Sufi masters to the confused terminology of "incarnationism." Hallaj played with the term *hulul* in his poetry, but rejected it in his Qur'an commentary.[110] As the process of dogmatizing proceeded, the *odium theologicum* attached to this term also grew, so when Sulami wrote an abridgement of a treatise on the errors of the Sufis, he concluded it with a section giving a refutation of the concept of *hulul*. He pointed out that none of the masters of Sufism ever held *hulul* as a theory, and that only a few people in Syria (Abu Hulman?) ever used the term, none of whom the shaykhs ever mention. As proof he cites the statements of five Sufi masters against *hulul*: Junayd, Dhu al-Nun, Ibn `Ata', Abu `Amr al-Dimashqi, and Hallaj. Sarraj likewise did not know of anyone who upheld the theory of *hulul*.[111] The issue of "incarnationism" is at best tangential to Sufism.

Aside from the doxographic reproaches against Sufism, the most frequent criticism was that Sufism seemed to be unconnected with traditional learning. There is no firm dividing line between Sufism and traditional scholarship, however; many of the leading Sufis have also been distinguished in the fields of *hadith, fiqh,* and so forth. When Ibn al-Jawzi says that Satan deceived the Sufis because of their lack of `*ilm*, he supports this contention by quoting various Sufi masters who emphasized the necessity of traditional religious learning. He not only cites conservative figures such as Junayd, Jurayri, and Sari al-Saqati, but also quotes pious remarks from Bayazid and Nuri, although he frequently castigates the latter two in other parts of the book.[112] As we have seen, novel terminology was also suspicious, since any innovation was by definition different from the practice of the Prophet and his companions. Therefore Ibn al-Jawzi is extremely critical of the technical terms of the Sufis, as found in such works as Qushayri's *Risalah*.[113]

In addition, he considered the reports of unusual experiences, such as seeing and conversing with angels or the prophets, to be highly dubious.[114] Worse still are those who claim to see and talk to God in this life. In this connection Ibn al-Jawzi cites with approval a treatise by the Mu`tazili theologian Abu al-Qasim al-Balkhi (d. 319/931), which demonstrates the impossibiliity of seeing God in this world.[115] The difficulty of clarifying the theoretical basis for critiques of Sufism is shown by the fact that here a Hanbali is quoting a Mu`tazili, with no concern for doctrinal purity.[116] The mystical states claimed by the Sufis are not totally imaginary, in Ibn al-Jawzi's view, but he is not inclined to accept these claims if there is anything unacceptable that accompanies the state. In his comment on Nuri's saying, "I love God and He loves me," Ibn al-Jawzi first points out that `*ishq* is an inappropriate word to use for God, since it has sexual connotations, and he further points out that the word is an innovation. His final comment is that there is no proof that God loves (*yuhibbu*) Nuri, because God would only love Nuri if he were destined to be saved, and no one can know if he is saved.[117] In any given case, a critic such as Ibn al-Jawzi may be unwilling to admit the genuineness of a mystic's claims, even if he acknowledges their theoretical possibility. This is probably the most telling attack that could be made against exotic statements by Sufis, since self-deception and God's ruse can scarcely ever be avoided on the path.

The jurists always tended to take refuge in dogmatic approaches, and the very resistence of Sufism to dogmatic reductionism was the cause of much frustration among traditional scholars. Ibn al-Jawzi has described Sufism as a school or teaching (*madhhab*), the same term that is used for the principal legal schools. What does this term signify? It is a distinction originally based on the different geographic origins of the early jurists, whose schools developed different methods and procedures as time went on. Eventually, Muslims had to choose which school they would follow in matters of law. Sufism is not an independent *legal* school in this sense, because individual Sufis adhered to all the different major schools of law. Therefore it is incorrect to think of Sufism as a separate school that rivals the standard *madhahib*. Yet Junayd said, "This *madhhab* of ours is tied to principles, scripture, and the example of the Prophet."[118] Here he clearly wants to show that Sufism is not separate from the legal principles (*usul*) on which all schools agree. His use of the term *madhhab* is at once very general, in the wide sense of a "teaching," and very specific, in that it evokes the acceptance to which all the conventional *madhahib* are entitled. Junayd's statement should be seen partly as an apologetic designed to disarm legalist critiques. According to Ibn `Ata', during the trial of Nuri and Abu Hamzah, Junayd "concealed himself (*istatara*) by jurisprudence according to the *madhhab* of Abu Thawr."[119] For Junayd, adopting a legal *madhhab* was equivalent to conceding that Sufism needed to be based on publicly acknowledged principles.

The most unusual application of the term *madhhab* in Sufism is that of Hujwiri, the fifth/eleventh century Sufi who died in Lahore. A major part of his *Kashf al-Mahjub* is devoted to an exposition of the differences between the twelve schools (*madhahib*) within Sufism. This classification, which is unique to Hujwiri, attempts to show the principle (*asl*) on which each school is based, according to the teaching of its founder. Thus from Muhasibi he derives the Muhasibis, and so forth. This arrangement is rather artificial, since Hujwiri himself mentions that of these twelve schools only one (the Sayyaris) has remained unchanged since its origin. The practices and exercises of the different schools are not exclusively theirs, so it is really a kind of abstract systematization of different psychological tendencies. Thus I would disagree with Nicholson when he sees here the "familiar process" of dogmatization that befell "the Mu`tazilites and other Muhammadan schismatics."[120] Hujwiri's use of the method of the heresiographers only creates that impression, as in his description of the two erring sects of the Hulmaniyah-Hululiyah and the Farisiyah-Hallajiyah, which he derived from the heresiographer al-Baghdadi. In the latter case, Hujwiri admits that he took his description of these two erring sects from a book, and that both the Sufi tradition and contemporary Hallajis rejected the book's condemnation of Abu Hulman and Hallaj.[121]

Hallaj himself had emphasized the anti-dogmatic tendency in Sufism. When asked to which *madhhab* he belonged, he replied, "The *madhab* is for you. I follow the *madhhab* of my Lord." We have previously alluded to `Ayn al-Qudat's development of this theme. For him, the school of love was the only one that mattered. Allegiance to the schools of Shafi`i and Abu Hanifah was of secondary importance.

Again, Hallaj said that he followed none of the leading jurists, but only took what was the most difficult from each school, and practiced that.[122] In an apparent reflection of the medieval heresiographer's attitude, Reuben Levy sees Hallaj's anti-school tendency as "antinomianism."[123] The Shi'i courtier Suli introduced Hallaj by saying that he pretended to belong to whatever sect he happened to encounter.[124] This frustrating habit of being difficult to classify is partly a result of the esoteric principle in Sufism, which recommends speaking with people in accordance with their understanding. Examples of this would be easy to multiply. Yahya ibn Mu'adh al-Razi (d. 258/871–2) spoke of *madhahib* as "satanic," and Qushayri counted it hateful in a novice that he associate with a non-Sufi *madhhab*.[125] Of course there were tendencies in the opposite direction, and to some extent the later history of the Sufi orders is based on the institutional and doctrinal factors that then became prominent. Still, the anti-dogmatic factor is a significant one that cannot be overlooked in interpreting these cases. As Massignon rightly pointed out, one of Hallaj's important contributions was a creed "of the heart," which for the Sufis replaced the dry and sterile creeds of the theological schools. Both Kalabadhi and Qushayri placed this creed (anonymously) at the beginnings of their treatises on Sufism, to indicate the primacy of experience over abstraction.[126]

2. ECSTATIC SAYINGS AND THE LAW

These general criticisms have so far not touched on the subject of *shathiyat*. In the three trials analyzed above, there were a number of points where the charges touched on statements that Sufis classified as *shathiyat*. In the case of Nuri, jurists saw "passionate love (*'ishq*)" of God and crying out "Here am I, Lord (*labbayk*)" as libertinism and incarnationism. Ruzbihan calls both sayings *shathiyat*. Likewise Hallaj's theory that God bears Himself witness by the tongue of His lover was called heresy (*zandaqah*), and the letter "from the Merciful, the Compassionate," which he ascribed to the state of essential union, was called pretension to divinity. These also Ruzbihan classifies as *shathiyat*.[127] 'Ayn al-Qudat's enemies saw his ecstatic expressions, which were apparently unknown to Ruzbihan, as pretension to prophecy. He himself called them instances of *shath*.[128] Ibn al-Jawzi collected a number of sayings that he found repugnant, mostly from the *Kitab al-Luma'* of Sarraj. These sayings are quoted from Bayazid, Sumnun, Nuri, Kharraz, Shibli, Ibn 'Ata', and Husri, and a number of them figure also in Ruzbihan's collection.[129] It is interesting to notice that Ibn al-Jawzi gives the opinion of the Hanbali jurist Ibn 'Aqil, that anyone who makes light of hellfire as Bayazid does deserves death as a *zindiq*. When Ibn 'Aqil heard

Shibli's remark that he and the Prophet would intercede for all the inhabitants of hell, he said, "By Him who has empowered my heart and tongue in the matter of these innovaters! If the sword were within my grasp, I would drench the earth with the blood of creatures!"[130] Here ecstatic utterances have been interpreted as giving the lie to the Prophet, especially in matters of eschatology.

The amazing thing, from the point of view of this study, is that none of the ecstatic sayings on faith and infidelity ever became an issue in the Sufi trials or in the critiques of Sufism. Why was this so? I would venture to say that a self-proclamation of infidelity by an eminent Sufi would have been seized upon eagerly by any opponents he had among the jurists. The explosive power of such a statement can be seen from a parallel instance involving the poet Abu Nuwas. Once in a mosque a preacher was reciting the Qur'an, and he came to a verse beginning, "O ye infidels!" Hearing these words, Abu Nuwas responded with a typically irreverent piece of buffoonery, shouting, "Here am I, Lord!" When the people around him heard this, they immediately took him to the police and reported that the man was a self-confessed infidel. The police turned him over to the inquisitor of *zindiq*s. This magistrate, realizing that Abu Nuwas was not a real heretic, was only able to calm the crowd by having Abu Nuwas destroy a portrait of Mani (here we see how heresy was automatically considered Manichaean). This task Abu Nuwas performed with alacrity, not only smashing the portrait but forcing himself to vomit over it. The crowd thereupon permitted him to go free.[131]

If Hallaj or 'Ayn al-Qudat had uttered publicly their statements on "real infidelity," this definitely would have formed part of the charges against them, since it would have been construed as a confession to infidelity and hence punishable. My conclusion is that the letters and writings of Hallaj and 'Ayn al-Qudat containing ecstatic sayings on faith and infidelity remained secret, and were never made available to the authorities. As far as I can tell, Hallaj's sayings on faith and infidelity were either spoken in private (and then transmitted orally for several generations) or written in letters addressed to his disciples. Some of his papers were saved when he entrusted them to Ibn al-Khafif shortly before his execution, and other papers may have been saved by his disciples in Khurasan, who were protected by the Samani wazir Bal'ami in spite of over twenty written demands for their extradition by Hamid.[132] In public, Hallaj's only recorded remark that might be seen as a confession of unorthodoxy was his verse on dying in the religion of the cross, which he recited in the marketplace. Yet his promptings of the people to kill him were not designed to provide evidence for the extraordinary court, but to plead with the people to share in his consciousness of absolute reponsibility before God. In the case of 'Ayn al-Qudat, it is clear that his Persian work, the *Tamhidat*, was not available to his judges, for the sayings contained there were far more likely to be viewed as outright heresy than the

relatively innocuous *Zubdat al-Haqa'iq*.[133] The apparent contradiction
between the self-conscious desire for martyrdom in `Ayn al-Qudat and
Hallaj and their protestations of innocence in court will be touched on in
the next section. Yet given the highly critical reception of the other
ecstatic sayings, I cannot believe that `Ayn al-Qudat and Hallaj could
have uttered their sayings on faith and infidelity publicly without some
record of this appearing in their trials. It is only in the orally transmitted
material (*Akhbar al-Hallaj*) and the privately circulated writings
(*Tamhidat*) that these sayings occur.

The legal interpretation of ecstatic utterances was conducted on very
different principles from the Sufi exegesis. Ruzbihan was insistent that
only those "firmly rooted in knowledge" were qualified to interpret
shathiyat, and this means only those who have been graced with divine
knowledge.[134] Others must accept on faith the interpretations of these
qualified masters. Likewise, `Ayn al-Qudat maintained that ecstatic say-
ings must be understood in context, just as in the case of the ambiguous
expressions of the Qur'an, which if taken out of context can be the source
of great misunderstanding. Like Ruzbihan, he spoke of those "firmly
rooted in knowledge" as the only ones able to treat these delicate sayings,
for "the words of lovers should not be bandied about."[135] But the
knowledge (`*ilm*) necessary for the interpretation (*ta'wil*) of these sayings
is equally essential for the interpretation of the Qur'an and *hadith*. It is
not identical with the learning (`*ilm*) of the jurists. Since the very word
`*ilm* was equivocal in this case, a dispute was inevitable. Sufis felt that in-
terpretation of the sayings and technical terms of Sufism was not within
the competence of other sciences, such as jurisprudence, grammar, etc.
`Ayn al-Qudat repeated the position that Sarraj had previously stated:
"It is appropriate for the wise and just man, when he hears these words,
that he refer their meanings to the speaker, and say to him, 'What do you
mean by these words?' And a judgment against the speaker in terms of
heresy and atheism, before asking his explanation of the meaning of
these words, is a shot made in the dark."[136] The Shaf`i jurist Subki (d.
773/1370-1) cites the view of Ibn al-Sam`ani that in the case of `Ayn al-
Qudat "they gleaned from his writings certain shocking phrases that were
beyond understanding and that required reference to their author for
clarification. . . ."[137] The Western humanistic scholar cannot but have
sympathy for this attitude. How else should speakers be judged, if not by
what they themselves mean? The jurists have another standard, which is
perhaps best symbolized by the principle of *istislah*, or general welfare,
whereby the strictly deduced legal decision is subordinate to pressing
concerns of the larger religious community. Regardless of how much
truth or sincerity may be contained in a particular formulation, if its
harm outweighs its good, it is to be rejected. The application of the law,
as formulated by Ibn al-Jawzi, is strictly impersonal. He feels that errors
can easily be committed by genuine saints, and are even more likely to

occur with their imitators. His aim in revealing these errors is not to attack anyone personally, but to purify the *shari`ah*. His is a jealousy for the law, directed against any compromise of the revelation as known through the tradition.[138] Thus Ibn Taymiyah, in spite of his great admiration for the Hanbali Sufi `Abd Allah Ansari, condemned passages in his writings that suggest an illumination of the saint by an immanent uncreated inspiration—this of course would be *hulul*.[139]

The literalist view of *shathiyat* was not typical of all jurists, however. The eleventh/seventeenth century Hanbali scholar Mar`i ibn Yusuf, whose works are still used in the law courts of Sa`udi Arabia, wrote a treatise examining the suspicious sayings of the Sufis. Mar`i admitted the principles of *shath*, provided they are applied in a rigorous manner to the internal meanings of technical terms and genuine ecstatic outbursts. In other words, it is necessary to use a proper spiritual hermeneutic on these sayings. If the speaker understands these expressions in a literal way, however, this is, on the contrary, infidelity and heresy punishable by death.[140] This remarkable about-face enables him to find defensible interpretations for the sayings of Bayazid, Ibn `Arabi, and Ibn al-Farid, and he achieves a sophisticated legal decision on the basis of this hermeneutical distinction.

The difficulty about deciding on the legal jurisdiction over ecstatic sayings is that there are no clear traditional principles for dealing with them. All the customary categories end up by taking the sayings literally and violating their intentions. The issue of literal understanding as opposed to spiritual interpretation is precisely the line of demarcation between those jurists who reject ecstatic sayings (Ibn al-Jawzi, Ibn `Aqil, Ibn Taymiyah) and those who accept them (Ansari, Subki, Mar`i). The decision to reject the independent inspiration attested by *shathiyat* cannot have been taken lightly. An investigation of the factors that led Ibn al-Jawzi and Ibn Taymiyah to take their stands against mystical excesses would assist in understanding this problem. The case of Ibn `Aqil is suggestive here: an outraged opponent of the blasphemy that he saw in some ecstatic sayings, he was nonetheless in 465/1072 forced publicly to recant a defense of the sanctity of Hallaj that he had writen in his youth.[141] The controversial problem of *shath* both fascinated and repelled these legal minds, who were basically in sympathy with the pietistic aims of moderate Sufism. In any case, it should be stressed that very few Sufis ever went to trial because of ecstatic sayings. The vast majority of Sufis (notably Ruzbihan) were able to express themselves freely, aside from self-imposed restraints. Since there was no appropriate legal category for *shathiyat*, jurists ordinarily preferred to ignore them, especially since the speakers were generally venerated persons. There was thus no juridical imperative to suppress mysticism. It was only in circumstances of political crisis or social disruption that Sufis were liable to be picked as scapegoats.

The last legal topic to be considered is the juristic reasoning that allows for a consideration of ecstatic sayings as a capital crime. The three trials analyzed above are unfortunately not helpful in determining the legal theory of heresy, because of the considerable political pressure involved. An authoritative view of this legal problem would require lengthy investigations into the handbooks of the various legal schools, but a basic overview can be given here. There are no clear Qur'anic verses on capital punishment for heresy or apostasy. In the *hadith* literature one finds descriptions of apostasy as a crime punishable by death. The apostate, one who publicly abjures his faith, is described as "one who strays from his religion and abandons his community," "one who rejects God (*kafara*) after submitting" "one who changes his religion (*din*)," "one who wars on God and His Prophet."[142] These descriptions were not adequate for dealing with those who hypocritically pretended to be faithful while actually rebelling against God in secret. To deal with this problem, the authorities introduced the category of *zandaqah* from Sasanian Iran to deal with the continued manifestation of Manichaean and Mazdaki influence within Islam (the word *zandaqah* is derived from the middle Persian *zand*, "commentary," hence the perverse allegorization of the sacred text attributed to the Manichaeans by Zoroastrian orthodoxy).

Massignon saw an infiltration of Manichaean ideas into the early Shi`i extremist circles of Mada'in (Ctesiphon, seat of the Manichaean pontiff), which produced the double phenomenon of incarnation of the spirit and liberation from the law for the first time in Islamic society.[143] This movement was seen as subversive because of its clandestine character, its hypocritical pretense of orthodoxy, and its disdain for social standards. This was the Shi`i *zandaqah*, with which peripheral figures in society (poets, free-thinkers, mystics) could be easily confused, because there is no obvious way to identify a hypocrite.

A useful analysis of the problem of *zandaqah* can be found in a treatise written by the Ottoman jurist of the Hanafi school, Kamalpasha-zadah, in response to a case of heresy that ended in an execution in 934/1527. Kamalpasha-zadah points out that although *zandaqah* refers primarily to adherents of a religion that authorizes communal possession of property and women (i.e., the religion of Mazdak), it by extension means anyone who puts himself beyond the pale of revealed religion by denying God's unity or repudiating his ordinances. He further quotes the opinion of Taftazani, that the *zindiq* is "one who is by common agreement an infidel." This declaration of infidelity must theoretically be by common agreement (*bil-ittifaq*) of the whole Muslim community, since the heretic's infidelity is dissimulated, unlike that of the apostate. The solidarity of consensus (*ijma`*) is necessary to counter the anti-social deception of the *zindiq*. The sixth/twelfth-century Hanafi jurist Tahir al-Bukhari is quoted as saying that the libertine (*ibahi*) is to be treated identically with the *zindiq*, and as seen above, this is also the view of Ghazali.

Kamalpasha-zadah states further that the punishment for the *zindiq* is equivalent to that for apostasy, that is, he is invited to repent, but if obdurate is executed. In fact, according to the Hanafi jurist and Sufi Abu al-Layth al-Samarqandi (d. 373/983), the Muslim *zindiq* must be technically viewed as having apostatized to the *zindiq* religion, and is thus legally defined as an apostate.[144] Therefore if a jurist encounters sayings that seem to call the Prophet a liar, insult God or the Prophet, claim divinity or prophethood, or claim freedom from the law, he can interpret them literally as infidelity by common consent, and the speaker may be charged as a *zindiq* and an apostate, a heretic who deserves only death.

3. SUFI RESPONSES: MARTYRDOM, CRIME, AND PERSECUTION

The Sufi reaction to heresy trials took several different forms. In some cases, such as Hallaj and `Ayn al-Qudat, there seemed to be an active desire for martyrdom. This had an element of self-blame (*malamah*) about it, and it also had to do with seeking God in affliction. Moderate Sufis considered these trials to have been necessary punishments for the sin of "revealing the secret of lordship (*ifsha' sirr al-rububiyah*)." This position gives a purpose to the condemnations of the Sufis that was certainly far from the intentions of the jurists. Another group sees these trials as a sinister persecution, in which the satanic powers continually harass the saints.

The desire for martyrdom, and the certainty of its occurrence, loom large in any description of Hallaj and `Ayn al-Qudat.[145] This fact makes it all the more intriguing that both men vigorously protested their innocence. Was it that they saw how badly the charges against them deformed their doctrine? The charge of crypto-Shi`ism, which implied that their teaching was merely a cunning hypocrisy advanced by ruthless conspirators, was an attack on their integrity. The strategies of Ghulam Khalil, Hamid, and Darguzini aimed at discrediting the mystical teaching by making it a cloak for Isma`ili subversion, the *zandaqah* of the extreme Shi`ah. Had this succeeded, the work and the preaching of Hallaj and `Ayn al-Qudat would have been nullified; their public revelation of their experiences would have been in vain. This, I suspect, was the fear that prompted them to deny their guilt, since these charges would have completely falsified their teachings. Massignon's meditation on Hallaj's protestation of innocence is quite interesting:

> There is, in effect, a sudden fright, before the reality when it appears, a compassion for his body, for the blood of this heart where he maintains that God dwells; Hallaj has not yet realized, accepted all the horror of the

sacrifice so much desired; he has no more the force to thank those who, wishing to kill him, consummate his offering. . . . He still believes that the divine presence that he feels within himself will protect his body, he no longer gives the law permission to execute him. . . .[146]

The desire for martyrdom is mysterious indeed. It must have required a faultless confidence. It is perhaps not so strange if this confidence showed itself in a new form as an unshakeable conviction of innocence.

The most popular legend explaining the "guilt" of Hallaj showed him stealing an esoteric book belonging to one of his first masters, `Amr al-Makki. His master is said to have cursed him, and his execution was the result of that curse. While Junayd developed his enigmatic literary style as a protection against his letters being opened, Hallaj spoke openly in the marketplaces. The great Persian poet Hafiz (d. 791/1389) expressed the feeling of many Sufis when he said of Hallaj, "That friend by whom the gallows was ennobled—his crime was this: he made the secrets public!"[147] In a similar vein, the later anthologist Taqi Awhad maintained that both Hallaj and `Ayn al-Qudat were killed for "revealing the secret of lordship."[148] This view reflected an important strand of Sufi thought. It was a pleasingly ambiguous position for some, since it enabled them simultaneously to approve Hallaj's execution (thereby showing solidarity with an apparent consensus of all Muslims) and to affirm his saintliness. This was a merely formal condemnation. In the generation immediately following Hallaj, it is difficult to tell whether the frequent denunciations of Hallaj were of this formal type or more substantial.[149]

Another popular interpretation of Hallaj's death is the legend of Junayd's condemnation of Hallaj, most familiar in Farid al-Din `Attar's version:

> On the day when the imams gave the *fatwa* requiring his (Hallaj's) execution, Junayd was in Sufi clothing and did not sign it. Since the caliph had said that Junayd's signature was necessary, Junayd put on the turban and robe (of the jurist), went to the *madrasah*, and (gave) the *fatwa* response, "We judge according to the external." That is, according to the external, he must be killed, and the *fatwa* is according to the external.[150]

This is, of course, a legend (Junayd died eleven years before Hallaj's trial), but it captures the ambiguous mood of a common Sufi response. Hallaj was in the right according to the authorities on mysticism, but in the wrong according to the jurists.

Sarraj and Ruzbihan took a different position, seeing the trials of the Sufis as a veritable persecution. In several chapters of the *Luma`*, Sarraj gives accounts of the sufferings of Dhu al-Nun, the trial of Sumnun and Nuri, and the charges of infidelity against Kharraz, Hallaj, Ibn `Ata', Junayd, Sahl, and Subayhi. The first such sufferer is said to have been the ascetic `Amir ibn `Abd al-Qays, who was persecuted under the caliph `Uthman on the charge of pretending to be greater than Abraham.[151] According to Sarraj, the opponents of Sufism are of two types: one group fails to understand the difficult sayings and makes no effort to inquire, and as a result encompasses their own destruction (Sarraj suggests that they may merit eternal damnation); the other consists of people who have dabbled in Sufism but failed to gain recognition, and therefore turned against the Sufis and laid charges against them. In the latter category Sarraj would place Ghulam Khalil and Ibn Yazdanyar, both of whom associated with Sufis but later became persecutors. In this connection Sarraj quotes some verses that the Sufi Qannad wrote in response to Ibn Yazdanyar's persecutions. Qannad refers to the sufferings of Bayazid, Nuri, Junayd, and others, and ends by affirming that God still speaks by the tongues of the mystics.[152]

Ruzbihan's analysis of persecution echoes Sarraj's description of the ignorant persecutors, but turns into a lament on the shameful behavior of these so-called learned men. He insists emphatically that the validity of mystical experience is demonstrated by unequivocal *hadith* reports attested by unbroken chains of witnesses going back to the Prophet. Scholars who deny the meaning of ecstatic expressions therefore have only the barest pretentions to `*ilm*, since they follow only the outward aspect and ignore the essential core.[153] At one time there existed a sizable literature on this subject. `Ayn al-Qudat refers to the works on "the persecutions of the saints (*mihan al-akhyar*)," and Ruzbihan speaks of the stories found in "the persecutions of the Sufis (*mihan al-sufiyah*)."[154] A later writer in this tradition, al-Sha`rani (d. 973/1565), violently protests the innocence of Hallaj and the many victims who have fallen by unjust persecution in later times.[155] The tradition of regarding the Sufi trials as a series of persecutions testifies to a keen sense of the injustice of the accusations against the Sufis, and a firm consciousness of the legitimacy of the independent spiritual life. It also constituted a historiography of martyrdom that dramatized and exaggerated the tension between the spirit and the letter into a struggle between Sufis and jurists. Thus Jurayri, describing Hallaj's first judicial persecutor, said that "Ibn Da'ud was a jurist, and it is in the nature of the jurist to deny Sufism, unless God wills otherwise."[156] But there was no basic opposition between mysticism and the law; neither a jurist like Ibn al-Jawzi nor a Sufi like Hallaj would have admitted such an interpretation. It would perhaps be best explained as in the fable of the blind men and the elephant: each one had jealously defended one part of the Truth.

Conclusion
Comparisons and Interpretations

The phenomenon of *shath* as a spiritual experience with a literary expression can profitably be compared with inspired speech as found in other religious traditions. Comparison furnishes a necessary criterion for the intelligibility of our analysis. By likening the phenomena under discussion to appropriate examples from traditions other than the Islamic, and at the same time taking account of significant differences, we are attempting to attain precision in our descriptions. The initial analysis, though couched in the terms used by the Sufi tradition itself, already contained implicit comparisons. The very phrases suggested as translations of *shath* are themselves comparative. Although it is always necessary to understand the unknown in terms of the known, this need not be a cause for despair, simply because of the limitations of the "hermeneutical circle." It should rather be an occasion for us to probe for further discoveries on the basis of traditionally grounded meanings (Eastern or Western), which provide an ensemble of actualities far beyond the capacity of any individual to anticipate. Just as it would have been wholly inappropriate to interpret *shathiyat* without reference to the Qur'an, *hadith*, and Islamic theology, so it would also be idiosyncratic and speculative to attempt an understanding of this phenomenon without making historically-based comparisons with other mystical traditions. Our comparisons may be subject to correction, but it is essential to the task of understanding that comparisons be made. By comparatively exploring the experiential and literary dimensions of *shathiyat*, we will be better equipped to comprehend the ecstatic expressions on faith and infidelity, not only according to Sufi interpretation, but also in terms of their impact on the wider Islamic society. We will therefore compare *shath* with the expressions of prophecy, paradox, and the Zen *koan*. In conclusion, we will attempt to reach a final balance between mystical interpretations and heresiographic reductions of the *shathiyat* on faith and infidelity, for these sayings decisively describe the limitations of inspired speech.

Let us begin by examining the prophetic aspect, with Massignon's translation of *shath* as "theopathic locution," a grandiose phrase which requires explanation. The classical Latin word *locutio* ordinarily meant any word, phrase, or conversation. It was thus a rhetorical term, and I do not know of any mystical significance for this term before St. John of the Cross. St. John uses the word *locución* to describe supernatural words that appear to the soul without proceeding through the senses. He distinguishes three kinds: the successive, which occurs in concentrated reasoning, when the Holy Spirit verbally prompts the intellect; the formal, which is uttered spiritually by another person (whether God, angel, or devil); and the substantial, which is a creative command from God that immediately impresses the nature of the word on the listening soul, as when God says, "Be good," and the soul is then good.[1] The phenomena to which St. John refers are considered to be purely spiritual conversations, as it were, between the soul and a spiritual being, not public expressions concerning one's spiritual state. The word "theopathic" is a modern one that William James introduced to describe the pathological condition of an impractical and anti-social excess of devotion; Evelyn Underhill, however, used the term "theopathetic" in just the opposite sense, to describe those great mystics who combined ecstasy with the "incessant power of good works," such as St. Paul, St. Francis, St. Joan of Arc, and St. Teresa of Avila.[2] Massignon, however, used the term strictly for its description of a mystical state.

Massignon's combined phrase "theopathic locution" refers to "a positive state of dialogical mental intermittence, which suddenly reveals to the isolated soul the supernatural visitation of a transcendent Interlocutor."[3] This is quite similar to the *locución* of St. John of the Cross, but Massignon goes on to add that *shath* is "the amorous inversion of roles" in which the soul speaks "in the first person" with the voice of the Beloved.[4] Is it possible that St. John's substantial locution would extend this far? Supposing that St. John, like Bayazid, had been told by God, "I am you and you are I," would he also have said, "Glory be to Me"? We do not find such statements in St. John of the Cross, although Meister Eckhart occasionally verges on speaking with the divine I, as when he says, "If I am to know God directly, I must become completely He and He I: so that this He and this I become and are one I."[5]

From the experiential point of view, "theopathic locution" implies a direct connection between the spiritual state of the mystic and the word of God. Given the focus on the divine word in Sufi devotion, this translation of *shath* would seem to be significant. There are, however, many *shathiyat* that refer to intermediate stages on the path, and do not presume direct conversation with God. If we keep the aspect of divine speech in mind, however, there are many comparisons that suggest themselves. The whole range of prophecy in the ancient world, both Biblical and Hellenistic, offers interesting similarities. Although there is usually no question of "deification" in prophecy, there is a parallel in the Biblical prophet's "being absorbed into the emotions of the Godhead," as a prerequisite for proclaiming the will of God.[6] There are, moreover, rhetorical similarities between the audacities of *shath* and certain sayings of the prophets; Gerhard von Rad had remarked on "the extreme boldness of their newly-minted rhetorical devices and of the comparisons they employed, which they chose solely to scandalize the people."[7] Just as some of the Sufis turned their audacity towards God, the prophets Jeremiah and Habakkuk voiced their complaints against God using "language audacious, almost blasphemous in sound."[8]

The sayings of Jesus are remarkably similar to some of the highest *shathiyat*, especially those that take the form of "I am" statements. I have heard a Muslim scholar advance just this suggestion, saying, "Who was the 'I' who said, 'Before Abraham was, I am'? It was certainly not the carpenter from Nazareth!"[9] At any rate, it is certainly true that both the Christian and Islamic traditions look back to the theophany of "I am who I am" (Exodus 4:14) as the revelation of God as the real I, the absolute subject. Another body of mystical sayings on divine selfhood is that found in the ancient Indian Upanishads. The *mahavakya* or "great saying" typically enunciated the unity of all things in the divine Brahman, as in the sayings, "I am Brahman," and "That thou art."[10] We cannot at the present time expand these comparisons beyond the merest suggestions, but they can serve as reminders of the importance of the categories of selfhood and testimony as expressed in *shathiyat*. If it is of the essence of the highest *shathiyat* that God speaks and bears witness to Himself by the tongue of man, then these *shathiyat* of prophetic character express the highest attainment of human consciousness.

There is another way of approaching *shath*, from a more literary perspective, and this is suggested by Henry Corbin's translation of *shath* as "inspired paradox."[11] The primary meaning of "paradox" is "contrary to received opinion," and in ancient Greek, *paradoxon* in an extended sense could mean "wonder" or "marvel." Modern senses of the term include the logical paradox, a formulation with two mutually contradictory conclusions. Here, however, we are concerned with the rhetorical and philosophical sense of paradox, which the Stoics first formulated as a literary form. For the Stoics, paradox was a way of summarizing moral insights expressed in opposition to the ways of the world. Among the more famous of these are the sayings, "only the morally noble is good;" "virtue is sufficient for happiness;" "only the wise man is free, and all fools are slaves."[12] Subsequent European writers in the paradox tradition were not typically mystical, but generally remained on a strictly rhetorical and logical plane, dealing with such paradoxes as the "praise of folly," or the liar's paradox of Epimenides.[13]

Nonetheless, according to Rosalie Colie, even the rhetorical paradox is "primarily a figure of thought," adorned though it may be with figures of speech, and it finds its source in "the paradoxical *topos* of *docta ignorantia* originated by Socrates and developed so brilliantly by St. Paul and a host of Christian thinkers."[14] This aspect of paradox is of course the topic of unknowing, which plays such an important role in ecstatic expressions on faith and infidelity. The Delphic motto, "Know thyself,' may have originally meant, "Know that thou art but a mortal," but in the Socratic and Platonic teaching, this saying increasingly came to mean knowledge of the higher divine self beyond the empirical human ego. When Socrates said that the wisest man is he who knows that he knows nothing, this insight not only expressed the limitations of human knowledge, but also implicitly assumed a standard of divine knowledge. The paradoxical "praise of folly" could be merely an ingenious excercise in the hands of the sophist like Gorgias, in his "Encomium on Helen." But the paradoxes of Zeno, which showed the inability of reason to account for phenomena, derived from the divinely-conferred knowledge of transcendent being, as expressed by his master in philosophy, Parmenides. Philosophers' insights into reality are the original paradoxes, since affirmation of transcendence is always contrary to the experience of the world. The logical form of paradox, detached from its original insight, can always be turned into a literary artifice, but the intuition of the nothingness of human knowledge in comparison to the divine can restore paradox to its original significance. The Christian mystical tradition has done precisely this in its formulations of "unknowing" and "learned ignorance," which Evelyn Underhill explains as follows:

> God in His absolute Reality is unknowable—is dark—to man's intellect . . . When, under the spur of mystic love, the whole personality of man comes into contact with that Reality, it enters a plane of experience to which none of the categories of the intellect apply. Reason finds itself, in a most actual sense, "in the dark"—immersed in the Cloud of Unknowing. This dimness and lostness of the mind, then, is a necessary part of the mystic's ascent to the Absolute. That Absolute . . . will not be "known of the heart" until we acknowledge that It is "unknown of the intellect" . . . This acknowledgment of our intellectual ignorance, this humble surrender, is the entrance into the "Cloud of Unknowing": the first step towards mystical knowledge of the Absolute.[15]

Paradox, then, is a useful technical term, which potentially conveys the contradictory symbol of mystical unknowing as the way to divine knowledge.

In using the term "paradox" to describe the ecstatic utterance, Corbin stressed the element of ambiguity and double meaning in *shath*, which he saw as a necessary result of the expression of the eternal through the temporal. He rightly observed that not all *shathiyat* appear to have been uttered in a state of exaltation. Moreover, if the difficult (and at first sight anthropomorphic) symbolism of the Qur'an is taken into account as the model for *shath*, then in both cases the interpreter is faced with the problem of assigning the appropriate inner meaning for each outward symbol. Since the correct inner meaning is reached by an exegetical effort presumably contrary to customary opinion, Corbin felt that result is best seen as paradox, not as ecstatic speech. Corbin's approach to *shath*, sensitive though it is, is largely colored by his understanding of Shi`i exegesis, with its typically gnostic outlook. This approach is not utterly inappropriate, but it tends to be schematic and overly systematic in the interpretation of these mystical texts, in spite of Corbin's insistence that *shath* is "inspired" paradox. Corbin initially missed the significance of paradoxical unknowing in Ruzbihan's text, and even tentatively suggested an alternate reading for the term "unknowings" where Ruzbihan first mentions it. Later on, though, familiarity with Ruzbihan's terminology led Corbin to recognize the importance of unknowing for *shathiyat*, though he did not pursue this line of meaning.[16]

In choosing the term "paradox," Corbin had in mind a comparison of Ruzbihan's *Sharh-i Shathiyat* with the *Paradoxa* of the Protestant mystic Sebastian Franck (1499–1542). In this book, Franck composed several hundred unusual sayings (both in Latin and German), accompanied by his own commentary, giving frequent references to the Bible as the supreme paradox. For Franck, the meaning of scripture is contrary to all the opinions of the world. "Now I have entitled this philosophy of mine 'Paradoxa,' and translated *paradoxon* into German as 'Wunderrede' or 'Wunderwort,' since theology, the true meaning of Scripture (which alone is God's word), is nothing but an eternal *paradoxon*, certain and true against all the delusion, seeming, belief, and respect of the whole world."[17] Out of all the literature of "paradox" in European history, the work of Franck is probably the closest to the *shathiyat* of the Sufis, because of his focus on the divine word of Scripture as the fundamental paradox. Some of Franck's paradoxes are actually near-replications of the Sufi *shathiyat* on faith and infidelity: "There is no faithful man on earth;" "The faith of the world is real infidelity."[18] There would seem to be some justice, then, in comparing the reflective variety of *shathiyat* with paradoxes, since on this level we are not concerned with the divine word but with "an earthbound view of transcendent knowledge, taken from the viewpoint of human understanding."[19] The

European paradox tradition, then, corresponds to the secondary class of *shathiyat*, which does not originate in a direct experience of God (selfhood, testimony), but in a mediated experience of the human situation in the cosmos. Paradoxical *shath* is a critique of the ways of the world, in that it reveals the nothingness of our condition. Although the background of the European paradox does not offer anything comparable to the boasting-contest of the Arabs, there is an essential similarity on the literary level: both paradox and *shath* rely on the wise folly of the Socratic praise of unknowing.

There is one further comparison that I would like to make, between *shath* and the Zen *koan*. Both are unusual kinds of expressions that are related to spiritual development; are there any other similarities beyond this? *Koan* is the Japanese form of the Chinese term *kung-an*, meaning literally "public records."[20] From the late ninth century on, this term denoted sayings in the forms of questions and answers and anecdotes, and were used by the Ch'an/Zen masters to test their disciples and to indicate obliquely the method of realizing the absolute. As a method, the *koan* is characteristic of the Lin-chi/Rinzai school, which is also famous for the use of shouting, beating, and unconventional behavior. There is something of the flavor of the Sufi boasting-match in the spontaneous dialogue, sometimes called "*dharma* combat," that used to take place between visiting novices and the master of a Zen monastery. Yet *shathiyat* in Sufism were never used in the kind of teaching method that developed with the *koan*; that is, *shathiyat* remained as statements produced in a spiritual state, but they were not systematically made into the subject of a course of meditation, as in Zen. Another difference between the two is that *shathiyat* described spiritual states, and could be analyzed in terms of a spiritual hermeneutic. *Koan*s, on the other hand, were used for a variety of purposes in Zen practice; though they contained meanings that could be disclosed in enlightenment, *koan*s could not themselves be deciphered as guides to the nature of enlightenment.[21]

Yet in spite of these differences, one cannot but feel that these two types of aphorism have much in common. At roughly the same time that Sarraj and Ruzbihan were collecting and commenting on the Sufi *shathiyat*, Yuan-wu was writing the *Pi-yen-lu* (1125), and Hui-k'ai the *Wu-men-kuan* (1228), as commentaries on the classical *koan*s.[22] Both *shath* and *koan* were anti-dogmatic, and sought to leap over the limits of the mind to attain intimate contact with reality. The anecdotes of the great Ch'an masters admittedly have a peculiarly Chinese flavor, informed by the spirit of Chuang Tzu and Mahayana metaphysics, and this naturally stands in contrast to the world of Sufism, with its inheritance of prophetic revelation, Hellenistic cosmology, and Arab manners. It is probably the prophetic element, the contact with the supreme "I am" of God, that most strongly differentiates the Sufi tradition from

Ch'an/Zen. One apparently does not find the exact equivalent of the *shathiyat* of selfhood and testimony in the Buddhist tradition. There are some *koan*s, however, that are tantalizing in their implications for selfhood, such as, "What was your original face before you were born?"

There are more obvious similarities between *shath* and *koan* on the paradoxical level. The topics of the transcendence of duality and the *coincidentia oppositorum* are central to the Mahayana teaching of the emptiness of all categories. This is evident in the proclaimed identity of *nirvana* and *samsara*, and in the teaching of "the five ranks," with its Taoistic symbolism of black and white circles to represent the different aspects of reality. Consider the famous *koan* of *mu*, "no." "A monk asked Master Joshu: 'Has the dog Buddha-nature or not?' Joshu answered: 'Mu!'"[23] *Mu* literally means "no," but Joshu's answer is not a literal one. This is a "no" that denies the ultimate validity of yes and no, which overturns the wrong-headed notion of separate "natures" by a transcendence of all categories. According to a modern Zen master, *mu* "has nothing to do with the dualistic interpretation of yes and no, being and nonbeing. It is Truth itself, the Absolute itself."[24] The Arabic negation *la* is identified with the spiritual state of annihilation and the black light of Iblis, which guards the divine threshold against all unworthy visitors. The *koan* and *shath* are alike in their negative approach to transcendence. In this respect they both fulfill the requirements of Dionysius' negative theology: since the infinite cannot be adequately symbolized, it is better to refer to it by the lowest of symbols, to avoid the possibility of confusing symbol with reality. So it is that Erigena can say that God is nothing (*nihil*). When the *koan* says that the Buddha is a dried dirt-scraper, this should not be surprising. It is simply the language of paradox. Like the paradox, the *koan* is an illumination of the condition of the finite in relation to the infinite. I am not prepared to follow Father Dumoulin in calling Zen a "natural mysticism" distinct from the "supernatural mysticism" possible only in an I-thou relationship with a personally conceived God.[25] At this point, the nature of mystical experience effectively disappears from the ken of the observers; what is the outsider to know of a state that traditionally can only be expressed by a negation? To criticize Buddhist mysticism in terms of Catholic theology is a reduction, not a true comparison. As different modes of paradox, however, *shath* and the *koan* may be legitimately compared.

What, then, was the significance of the ecstatic experessions on faith and infidelity in Sufism? Do they partake of both the prophetic and paradoxical aspects of *shath*? To recapitulate, in their theological discussions of *iman* and *kufr*, the Sufis sought to reverse the rationalizing trend in theology by recovering the personal orientation toward God. Although this effort had some success, the linguistic devaluation of *iman* and *kufr* was to some extent irreversible. No longer was it possible for *iman* to serve as the all-embracing term for the religious life. The heightened spiritual sensitivity cultivated in Sufism found the dogmatized version of *iman* incapable of encompassing the ultimate goals of the path. Further extensions of faith had to be differentiated in terms of certainty (*yaqin*) and gnosis (*ma`rifah*), in order to accomodate the urge for transcendence. In the same way, the intellectualized concept of *kufr* was rejected by the Sufis, in favor of an existential interpretation of infidelity as the denial of the divine unity. This led to the employment of spiritual *takfir*, the condemnation of created duality as infidelity. It is nothing but the mirror image of *tawhid*, the confession of the divine unity.

   Shathiyat emphasized infidelity more than faith, probably because *kufr* now had a more powerful semantic aura than *iman*. The negative implications of *kufr* were also more suited to the rhetoric of paradox, as a praise of folly. In experiential terms, *kufr* was a negative symbol for annihilation (*fana'*) and unknowing (*nakirah*), the inadequacy of the creature to comprehend the creator. This experience has been communicated in many metaphors: astonishment, wandering in the desert, the black light, even the word "no." To get another comparative insight into the significance of mystical infidelity, we can, paradoxically, turn to a Christian formulation of faith, Anselm's "faith in search of understanding." Here by faith the soul perceives the nothingness of creation just as it realizes that it cannot possibly comprehend God:

> O Lord my God, who formed me and reformed me, tell my soul, which so desires thee, what thou art beyond what it has seen, that it may see clearly what it desires. It strains itself to see more, and sees nothing beyond what it has seen, save darkness. Or rather, it does not see darkness, since there is no darkness in thee, but it sees that it can see nothing more, because of its own darkness. Why is this, O Lord, why is this? Is its eye darkened by its own weakness, or dazzled by thy glory? In fact, it is both darkened in itself and dazzled by thee.[26]

Anselm has expressed his delicate formulation in a style quite different from the poetic enthusiasm of a Hallaj or an `Ayn al-Qudat, but the insight is substantially the same. The soul is dark in itself just as it is dazzled by the light of God, the excess of light that is called the divine dark of unknowing. For the Sufis, this soul becomes the "infidel heart" that is never satisfied with any created thing, and so gives itself the despised name of "infidel" from a sense of blame. As `Ayn al-Qudat says of the stage of "real infidelity," "One sees the Lord, and one becomes ashamed. Here, *tawhid* and faith begin."[27]

   Beyond this intuition of unknowing, however, the ecstatic sayings also imply that faith and infidelity are finally united in God's Essence, in the *coincidentia oppositorum*. The Sufis seem also to refer to a final union with the Essence, and this is surely the most tantalizing of symbols (as well as the origin of the accusations of *hulul*). What is really meant by terms such as "gnosis" and "union"? Do these terms refer to an actual attainment? They are formulations of a relationship that is, strictly speaking, inconceivable. It is not possible to explain how a limited being can possess omniscience or be united with an Essence that is, by definition, independent and absolute. Anselm's formulation does not attain an end; it is always striving for an understanding. The Sufi expression differs formally in that it posits gnosis and union as limiting functions, as intuitive symbols for a relationship that is incapable of being adequately symbolized. It would be a mistake to think that gnosis and union in this sense are "things" that one could appropriate. There is an ineffable mystery of participation, but as Hallaj concludes in his *Bustan al-Ma`rifah* ("Garden of Gnosis"), "God is Real (*al-haqq haqq*), and creation is created (*al-khalq khalq*), and there is nothing to fear."[28] The ecstatic expressions on faith and infidelity are paradoxical, but they verge on prophecy.

No matter how subtle and ingenious the Sufi interpretations of *shathiyat* may have been, it has been customary to suppose that the normal public reaction would have been shocked outrage. Nonetheless, the ecstatic sayings on faith and infidelity apparently had nothing to do with Sufi trials. This is especially surprising, since it would seem obvious that such evident admissions of apostasy, taken literally, would have been ideal material for prosecutors. I have inferred that these sayings must not have been made public by any of the Sufi martyrs. But why would Hallaj and `Ayn al-Qudat conceal their sayings on *kufr* and *iman*? Hallaj had proclaimed that the day of his martyrdom would be the happiest day in his life, and `Ayn al-Qudat knew that his own execution was inevitable. Why, then, would they protest their innocence to their judges, if they both sought martyrdom?

For the Sufis, mystical infidelity was an indication of the spiritual state of annihilation (*fana'*). In terms of the subject matter of *shathiyat*, the sayings on faith and infidelity were of secondary importance, less prophetic than paradoxical. They were statements about the nothingness of creation, not about the word of God. Since the sayings on faith and infidelity refer to finite and creation-bound experiences, they are of the reflective type of *shath*, impersonal observations rather than the witnessing of God in the first person. Their sayings were technical in nature, designed for advanced wayfarers rather than the general public. To use Evelyn Underhill's categories, the "divine darkness" does not easily lend itself to public disclosure, because of its very obscurity. It is rather the ecstasy of the "spiritual marriage" of union that the mystic will preach in public.[29] As an example, the revealing report of the geographer Ibn Hawqal (d. 367/977) stated that in Iran, Hallaj was known for publicly preaching purification from all desire, to allow the spirit of God to dwell within the heart, as it had done with Jesus.[30] There was no report of his preaching "unknowing" or "infidelity" in public. Neither Hallaj nor 'Ayn al-Qudat attempted to supply the judges with ready-made materials for the case-books. Martyrs understandably want to be understood on their own terms, just as those who practise civil disobedience want to be understood on their own terms; neither wishes to be treated as a common criminal. But in the Sufi trials, the intentions of the mystics and the jurists bypassed each other in mutual incomprehension.

Ecstatic expressions frequently gave rise to accusations of crypto-Shi'ism, so it must be asked whether there was any reason for this suspicion. Certainly the authorities thought they had good reasons to fear the revolutionary ambitions of the Qarmatis and the Nizari Isma'ilis. The Saljuq wazir Nizam al-Mulk (himself murdered by an Assassin) had traced the lineage of the Isma'ilis back to Mazdak, the leader of the great *zindiq* revolution of the late Sasanian period. The Mazdakis were hated and feared for their teachings regarding property and marriage. Although the sexual anarchism attributed to Mazdak may have been a heresiographic invention, other "spirituals" among the ancient Gnostics had developed a deliberate theory of libertinism.[31] It is not improbable that Mazdaki Manichaeans carried forward libertine attitudes into the Shi'i *zandaqah*, as Massignon suggested, but there is no evidence available to support this contention. We have already seen how mysticism also called forth denunciations of libertinism and incarnationism, terms frequently applied to certain extreme Shi'i positions. The accusations of immorality do not help us to understand either position, nor whether they have anything in common; such charges belong rather to the literature of invective, which attacks the person rather than the teaching in question. In this manner, even noted ascetics were identified as libertines, from the sheer momentum of this heresiographical impulse. Thus the jurists al-Tanukhi and Ibn al-Jawzi were ready to believe that the stern Ibn al-Khafif had participated in nocturnal orgies.[32] It is impossible to establish the truth of such charges, based as they always are on hearsay evidence. They belong to that class of imaginary themes, like the "extinguished lights" orgy, which was inevitably ascribed to heretics and witches by Christian writers.[33] We can conclude nothing about the connection between Sufism and Shi'ism from these accusations of libertinism.

A remarkable example of the reduction of unorthodoxy to Isma'ili "heresy" occurred in northern India during the reign of Firuz Shah ibn Tughluq (d. 790/1388). Firuz Shah executed several Sufis during his reign for uttering *shathiyat* (or pseudo-*shathiyat*) that he saw as posing a danger to state and religion. In the triumphal inscription that recorded these events, Firuz Shah also mentioned a number of other heretics whom he executed, including some Shi'is (who were incidentally accused of sodomy), a false mahdi, and a group of "heretics and libertines."[34] Modern research has indicated, however, that the libertines were in fact a Hindu Tantric group, although one of the two manuscript readings explicitly identifies them as Shi`is! Apparently there was an irresistible temptation to regard all detestable behavior as Isma`ilism, since the Isma`ilis were, by doxographic definition, detestable. Again in these cases, fears of Isma`ili influence played their part; certain disturbances and revolts in Delhi in the seventh/thirteenth century had been attributed to well-trained groups of Isma`ili assassins.[35] Heresiography handily lumpted together Sufis, messiahs, and Hindu Tantrists with the hated Isma`ilis, without seeing any essential distinctions.

Though accusations of immorality tell us nothing of the relation between Sufism and radical Shi`ism, perhaps there is some common ground in their attitude to the word of God. Sufi devotion to the Qur'an was, as we have seen, a development of one of the primary qualities of faith, but this openness to the divine word could be misconstrued as the perverse allegorization of the Shi`i *zandaqah*. Disrespect for the literal meaning of the Qur'an was popularly ascribed to the literary *zindiq*s of `Abbasi Baghdad, who were supposed to prefer their own poetry to the inimitable Qur'an.[36] These literary *zindiq*s were dabblers in Manichaeism rather than committed Isma`ilis, but the doctrinal handbooks are not concerned to distinguish these two forms of *zandaqah*. An instructive story is told about Hallaj in this regard. It is said that one day he was walking along with his teacher `Amr al-Makki, while the latter was reciting from the Qur`an. Hallaj remarked that he could say things like that, too—meaning that he could write things to rival the word of God. Here Hallaj appears in the role of a literary *zindiq* who sneers at the Qur'an and produces his own private "revelation." This is one of the tales, emanating from moderate Sufi circles, which tried to explain the true reason for Hallaj's execution—in this case, displaying heretical arrogance before a Sufi master. Although the story is not historical, may we not see here a veiled critique of *shath*, which pretends in some way to continue the process of revelation by inspired speech? In this way, ecstatic expressions may also have encouraged the assimilation of Sufism to Isma`ilism in the eyes of the authorities. It is also likely that the tendency of some Sufis to court blame (*malamah*) encouraged suspicions of Isma`ilism, not only because of the implied separation of personal from societal values, but also because blame, once aroused, tends to flow into familiar channels. But once again, this equation of Sufism with literary *zandaqah*, and hence with Isma`ili *zandaqah*, is nothing but a procession of confusions. All that these examples reveal is that Sufis, Manichaeans, and Isma`ilis were equally suspicious in the eyes of literalists.

But after so many instances over the centuries, in which Sufis were accused of secret Shi`i sympathies and *zandaqah*, can we assume that the resemblances between Sufism and Shi`ism were only superficial? This would probably be too simplistic. Certainly, Sufism has absorbed features typical of extreme Shi`ism, and there have been movements such as the Safawis that seemed to combine Sufi and Shi`i qualities. The thought of Hallaj, too, cannot be understood without reference to the Qarmati terms that he employs. Hermann Landolt even suggests that the Isma`ili element in `Ayn al-Qudat's thought has been underestimated.[37] It is particularly in the esoteric approach that one finds a close resemblance between Sufism and Shi`ism. Like the Sufis, the fourth/ tenth century Isma`ili authors of the encyclopedia of the Pure Brethren (Ikhwan al-Safa') distinguished a further stage of certainty (ya-qin) beyond ordinary religious faith.[38] The Isma`ilis also spoke in terms of internal and external meanings, and their theory of allegorization used the same scriptural support that Ruzbihan cited in his exegesis of shathiyat: this is Qur. 3.7, in the version that reads, "and none knows the exegesis of it save God and those who are rooted in knowledge." This Qur'anic verse was not only a proof-text for the philosophers (Averroes), but also for the Syrian Isma`ilis, who quoted it in a text on the allegorical interpretation of the Qur'an.[39] Unlike the esoteric Shi`is, however, Sufis like Hallaj and `Ayn al-Qudat tried to reveal the highest truth to the public. For the Qarmatis, revelation of the secret (ifsha' al-sirr) constituted adultery and was punishable by death, while dissimulation (ta-qiyah) was elevated into a principle for action.[40] The attitude of the mystic is quite different. "If ignorant people are not taught, they will never learn, nor will they ever know how to live or die. . . If these words are misconstrued, what can one who puts their right construction on them do about it? . . . indeed the words of our Lord, are often misconstrued."[41] These are the words of Meister Eckhart, in response to critics who blamed the excesses of the Beghards and the Brethren of the Free Spirit on his public mystical sermons. `Ayn al-Qudat could easily have made the same protest.

There was no inherent connection between the Sufi spiritualization of ritual and the radical Isma`ili abolition of the law, yet the Sufi attitude remained ambiguous. From a legalistic point of view, however, there was no appreciable difference between spiritualization of the law and antino-mianism. In any case, to decide the nature of the relationship between Sufism and Shi`ism is a question too large to be decided here. Though the two movements certainly diverged after the third/ninth century, the early period of Shi`ism had much in common with Sufism, and this is surely a promising field for further investigation. In the hadith of the Shi`i imams there is an important body of inspired sayings that may be comparable to shathiyat.[42] The legalistic reaction to shathiyat as a form of Isma`ilism, however, was simply a projection.

There have been, then, two possible modes of interpretation of the ecstatic expressions on faith and infidelity. One is the mystical interpretation of true infidelity as a paradoxical formulation of the nothingness of creation in the light of the experience of divine reality. This interpretation contains the further intuition that faith and infidelity are one in the divine coincidentia oppositorum. The negative formulation of infidelity powerfully emphasizes the inadequacy of symbols to express the nature of such a mystical experience. The juristic interpretation would presumably have been an accusation of *zandaqah*, the worst heresy. Yet this entire symbolism seems to have remained esoteric, so that in no case do we find either unambiguous public affirmation or rejection of the *shathiyat* on faith and infidelity. There is a good reason for this silence. *Shath* ultimately is meant to throw us back on our own resources, not to hold us fascinated in either admiration or disgust. Preoccupation with either the mystical symbolism or the shocking heresy of *shath* ignores the reality that inspired such speech. Hallaj himself described the two main reactions to his mission: on the one hand, enthusiastic partisans who called him divinely inspired, and on the other, furious opponents who called him a *zindiq*. Both of these reactions were off the mark, he says, since they confused him with the message that he presented. For one who truly understood what Hallaj was saying, the issue of his innocence or guilt would have been unimportant. Hallaj drew a figure containing four concentric circles to explain this:

> The denier remains in the outermost circle. He denies my state since he cannot see me, he charges me with *zandaqah*, and accuses me of evil. The inhabitant of the second circle thinks that I am a divine master (`alim rabbani`). And he who attains to the third reckons that I am in my heart's desires. But he who attains to the circle of reality forgets, and is hidden from my sight.[43]

After presenting his *shath*, Hallaj wishes to be removed from in between; when the king's message has been proclaimed, the messenger is no longer needed.

Notes

INTRODUCTION

1. Abu al-Hasan Fushanjah, in ʿAli Hujwiri, *Kashf al-Mahjub*, ed. Ahmad ʿAli Shah, Lahore, 1342/1923, p. 32.
2. Hallaj, *Diwan,* ed. Massignon, p. 106.
3. Hallaj, *Akhbar,* no. 41.
4. ʿAli Akbar Dihkhuda et al., *Lughat Namah,* Tehran, fasc. 156, pp. 381-2 (1348/1970), s.v. *"shath."*
5. *Essai,* Paris, 1922; new ed., Paris, 1968, p. 15.
6. Massignon, "Shath", EI¹ (1938), IV, 335-6.
7. Paul Nwyia, *Exégèse coranique et langage mystique,Nouvel essai sur le lexique technique des mystiques musulmans,* Beirut, 1970, p. 4.
8. Corbin, Introduction to *Sharh,* p. 31.
9. Gerardus van der Leeuw, *Religion in Essence and Manifestation,* trans. J. E. Turner, New York, 1963, II, 680-1.

CHAPTER ONE

1. Annemarie Schimmel, *Mystical Dimensions of Islam,* Chapel Hill, N.C., 1976, pp. 24-6, quoted by permission of the University of North Carolina Press.
2. Louis Massignon, "Shaṭh," EI¹, IV, 336.
3. William A. Graham, *Divine Word and Prophetic Word in Early Islam, A Reconsideration of the Sources, with Special Reference to the Divine Saying or "Hadîth Qudsî,"* Religion and Society 7, The Hague, 1977, p. 70, quoted by permission of Mouton.
4. Trans. Graham, p. 127, no. 12.
5. Trans. Graham, p. 142, no. 19a.
6. Trans. Graham, p. 173, no. 49.
7. Schimmel, *Dimensions,* p. 43; cf. pp. 133, 277.
8. Jaʿfar al-Sadiq, trans. Nwyia, *Exégèse,* pp. 179-80; cf. Massignon, *Essai,* pp. 201-5.

9. Abu Sa`id al-Kharraz, in Nwyia, pp. 248–50; Abú Nasr `Abdallah b. `Alí al-Sarráj al-Túsí, *The Kitáb al-Luma` fi'l-Tasawwuf*, ed. Reynold Alleyne Nicholson, "E. J. W. Gibb Memorial" Series, Vol. XXII, London, 1963, pp. 31–2.

10. Schimmel, *Diemnsions*, p. 44; *Essai*, p. 202.

11. Nwyia, p. 181.

12. Schimmel, *Dimensions*, pp. 47–51, esp. p. 48; GAS I, 645–6.

13. `Abd al-Rahman Badawi, ed., *Shatahat al-Sufiyah*, Part 1, *Abu Yazid al-Bistami*, Darasat Islamiyah, 9, Cairo, 1949, pp. 44–148.

14. Sarraj, *Luma`*, pp. 375–6.

15. *Ibid.*, p. 378.

16. *Ibid.*, p. 378.

17. *Ibid.*, p. 380.

18. *Ibid.*, p. 383.

19. A. J. Arberry, "Khargushi's Manual of Sufism," *Bulletin of the School of Oriental and African Studies* 9 (1937–39), pp. 345–9. Cf. GAS I, 670 for MSS; Massignon, *Passion* IV, 21 (bibliographie hallagienne, no. 180a); *idem*, "Shath," EI¹, IV, 337b.

20. Abu `Abd al-Rahman al-Sulami, *Ghalatat al-Sufiyah*, MS 178/8 Majami`, Dar al-Kutub al-Misriyah, Cairo, fol. 79a, lines 8–18 = Sarraj, *Luma`*, p. 375. See also A. J. Arberry, "Did Sulami Plagiarize Sarraj?" *Journal of the Royal Asiatic Society* (1937), pp. 461–5.

21. Abu Hamid al-Ghazali, *Ihya' Ulum al-Din,* Cairo, n.d., I, 60–62.

22. Abu al-Ma`ali `Abd Allah ibn Muhammad ibn `Ali ib n al-Hasan ibn `Ali al-Miyanji al-Hamadani (`Ayn al-Qudat), *Risalat Shakwa al-Gharib*, ed. `Afif `Usayran, Intisharat-i Danishgah-i Tihran, 695, Tehran, 1962, pp. 32, 35–6.

23. See the dual introductions by Henry Corbin and Muhammad Mu`in to their edition of Ruzbihan Baqli Shirazi, `*Abhar al-`Ashiqin*, Bibliothéque Iranienne 8, Tehran, Paris, 1958; Louis Massignon, "La Vie et les oeuvres de Rûzbehân Baqlî," *Opera Minora*, ed. Y. Moubarac, Beirut, 1963, II, 451–65.

24. The original version is Ruzbihan ibn Abi Nasr Baqli Shirazi, *Shathiyat (Mantiq al-Asrar)*, MSS 156, 871 `Irfan, Kitabkhanah-i Asitan-i Quds-i Ridawi, Mashhad (catalog I, 48; IV, 199); MS in collection of Louis Massignon, Paris. None of these were available to me, although excerpts have been given by Massignon in his *Essai*, pp. 445–7; cf. Massignon, "Rûzbehân," pp. 459–61, *Passion* II, 406–414, 498–501.

25. Corbin, introduction to *Sharh*, p. 23. Corbin has therefore given in several footnotes the Arabic original of some of the more puzzling passages.

26. Schimmel, *Dimensions*, p. 298.

27. Ruzbihan, *Sharh*, p. 12.

28. Ruzbihan, *Sharh*, p. 45; cf. Qur. 51.52.

29. Hallaj, *Akhbar*, no. 7; *Tawasin*, ed. Nwyia, VI.26. Massignon's reading *an-niyah* (*Tawasin*, p. 162; *Diwan*, p. 90) is incorrect; cf. Sarraj, *Luma`*, pp. 31–2; Soheil M. Afnan, *A Philosophical Lexicon in Persian and Arabic,* Beirut, 1969, p. 12; Ruzbihan, *Sharh*, p. 421, line 9 ff.

30. Junayd, in Sarraj, *Luma`*, p. 372; Ruzbihan, *Sharh*, p. 477, also index, s.v. "*hulul*." The heresiographic importance of the term *hulul* is discussed in part III below.

31. Ruzbihan, *Sharh*, p. 57.

32. *Ibid.*, pp. 57–8. I translate *mutashabih* as "symbolic" to reflect the position of Ruzbihan.

33. *The Glorious Qur'an,* trans. Abdullah Yusuf Ali, U.S.A., 1395/1975, p. 123, n. 348. Cf. GAS I, 29 on Muhahid.

34. Averroes, "The Decisive Treatise, Determining what the Connection is between Religion and Philosophy," trans. George F. Hourani, in *Medieval Political Philosophy, A Sourcebook*, ed. Ralph Lerner and Muhsin Mahdi, New York, 1963, pp. 170, 172, 177.

35. Ruzbihan, *Sharh*, pp. 58–9. On *iltibas* in the sense of clothing with divinity, cf. Bayazid (in *Luma`*, p. 382; *Sharh*, ch. 35); Hallaj, *Akhbar*, no. 74; Ruzbihan, *Sharh*, pp. 63, 435. Elsewhere *iltibas* means "covering up," "confusion," cf. Hallaj, *Akhbar*, nos. 8, 53; Ruzbihan *Sharh*, pp. 508–9, 513. Corbin's translation of *iltibas* as "ambiguity" does not do justice to the rich nuances.

36. *Aqwal al-A'immah al-Sufiyah*, MS 12632 Or., British Museum, London, fols. 241a–243b on *shathiyat*, quoting *Luma`*, pp. 381, lines 1–2; 382, lines 1–8; 375, lines 4–5. A longer version is given of *Diwan al-Hallaj*, ed. Massignon, no. M 75, ed. Shaybi, p. 242. The biography of Hallaj (inclined toward rejection of him) is on fol. 145b. For other citations of this MS, see Nwyia, pp. 251, 263, 272, 297.

37. S. Guyard, ed. and trans., *Fragments relatifs à la doctrine des Ismaélîs,* Paris, MDCCCLXXIV, p. 33.

38. Marshall G. S. Hodgson, *The Order of Assassins, The Struggle of the Early Nizârî Ismâ`îlîs against the Islamic World*, 's-Gravenhage, 1955, pp. 250, 179. For *ta'yid*, see pp. 173, 195, 199, 215.

39. Ibn `Arabi, in `Ali al-Jurjani, *Kitab al-Ta`rifat*, ed. Gustavus Fluegel, Leipzig, MDCCCXLV, p. 285 (cf. p. 132, Jurjani's definition); Kamal al-Din Abu al-Ghanayim `Abd al-Razzaq al-Kashi al-Samarqandi, *Istilahat al-Sufiyah*, ed. Aloys Sprenger, Calcutta, 1845, p. 151, quoting *Luma`*, p. 375, lines 14–15.

40. al-Dhahabi, in Abu al-`Abbas Ahmad ibn Muhammad al-Maqqari, *Kitab Nafh al-Tib min Ghusn al-Andalus al-Ratib wa Dhikr Waziriha Lisan al-Din ibn al-Khatib*, ed. R. Dozy et al., Leiden, 1855–61, I, 569. See the rare use of the term *shath* by Da'ud al-Qaysari, *Sharh Fusus al-Hikam,* Tehran, 1299/1882, p. 173, trans. Henry Corbin, *Creative Imagination in the Sufism of Ibn `Arabi*, trans. Ralph Mannheim, Bollingen Series XCI, Princeton, 1969, p. 121, n. 47 (reading *naw` min al-shath* for *nu'min*).

41. Sharaf al-Din Yahya Maneri, *Ma`din al-Ma`uni*, comp. Zayn Badr Arabi, MS 425 Curzon Persian, Asiatic Society Library, Calcutta, fols. 169b–170a. See also his *Maktubat-i Jawabi*, Cawnpore, n.d., letter no. 15, pp. 21–22, for Hallaj. On Maneri, see Bruce Lawrence, *Notes from a Distant Flute: The Extant Literature of pre-Mughal Indian Sufism*, Tehran, 1978, pp. 72–77; Sharafuddin Maneri, *The Hundred Letters*, trans. Paul Jackson, The Classics of Western Spirituality, New York, 1980.

42. Nur Qutb-i `Alam Pandawi, *Maktubat*, MS 297671/18 Farsi, Subhanullah Collection, Maulana Azad Library, Aligarh Muslim University, Aligarh, fol. 3b, cf. 23a. See also Lawrence, pp. 55–7.

43. Ashraf Jahangir Simnani, *Maktubat-i Ashrafiyah*, MS 166 Farsi, Subhanullah Collection, History Department Library, Aligarh Muslim University, letter no. 49, fols. 145a–147a; supplement, fol. 257a. This *Tafsir-i Nurbakhshiyah* is not extant. For Simnani see Lawrence, pp. 53–5.

44. Ashraf Jahangir Simnani, *Lata'if-i Ashrafi*, comp. Nizam Gharib Yamani, Delhi, 1295, II, 1–21. His definition of *shath* (I, 232) is a translation of that given by Simnani's teacher, `Abd al-Razzaq al-Kashani, cited above, n. 39.

45. Adhari Isfara'ini, *Jawahir al-Asrar*, MS 429 Curzon Persian, Asiatic Society, Calcutta, fol. 65b.

46. *Ibid.*, fol. 66a, quoting the *khutbat al-bayan* from *Nahj al-Balaghah*.

47. Dara Shikuh, *Hasanat al-`Arifin*, ed. Makhdum Rahin, Tehran, 1352/1973, p. 3.

48. Ruzbihan, *Sharh*, ch. 117, p. 202, line 11, *anja ki barmad*, is corrected by *Hasanat*, p. 14, to read *nukhalah ba ramad* ("bran with ashes"), also confirmed by Sarraj, *Pages*, p. 6.

49. Dara, *Hasanat*, p. 79.

50. Fansuri's *shath* is discussed by Syed Muhammad Naguib al-Attas, *Raniri and the Wujudiyyah of 17th Century Acheh*, Monographs of the Malaysian Branch of the Royal Asiatic Society, III, Singapore, 1966, pp. 16, 19, 112–114. Nabulusi's defense is printed as an appendix to Badawi's *Shatahat*, pp. 148–158. On Kawrani, who had many disciples in Java, see *Passion,* index, s.n.

51. `Aziz Allah ibn Sayyid Asad Allah al-Hasani al-Husayni al-Hindi, *Durr-i Maknun*, MS Or. 4382, British Museum, London.

52. This is Ja`far ibn Muhammad `Uthman al-Mirghani's *Qussat al-Mi`raj*, cited by J. Spencer Trimingham, *The Sufi Orders in Islam*, London, 1973, p. 209.

53. Bayazid, in *Sharh*, ch. 76.

54. Bayazid, in *Shatahat*, p. 111.

55. Massignon, ed., *Tawasin*, pp. 129–131.

56. Bayazid, in *Sharh*, ch. 65; *Shatahat*, p. 23, no. 22.

57. Bayazid, in *Sharh*, ch. 54.

58. Bayazid, in *Recueil*, p. 28; *Sharh*, ch. 57, where the nuance has been lost: "God, you became a mirror for me, and then I became a mirror for You."

59. Bayazid, in *Luma`*, p. 382; *Sharh*, ch. 35.

60. Bayazid, in *Shatahat*, p. 77.

61. Hallaj, in *Sharh*, ch. 230; *Diwan*, ed. Massignon, no. Q 9, pp. 30–1; ed. Shaybi, pp. 285–6. Ruzbihan translates verses 1a, 3b, 2a, 2b, out of a total of five verses.

62. Ruzbihan, *Sharh*, p. 387.

63. Hallaj, in *Sharh*, ch. 228, with apparatus to p. 385, line 6.

64. *Diwan*, ed. Massignon, no. M 48, p. 82; ed. Shaybi, p. 251.

65. Hallaj, in *Sharh*, ch. 267, with preference for the text in *Diwan*, ed. Massignon, no. M 5, p. 41; ed. Shaybi, pp. 150–1.

66. Ibn Taymiyah, in *Diwan*, ed. Shaybi, p. 153; Ibn al-Khafif, in *Sharh*, p. 433.

67. Ruzbihan, *Sharh*, p. 433.

68. Hallaj, in *Sharh*, ch. 266.

69. Hallaj, in *Sharh*, ch. 259; *Diwan*, ed. Massignon, no. M 55, p. 90; ed. Shaybi, pp. 298–9; *Akhbar*, no. 50.

70. Junayd, in *Sharh*, ch. 91.

71. Junayd, in *Sharh,* ch. 92.

72. Junayd, in Ali Hassan Abdel-Kader, ed. and trans., *The Life, Personality and Writings of Al-Junayd*, "E. J. W. Gibb Memorial" Series, N.S. XXII, London, 1976, p. 70.

73. Ruwaym, in *Sharh*, ch. 107; *Luma`*, p. 31.

74. Sarraj, *Luma`*, pp. 31–2.

75. Hallaj, in *Sharh*, ch. 254.

76. Hallaj, in *Sharh*, ch. 274.

77. Bayazid, in *Sharh*, ch. 68.

78. Shibli, in *Sharh*, ch. 144; *Luma`*, p. 402.

79. Husri, in *Sharh*, ch. 468.

80. Shibli, in *Sharh*, ch. 147; *Luma`*, pp. 404–5.

81. Husri, in *Sharh*, ch. 466.

82. Schimmel, *Dimensions*, pp. 72, 146.

83. Muzayyin, in *Sharh*, ch. 126.

84. Bayazid, in *Sharh*, ch. 51.

85. Bayazid, in *Shatahat*, p. 77.

86. Husri, in *Sharh*, ch. 470.

87. Bayazid, in *Luma`*, p. 384.

88. Junayd, in *Luma`*, pp. 375, 377.

89. Ruzbihan, *Sharh*, p. 81; `*Ara'is*, cited by Reynold A. Nicholson, ed. and trans., *The Mathnawi of Jalalu'ddin Rumi*, "E. J. W. Gibb Memorial" Series IV, 8, London, 1940, VIII, 56. Cf. R. C. Zaehner, *Hindu and Muslim Mysticism*, New York, 1972, pp. 214–6, lines 342–369. See also the discussion in the Appendix.

90. Bundar ibn Husayn, in *Sharh*, ch. 189.

91. Husri, in *Sharh*, ch. 478, reading *khawf* for *harf*.

92. Wasiti, in *Sharh*, ch. 168.

93. Yusuf ibn Husayn al-Razi, in *Sharh*, ch. 113.

94. Kattani, in *Sharh*, ch. 124.

95. Sahl al-Tustari, in *Sharh*, ch. 121.

96. Ruzbihan, *Sharh*, p. 209.

97. Tinati, in *Sharh*, ch. 137.

98. Shibli, in *Sharh*, ch. 162 reading *siyanat* for *jinayat*, cf. Hujwiri, trans. Reynold A. Nicholson, *The Kashf al-Mahjúb, The Oldest Persian Treatise on Sufiism (sic)*, "E. J. W. Gibb Memorial" Series, vol. XVII, new ed., London, 1936, reprint ed., 1976, p. 38.

99. Abu Bakr al-Siddiq, in *Sharh*, ch. 21: *al-`ajz `an dark al-idrak idrak*.

100. Sahl, in Abu Bakr al-Kalabadhi, *The Doctrine of the Sufis (Kitab al-Ta`arruf li-madhhab ahl al-tasawwuf)*, trans. Arthur John Arberry, reprint ed., Lahore, 1966, p. 57; Hallaj, *Tawasin*, ed. Massignon, pp. 71, 105–6, 192–4. The saying is elsewhere attributed to the fourth caliph, `Ali.

101. *Luma`*, p. 124; Hujwiri, trans. Nicholson, p. 276, attributed to Shibli; *Tamhidat*, p. 58.

102. See also Alexander Altmann, "The Delphic Maxim in Medieval Islam and Judaism," in *Studies in Religious Philosophy and Mysticism*, Plainview, New York, 1969, pp. 1–40.

103. Dionysius the Areopagite, *The Mystical Theology and the Celestial Hierarchies*, trans. by the editors of the Shrine of Wisdom, 2nd ed., Fintry, Surrey, England, 1965, p. 11.

104. Ruzbihan, *Sharh*, pp. 66–7.

105. Badi` al-Zaman Furuzanfarr, *Ahadith-i Mathnawi*, Intisharat-i Danishgah-i Tihran, 283, Tehran, 1334, p. 2, no. 3.

106. Wasiti, in *Luma`*, pp. 369–70; *Sharh*, ch. 163.

107. Shibli, in *Sharh*, ch. 155.
108. Ja`far al-Hadhdha', in *Sharh*, ch. 183.
109. Wasiti, in *Sharh*, ch. 175.
110. Abu Yahya al-Shirazi, in *Sharh*, ch. 184.
111. Husri, in *Sharh*, ch. 465, reading *payda* for *bayda*.
112. Hallaj, in *Sharh*, ch. 264; *Tawasin*, ed. Massignon, XI.1; *Tawasin* V.36 with Ruzbihan's comment, in *Sharh*, p. 507.
113. Ruzbihan al-Baqli al-Shirazi, *Mashrab al-Arwah, wa huwa Mashhur bi-Hazar-u-Yak Maqam (bi-Alf Maqam wa Maqam)*, ed. Nazif Muharram Khwajah, Istanbul, 1973, p. 199. For "obliteration of the eye (*intimas al-`ayn*)," cf. Qur. 36.66.
114. Ruzbihan, *Sharh*, p. 528. Iblis is quoting Hallaj's own dictum.
115. *Passion* II, 88–9; *Essai*, p. 101.
116. Ruzbihan, *Sharh*, p. 450.
117. Nuri, in *Sharh*, ch. 98; *Pages*, p. 5.
118. Ruzbihan, *Sharh*, ch. 185.
119. *Ibid.*, ch. 190.
120. *Ibid.,* ch. 195.
121. *Ibid.,* ch. 197.
122. Hellmut Ritter, "Muslim Mystics Strife with God" (*sic*), *Oriens* 5 (1952), pp. 8 ff.
123. Ruzbihan, *Sharh*, ch. 462.
124. Abu Hamzah, in *Sharh*, ch. 117; *Pages,* p. 6; Nuri, in *Sharh*, ch. 96; *Pages,* p. 5.
125. Hallaj, in *Sharh*, p. 261.
126. Ruzbihan, *Sharh*, p. 425.
127. *Ibid.*, ch. 159. The text says that the man gave a shout, *za`qah-i bi-zad*, but it is not clear why this should have called forth Shibli's wrath. Since in line 12 Ruzbihan compares this with a case of fainting during an inspiring sermon, I suggest the emendation of *sa`qah-i bi-zad*, "he fell into a faint," recalling that Moses fainted before God, *fa-kharra Musa sa`qan* (Qur. 7.143), though there is no other textual support for this reading.
128. Ruzbihan, *Sharh*, pp. 273–4; cf. Schimmel, *Dimensions*, pp. 22, 79.
129. Wasiti, in *Sharh*, ch. 172; *Recueil*, p. 29.
130. Shibli, in *Sharh*, ch. 143; *Luma`*, p. 397.
131. Bayazid, in *Sharh*, ch. 74; *Recueil*, p. 29.
132. Hallaj, in *Sharh*, ch. 269.
133. Shibli, in *Sharh*, ch. 151; *Luma`*, p. 406.
134. Kharaqani, in *Sharh*, ch. 182.
135. Bayazid, in *Sharh*, ch. 53.
136. Bayazid, in *Shatahat*, p. 111; *Sharh*, ch. 71.
137. Hellmut Ritter, "Die Aussprüche des Bāyezīd Bisṭāmī," *Westöstliche Abhandlungen Rudolf Tschudi zum siebzigsten Geburtstag überreicht von Freunden und Schulern*, ed. Fritz Meier, Wiesbaden, 1954, p. 243, quoted by permission of Otto Harrassowitz Verlag.
138. Bayazid, in *Sharh*, ch. 40; *Luma`*, p. 391; Harawi, in Ritter, "Aussprüche," p. 232.
139. Bichr Farès, "Mufākhara", EI[1], Suppl., p. 151 (1938), quoted by permission of E. J. Brill.

140. 'Abd al-Qahir ibn 'Abd Allah al-Suhrawardi (*sic*), *Adab al-Muridin*, ed. Menahem Milson, typescript, Widener Library, Harvard University, p. 88, no. 193. Cf. Abu al-Najib al-Suhrawardi, *A Sufi Rule for Novices: Kitab Adab al-Muridin*, trans. Menahem Milson, Cambridge, 1975, p. 81, no. 205. See also the definition of *shath*, p. 23, no. 50 (text); p. 40, no. 57 (trans.).

141. Muhammad Taqi Danish-Puzhuh, ed., *Ruzbihan Namah*, Silsilah-i Intisharat-i Anjuman-i Athar-i Milli, 60, Tehran, 1347/1969, pp. 197–8; cf. the similar story on pp. 195–6.

142. Ibn 'Arabi, *Futuhat* II, 2, 338, in Rahin, Introduction to *Hasanat al-'Arifin*, p. 19; cf. p. 22.

143. Hallaj, in *Sharh*, ch. 253, reading *habbat* for *jannat*, cf. p. 415, line 3.

144. Abu Bakr Ahmad ibn 'Ali al-Khatib al-Baghdadi, *Ta'rikh Baghdad*, Cairo, 1349/1931 (cited hereafter as Khatib), VIII, 128–9; *Sharh*, ch. 249; *Passion* I, 568–71.

145. *Akhbar*, p. 164, n. 1.

146. Ruzbihan, *Sharh*, p. 410.

147. Louis Massignon and Paul Kraus, Introduction to *Akhbar*, p. 76.

148. Hallaj, *Akhbar*, no. 2. Cf. trans., pp. 10–14; revised trans. pp. 163–5; Introduction, pp. 53–6, 76–81; *Sharh*, ch. 257.

149. Hallaj, in *Sharh*, ch. 257. Cf. Arabic original in apparatus to p. 418, lines 15–17; *Akhbar*, p. 165, nn. 12, 13, 15, 16. Emphasis indicating the inversions is mine.

150. Ruzbihan *Sharh*, p. 419.

151. Bayazid, in *Shatahat*, pp. 138–141, *Sharh*, ch. 63; trans. A. J. Arberry, *Revelation and Reason in Islam*, London, New York, 1957, pp. 99–103, cf. 107–8. Zaehner, pp. 198–210, has also translated this text, with 'Attar's Persian version alongside. But his perverse attempt to see Bayazid as a transmitter of Vedanta to Sufism distorts his interpretation badly (pp. 93–134). See the refutation by A. J. Arberry, "Bistamiana," *Bulletin of the School of Oriental and African Studies* 25 (1962), pp. 28–37.

152. Ruzbihan, *Sharh*, p. 116.

153. Bayazid, in *Shatahat*, p. 139; cf. Arberry's trans., *Revelation*, pp. 100–1.

154. Bayazid, in *Shatahat*, p. 141.

155. Hallaj, *Tawasin* X.15–16, ed. Nwyia (cf. Nwyia's translation, p. 226).

156. Bayazid, in *Shatahat*, p. 60.

157. Bayazid, trans. Ritter, "Aussprüche," p. 238.

158. Bayazid, in *Shatahat*, p. 122; Ritter, "Aussprüche," pp. 238–9, cf. *Sharh*, ch. 50, for a different version that makes the motive out to be Bayazid's desire to be left in peace.

159. Ritter, "Aussprüche," p. 238.

160. Hallaj, *Akhbar,* no. 62.

161. *Passion*, I, 663–5.

162. *Passion* III, 260; Ritter, "Aussprüche," p. 241.

163. Sarraj, *Luma'*, p. 303, but cf. p. 310.

164. On the divine deception (*makr*) see Hallaj, in *Essai*, p. 368, nos. 45–6, p. 375, no. 72; Bayazid, in *Shatahat*, p. 101; Sarraj, *Luma'*, p. 311; Nwyia, *Exégèse*, pp. 126, 284.

165. Hallaj, in *Sharh*, ch. 244, also *Essai*, p. 446; trans. *Passion* III, 314, n.

166. *Passion* II, 410–411. Herbert Mason's English translation, *The Passion of Hallaj* (Princeton, 1982), appeared too late to be used in this study, but in the interests of accuracy, I have checked my translations from the second French edition against Prof. Mason's version.
167. Abu Sa`id ibn al-A`rabi, *Kitab al-Wajd*, in *Luma`*, p. 309.
168. Ruzbihan, *Sharh*, p. 425, cf. *Luma`*, pp. 340–1; Ruzbihan, *Mashrab al-Arwah*, p. 122.
169. `Abd al-Rahman ibn Muhammad ibn Khaldun, *Muqaddimat Ibn Khaldun*, ed. `Ali `Abd al-Wahid Wafi, n.p. (Cairo), 1379/1960, III, 1081.
170. `Abd al-Qadir al-Jilani, quoted by Rahin, introduction to *Hasanat al-`Arifin*, p. 27.
171. Hujwiri, trans. Nicholson, p. 153, in reference to a "mischievous" saying of Hallaj. Cf. also pp. 168, 184–9.
172. Massignon, *Passion* II, 189–90, 364; "Rûzbehân," *Opera Minora* II, 463–4.
173. Hujwiri, trans. Nicholson, p. 189.
174. Shibli, in `Ali Hujwiri, *Kashf al-Mahjub*, p. 120; trans. Nicholson, p. 151.
175. Sarraj, *Luma`* p. 382.
176. Junayd, in *Shatahat*, pp. 103, 68. Sarraj explains away Bayazid's "Glory be to Me!" as a quotation from God also, *Luma`*, p. 391. The story of Majnun and Layla is one of the most popular allegories of mystical love in the Islamic tradition.
177. Sarraj, *Luma`*, p. 390.
178. *Ibid.*, p. 391.
179. Ritter, "Aussprüche," p. 232.
180. Henry Corbin, introduction to *Sharh*, p. 41.

CHAPTER TWO

1. Abu `Abd Allah ibn Muhammad ibn Hanbal al-Shaybani al-Marwazi, *(al-)Musnad*, Egypt, 1306, I, 107 (henceforth cited as Ibn Hanbal); cf. Muhammad ibn Isma`il ibn Ibrahim ibn al-Mughira al-Bukhari, *(al-)Sahih*, Egypt, 1306, Maghazi 23, III, 9 (henceforth cited as Bukhari), also Abu `Isa Muhammad ibn `Isa ibn Sura al-Tirmidhi, *(al-)Jami`*, ed. Ashraf `Ali al-Wasiti, Delhi, 1265, Tafsir Sura 2, p. 487 (henceforth cited as Tirmidhi) for similar incidents.
2. Ibn Hanbal III, 439.
3. Bukhari, Iman 18.
4. Ahmad ibn Shu`ayb ibn `Ali al-Nasa'i, *(al-)Sunan*, Cawnpore, 1290, Zakat 1, p. 383 (henceforth cited as Nasa'i), on ablution; Tirmidhi, Iman 11, p. 431, on caring for mosques; Bukhari, Iman 25, 26, 28, on prayers of Ramadan and *laylat al-qadr*; Bukhari, Iman 35 on funerals; Bukhari, Iman 26, also Jihad 45 (II, 100) on *jihad*.
5. Ibn Hanbal III, 135.
6. Bukhari, Fada'il (Haram) Madinh 1, I, 222; cf. Ibn Hanbal I, 174 and IV, 73 for variations. Here we might suspect a tendentiousness in favor of the supremacy of Medina in the interpretation of the law, directed against the speculative schools of Iraq.

7. Ibn Hanbal III, 276; cf. Ign. Goldziher, "Zwischen den Augen," in *Der Islam* XI (1921), p. 178.

8. Examples are found in Bukhari, Iman 10, "The sign of faith is the love of the Ansar"; Bukhari, Fada'il al-Qur'an 36, III, 147, anti-Khariji; Ibn Hanbal II, 133, anti-Shi`ah; Ibn Hanbal V, 199, pro-Marwani ("When schisms occur, faith will be in Syria.").

9. Louis Gardet and M.-M. Anawati, *Introduction á la théologie musulmane, essai de théologie comparée*, Études de philosophie médiévale, XXXVII, Paris, 1948, p. 433–5.

10. Gardet and Anawati, *Introduction*, pp. 439–440.

11. Abu Hamid al-Ghazali, *Faysal al-Tafriqah bayn al-Islam wa al-Zandaqah*, trans. Toshihiko Izutsu, *The Concept of Belief in Islamic Theology—A Semantic Analysis of "Iman" and "Islam"*—Studies in the Humanities and Social Relations, vol. VI, Tokyo, 1965, p. 25. The following discussion is a summary of Izutsu's analysis, *Ibid.*, pp. 25–34.

12. Ruzbihan al-Baqli, `Ara'is al-Bayan fi Haqa'iq al-Qur'an, Calcutta, 1883, II, 208, *in Qur.* 40.35.

13. Abu Bakr Muhammad al-Kalabadhi, *al-Ta`arruf li-Madhhab Ahl al-Tasawwuf*, ed. `Abd al-Halim Mahmud and Taha `Abd al-Baqi Surur, Cairo, 1380/1960, p. 79.

14. L. Gardet, "Iman," EI^2, III, 1170b-1174a (1971); Muhammad A`la ibn `Ali al-Thanawi, *Kashshaf Istilahat al-Funun*, Beirut, 1962 (reprint of 1855-62 ed.), pp. 94–98.

15. Ibn al-Khafif, *Mu`taqad*, in Abu al-Hasan `Ali ibn Muhammad al-Daylami, *Sirat al-Shaykh al-Kabir Abu `Abd Allah ibn al-Khafif al-Shirazi*, trans. Rukn al-Din Yahya ibn Junayd al-Shirazi, ed. Annemarie Schimmel, Ankara, 1955, p. 297.

16. Ibn al-Khafif, in Abu al-Qasim `Abd al-Karim al-Qushayri, *al-Risalah al-Qushayriyah*, ed. `Abd al-Halim Mahmud and Mahmud ibn al-Sharif, Cairo, 1974, p. 35; cf. Schimmel, introduction to al-Daylami, p. 27.

17. Qushayri, p. 36.

18. Nicholas Heer, trans., "A Sufi psychological treatise, A translation of the *Bayan al-Farq bayn al-Sadr wa al-Qalb wa al-Fu'ad wa al-Lubb* of Abu `Abd Allah Muhammad ibn `Ali al-Hakim al-Tirmidhi," *Muslim World* 51 (1961), p. 88.

19. Josef van Ess, *Die Gedankenwelt des Ḥārit al-Muḥāsibī*, Bonner Orientalistische Studien, new series, vol. 12, Bonn, 1961, p. 185. For the whole problem, cf. A. J. Wensinck, *The Muslim Creed, Its Genesis and Historical Development*, London, 1965, p. 138–140.

20. Ibn al-Khafif, in Daylami, p. 297.

21. Kalabadhi, p. 82. See also Sarraj, *Luma`*, p. 350; Nwyia, p. 272 (Kharraz).

22. Kalabadhi, p. 80.

23. Ibn al-Khafif, in Daylami, p. 298, reading *lil-iman* for *al-iman* (cf. the Persian, *iman wa tawhid wa ma`rifat-ra*).

24. Kalabadhi, p. 83.

25. Ibn al-Khafif, in Daylami, p. 298.

26. Muhasibi, trans. van Ess, p. 160.

27. Ibn al-Farra', *Kitab al-Mu`tamad fi Usul al-Din*, ed. Wadi` Z. Haddad, "Al-Qādi Abū Ya`lā ibn al-Farrā': His Life, Works and Religious Thought, Muslim Jurisconsult and Theologian, Died in Baghdad in 458/1066," Ph.D. Thesis, Harvard University, 1969, pt. II, p. 105, no. 347 (text), pt. II, p. 159. no. 347 (trans.).

28. Massignon, *Passion* III, 146; Ibn al-Farra`, ed. Haddad, pt. II, p. 105, no. 346, trans. pt. II, pp. 158–9, no. 346; Hallaj, in Sulami, *in Qur.* 3.16, in Massignon, *Essai*, p. 362, no. 12; *in Qur.* 7.171, in *Essai*, p. 370, no. 50.

29. Kalabadhi, p. 81.

30. Sahl al-Tustari, *in Qur.* 58.22, in Ruzbihan, `Ara'is al-Bayan* II, 315. This primordial distribution of faith is also assumed by *Fiqh Akbar* II, trans. Wensinck, *Creed*, pp. 190–1.

31. Sahl, in Qushayri, p. 446. Sarraj criticizes a Sufi who placed faith above certainty (*Luma`*, p. 369). According to Muhasibi, certainty is the basis of faith (van Ess, p. 160).

32. Kalabadhi, p. 82.

33. Ibn al-Khafif, in Daylami, p. 298.

34. Massignon, *Passion* III, 162.

35. *Ibid.*, III, 46.

36. Kalabadhi, p. 82.

37. *Kufr ahl al-himmah aslamu min iman ahl al-minnah*, in Sulami, *Tabaqat al-Sufiyah*, ed. J. Pedersen, Leiden, 1960, p. 64; also in Badawi, *Shatahat*, p. 178.

38. Hallaj, in Sulami, *Jawami` Adab al-Sufiyah*, in *Essai*, p. 428; in Ruzbihan, *in Qur.* 4.85, in *Essai*, p. 414, no. 5.

39. Hallaj,in Sulami, *Tabaqat*, p. 313; also in Ruzbihan, *Sharh*, no. 275, and Harawi, in *Essai*, p. 442.

40. Hallaj, in Sulami, *in Qur.* 17.110, in *Essai*, p. 377, no. 79.

41. *Ibid., in Qur.* 3.96 ("III.89"), in *Essai*, p. 363, no. 17; *ibid., in Qur.* 7.158, in *Essai*, p. 370.

42. Hallaj, in Ruzbihan, *in Qur.* 48.10, in *Essai*, p. 417, no. 24; also *Akhbar*, no. 47.

43. Hallaj, in Ruzbihan, *Sharh*, no. 238.

44. Hallaj, *Akhbar*, no. 41.

45. Hallaj, in Kalabadhi, in *Essai*, p. 348, no. 8. Cf. *Tawasin* 6.19; *Essai*, p. 301 (Kharraz).

46. Hallaj, *Akhbar*, no. 35.

47. Shibli, in `Ayn al-Qudat, *Tamhidat*, p. 332.

48. Shibli, in Ruzbihan, *Sharh*, ch. 162, reading *siyanat* for *jinayat* (cf. Hujwiri, trans. Nicholson, p. 38).

49. Hallaj, *Akhbar*, no. 25; cf. also nos. 49, 57, 63.

50. *Ibid.*, no. 43. This verse attracted the particular wrath of ibn Taymiyah, who called it "not only infidelity but also the word of an ignoramus who does not understand what he is saying"; cf. *ibid.*, pp. 66–7.

51. *Ibid.*, no. 3.

52. *Ibid.*, no. 5.

53. *Ibid.*, no. 50, also no. 54, in which Hallaj agrees to heal a man's sick brother only on condition that the man continue vilifying Hallaj, accusing him of infidelity, and urging that he be killed. Cf. Schimmel, *Al-Halladsch*, p. 102.

54. Massignon, *Passion* I, 67, cf. *ibid.*, I, 265–7, 533, 586–8.

55. Hallaj, in `Attar, *Tadhkirat al-Awliya'* II, 139, in *Akhbar*, no. 14*, p. 145.

56. Hallaj, *Diwan*, ed. Massignon, no. 51.

57. Hallaj, *Akhbar*, no. 52.

58. *Ibid.;* for Christianizing tendencies in Massignon, see, e.g., Massignon, "Étude sur une courbe personelle de vie: le cas de Hallaj, martyr mystique de l'Islam," *Opera Minora*, ed. Y. Moubarac, Beirut, 1963, II, 190, and the overly negative complaint of Edward Said, *Orientalism*, New York, 1979, pp. 104, 268–9, 272.

59. Hallaj, *Akhbar*, no. 66; cf. translation by Schimmel, *Al-Halladsch*, p. 101. `Ayn al-Qudat renders the Arabic *kafartu* into Persian as *kafir shudam*, "I became infidel" (*Tamhidat*, p. 215, no. 275).

60. Hallaj, *Tawasin*, ed. Nwyia, p. 188 (title page).

61. Hallaj, *Akhbar*, no. 6.

62. Hallaj, in Sulami, *Tabaqat*, p. 311; also in *Akhbar*, no. 1*/12, p. 115 (*ya' ba'*).

63. Hallaj, *Akhbar*, no. 47. Massignon's translation misses the astral opposition between the verbs of setting (*saqatat*) and rising (*al-tali'ah*). The phrase *la `ayn wa la athar* means annihilation of humanity in divinity, cf. *Akhbar*, no. 10, line 11.

64. *Ibid.*, no. 48.

65. Paul Kraus and Louis Massignon, eds., *Akhbār al-Hallāj, Texte ancien relatif à la prédication et au supplice du mystique musulman al-Hosayn b. Mansour al-Hallāj*, 2nd ed., Paris, 1936, pp. 50–1. This section (pp. 44–52 of the introduction) was not included by Massignon in the third edition, and may be attributed to the more cerebral Kraus.

66. Hallaj, *Akhbar*, no. 2, and in Ibn al-Khatib, *Rawdat al-Ta`rif*, in *Akhbar*, no. 8*, p. 143.

67. `Abd al-Rahman ibn Ahmad Jami, *Nafahat al-Uns min Hadarat al-Quds,* ed. Mahdi Tawhidipur, Tehran, 1337, p. 414. Cf. also Schimmel, *Dimensions*, pp. 295–6; *Passion* II, 176–8.

68. `Ayn al-Qudat, *Tamhidat*, p. 115, no. 162.

69. *Ibid.*, p. 295, ch. 387.

70. *Ibid.*, p. 369.

71. Alessandro Bausani, *Persia Religiosa da Zarathustra a Baha'u'llah*, La Cultura, IV, Milan, 1959, pp. 301–11, 318–336, 342; *idem*, "Ghazal.II. — In Persian Poetry," EI2, II, 1036a (1965), in both places following Muhammad Mu`in, *Mazdayasna wa Ta'thir-i An dar Adabiyat-i Parsi*, Tehran, 1326/1948, pp. 507 ff.

72. `Ayn al-Qudat, *Tamhidat*, p. 210, no. 270.

73. *Ibid.*, pp. 115–6, no. 163.

74. Toshihiko Izutsu, "Creation and the Timeless Order of Things: A Study in the Mystical Philosophy of `Ayn al-Qudat," *Philosophical Forum* (1972), p. 133.

75. Schimmel, *Dimensions*, pp. 214–7.

76. *Ibid.*, pp. 224, 419.

77. `Ayn al-Qudat, *Tamhidat*, pp. 116–8, nos. 164–5.

78. *Ibid.*, pp. 117–8, no. 166.

79. *Ibid.*, pp. 119–20, no. 167. For Iblis as the watchman of the unpointed word *la*, see Ahmad al-Ghazali's *Kitab al-Tajrid fi Kalimat al-Tawhid*, in Abu Muhammad al-Ghazali, *Kitab Faysal al-Tafriqah bayn al-Islam wa al-Zandaqah*, ed. Muhammad Badr al-Din al-Naz`ani al-Halai, Egypt, 1325/1907, p. 82. See further *Tamhidat*, pp. 73–5, nos. 101–4; Hellmut Ritter, *Das Meer der Seele*,

Mensch, Welt und Gott in den Geschichten des Fariduddin `Attar, 2nd ed., Leiden, 1978, pp. 541-2, quoted by permission of E. J. Brill.

80. Cf. the phrase "black light" as used by the early Shi`i theologian Hisham ibn Salim al-Jawaliqi, in al-Shahrastani, *Kitab al-Milal wa sl-Nihal,* ed. Muhammad ibn Fath Allah Badran, Silsilah fi al-Darasat al-Falsafiyah wa al-Akhlaqiyah, Cairo, n.d., I, 165. For the symbolism of the black light according to Najm al-Din al-Kubra, see Henry Corbin, *L'homme de lumière dans le soufisme iranien,* Collection Le Soleil dans le coeur, Paris, 1971, p. 60, n.; index, s.v. "lumière noire."

81. `Ayn al-Qudat, *Tamhidat,* pp. 204-5, no. 263.

82. *Ibid.,* p. 205, no. 264.

83. *Ibid.,* pp. 205-6, no. 265.

84. *Ibid.,* pp. 206-7, no. 265.

85. *Ibid.,* pp. 208-212, nos. 266-271.

86. *Ibid.,* p. 214, no. 274; cf. pp. 48-9, no. 67.

87. *Ibid.,* pp. 214-5, no. 275.

88. *Ibid.,* p. 215, no. 275, citing Hallaj, *Akhbar,* no. 66. For *faqr* as *fana',* see Schimmel, *Dimensions,* pp. 123-4.

89. `Ayn al-Qudat, *Tamhidat,* pp. 349-50, no. 463; *Recueil,* pp. 189-90. See also Fritz Meier, *Abu Sa`id-i Abu l-Ḥayr,* Acta Iranica 11, third series, vol. 4, Leiden, 1976, pp. 26-9.

90. Gisu Daraz, in *Tamhidat,* pp. 412-3.

91. `Ayn al Qudat, *Tamhidat,* pp. 227-8, no. 295.

92. *Ibid.,* pp. 232-3, no. 302.

93. *Ibid.,* pp. 122-3, no. 171, reading *ba du hijab* for *dar hijab* on p. 123, line 3. The "great man" is identified in the index (p. 513) as Hallaj.

94. *Ibid.,* p. 340, no. 451.

95. Ruzbihan, *Sharh,* ch. 200.

96. Danish-Puzhuh, *Ruzbihan Namah,* p. 280.

97. Ruzbihan, *Sharh,* ch. 272, p. 446.

98. *Idem, `Ara'is* I, 128, *in Qur.* 3.193.

99. *Idem, Sharh,* ch. 29, pp. 74-5.

100. Ibn Hanbal, *Musnad* V, 447.

101. Ruzbihan, *Sharh,* ch. 156, p. 270.

102. *Ibid.,* ch. 130, p. 224.

103. *Ibid.,* ch. 149, pp. 252-3.

104. *Ibid.,* ch. 130, p. 224; ch. 105, p. 185.

105. *Idem, `Ara'is* I, 173, *in Qur.* 5.5. *Wajd* here also means ecstasy.

106. *Ibid.*

107. Ruzbihan, *Sharh,* ch. 50, p. 111; cf. ch. 176, p. 311, also ch. 129, p. 222.

108. *Ibid.,* ch. 115, p. 197 f.

109. Hallaj, *Akhbar,* no. 47.

110. Ruzbihan, *Sharh,* p. 451.

111. The verse is from the exordium to Sana'i's *Hadiqat al-Haqiqah,* cf. *The First Book of the Hadiqatu' l-Haqiqat or the Enclosed Garden of the Truth,* ed. and trans. J. Stephenson, reprint ed., New York, 1972, p. 1, line 12 (text). Ruzbihan wrote a treatise (not extant) on opposites, called *Kitab al-Mirsad fi al-Addad* (cf. Muhammad Taqi Danish-Puzhuh, *Ruzbihan Namah,* p. 342, no. 33).

112. Ruzbihan, *Sharh,* ch. 141, pp. 240-1.

113. *Idem.,* `*Ara'is* I, 203, *in Qur.* 6.28.
114. *Idem., Mashrab,* p. 306.
115. *Idem, Sharh,* ch. 3, p. 23.
116. *Ibid.,* ch. 174, p. 309.
117. *Ibid.,* ch. 347 (on *Tawasin* 6.15–17), p. 521.
118. The titles are: *Kitab al-Muwashshah fi `Ilm al-Fiqh,* a small section preserved in Danish-Puzhuh, *Ruzbihan Namah,* pp. 317–318 (questions on ritual prayer); *Kitab al-Haqa'iq fi al-I'tiqad,* cf. *ibid.,* p. 280; *Kitab al-Miftah fi `Ilm Usul al-Fiqh, Kitab al-Intiqad fi al-I`tiqad, ibid.,* p. 342. Ruzbihan was a Shafi`i.
119. Ruzbihan, *Sharh,* ch. 137, p. 232.
120. *Ibid.,* ch. 223, pp. 395–6.
121. *Idem, Mashrab,* p. 315.
122. *Idem,* `*Ara'is* II, 192, *in Qur.* 39.7. This comment is quoted by Dara Shikuh, *Hasanat,* p. 36.
123. Ruzbihan, *Sharh,* ch. 154, p. 265.
124. *Idem, Sharh al-Hujub wa al-Astar fi Maqamat Ahl al-Anwar wa al-Asrar,* Silsilah-i Isha`at al-`Ulum, No. 41, Hyderabad, 1333, p. 21.

CHAPTER THREE

1. Georges Vajda, "Les Zindîqs en pays d'Islam au debut de la période abbaside," *Revista degli Studi Orientale* (1937), pp. 173–229; L. Massignon, "Zindīk," SEI, pp. 659–660.
2. Sarraj, *Pages,* p. 6; cf. Sulami, *Tabaqat,* pp. 151–8.
3. Schimmel, *Dimensions,* p. 61.
4. Abu Nu`aym Ahmad ibn `Abd Allah al-Isfahani, *Hilyat al-Awliya' wa Tabaqat al-Asfiya',* Cairo, 1936–38, X, 252.
5. Ghulam Khalil, in *Recueil,* pp. 213–4; Sarraj, *Pages,* p. 5; GAS I, 511, no. 7; Khatib V, 78–80.
6. GAS I, 475–6.
7. Abu Nu`aym, X, 251. Sarraj (*Pages,* p. 5) says that al-Muwaffaq himself broke into tears, but it seems more likely that the qadi performed the examination alone or with the wazir.
8. Abu Nu`aym, X, 249–50.
9. Massignon, *Passion* I, 120, n. 6.
10. Sulami, p. 169, begins his account: "and Nuri was summoned to a session with the sultan . . . ," where Abu Nu`aym says, "One day the sultan asked him . . . " (X, 251, also Khatib, V, 133). The plural verb *ta'kuluna* implies others included in the question, and in both accounts the question directly follows the trial.
11. Nuri, in Sarraj, *Pages,* p. 5; Ruzbihan, *Sharh,* ch. 95, p. 165, line 19 should read *mutamatti`*, not *mumtani`* (cf. *Passion* I, 121, no. 8, *mutamati`*).
12. Nwyia, *Exégèse,* pp. 317–8 has an excellent commentary on this.
13. Sarraj, *Pages,* p. 5. Ruzbihan, in *Sharh,* ch. 96 p. 168, lines 5, 17, confirms Sarraj's MS reading *samm al-mawt* against Arberry's emendation *shamm.*
14. Sarraj, *Pages,* p. 5. Cf. Nwyia, p. 319.

15. Abu Hamid al-Ghazali, *Ihya' `Ulum al-Din*, Cairo, n.d., part 7, pp. 1273-4; Massignon, *Passion* I, 121; Nwyia, p. 317, n. 1.

16. Sarraj, *Luma`*, p. 195.

17. Sarraj, *Pages*, p. 8.

18. Ghulam Khalil in *Recueil*, p. 214.

19. Richard N. Frye, *The Heritage of Persia*, History of Civilization, London, 1962, p. 221-2; Khushaysh, in *Recueil*, p. 211, where *mazdakiyah* is a subsect of *zanadiqah*.

20. al-Hasan al-Basri, in *Recueil*, p. 3.

21. Khushaysh, in *Recueil*, p. 7; cf. *ibid.*, pp. 211-2, *Essai*, pp. 114-5, 217-8; *Passion*, III, 219 for other sub-sects of the *ruhaniyah*.

22. Ruzbihan, *Sharh*, ch. 117; Abu Nu`aym, X, 321.

23. Ruzbihan, *Sharh*, ch. 246.

24. Massignon, *Passion*, I, 121 (source not named).

25. Dominique Sourdel, *Le vizirat `abbâside de 749 à 936, 132 à 324 de l'Hegire*, Damascus, 1959-60, p. 643.

26. *Ibid.*, p. 326.

27. Sarraj, *Luma`*, p. 210.

28. Massignon, *Passion*, ch. V, "L'Accusation, le tribunal et les acteurs du drame" (I, 385-500); ch. VI, "Les procès" (I, 501-606).

29. Khatib, VIII, 129; cf. *Quatre Textes*, p. 32*, trans. *Passion* I, 52. This may have taken place as early as 288/900 (*ibid.*, I, 378).

30. *Ibid.*, I, 394.

31. Preachers (*qussas*) had been prohibited from public speaking by a caliphal edict of 284/897 (*ibid.*, I, 395).

32. *Ibid.*, I, 387-91; cf. Schimmel, *Al-Halladsch*, pp. 20-21.

33. Ruzbihan, *Sharh*, ch. 272. pp. 441-5, where *mahabbah* replaces Hallaj's controversial term `*ishq*; Hallaj, in Sulami, in *Essai*, pp. 428-9, no. 8, cf. *Passion* I, 389.

34. Ibn Da'ud, *Zahrah*, in Massignon, *Passion* I, 389.

35. Ibn Surayj, in Ibn Khallikan, in *Akhbar*, no. 72, apparatus, p. 107; Massignon's translation of this terse statement (*Passion* I, 417) is inflated, inserting the words "inspiration" and "doctrinalement."

36. *Akhbar*, no. 72; cf. *Passion* I, 418.

37. *Akhbar*, no. 72, notes to line 3, also *Recueil*, p. 60, no. 6. Emphasis mine.

38. Ruzbihan, *Sharh*, p. 46, where the text mistakenly has Sharih for Surayj.

39. Massignon, *Passion* I, 514-5.

40. *Ibid.*, I, 518.

41. `Ali ibn `Isa, in Abu Bakr Muhammad ibn Yahya al-Suli, *Kitab al-Awraq fi Akhbar Al `Abbas wa Ash`arihim*, ed. I. Kratchkovsky, "Razskaze sovremennika obe Al-Halladsche," *Zapiski Vostochnago Otdyeleniya Imperatorskago Russkago Arkheologicheskago Obshchestva* XXI (1911-12), p. 139, lines 12-14; cf. the slightly differing composite version translated by Massignon, *Passion* I, 520.

42. *Ibid.*, I, 523-534.

43. Ibn Dihya, trans. Massignon, *Passion* I, 539.

44. Hallaj, *Akhbar*, no. 7 ("there is no difference betwen my 'I-ness' and Your 'He-ness' save for the temporal and the eternal"); on Ibrahim ibn Adham, see Massignon, *Essai*, p. 57, n. 5, and *Passion* III, 15 (no source given).

45. *Ibid.*, I, 558-60, 572; Hamid, in Ibn Sinan, in *Quatre Textes*, p. 10*, n. 1.

46. *Ibid.*, I, 573.

47. Khatib, VIII, 127-8; Massignon, *Passion* I, 574-8.

48. *Quatre Textes*, p. 7*, lines 1-5; trans. *Passion* I, 561-2.

49. *Quatre Textes*, pp. 10*-11*.

50. Massignon, *Passion* I, 593-5. The inconsistencies in the three versions of Hallaj's trial could also be explained simply as differing accounts of a single interrogation without the assumption of duplicity.

51. Sourdel, p. 400.

52. Hamid, in Ibn `Ayyash, trans. Massignon, *Passion* I, 602.

53. M. T. de Goeje, "Carmaṭians," *Encyclopaedia of Religion and Ethics*, ed. James Hastings, Edinburgh, 1910; reprint ed., 1953, III, 223b.

54. Suli, p. 140, line 19; cf. *Passion* I, 560-1.

55. *Ibid.*, p. 140, lines 12-14; cf. *Passion* I, 540, with n. 2.

56. Hamzah ibn Hasan al-Isfahani, trans. Massignon, *Passion* I, 534.

57. Massignon, "Étude sur une courbe personelle de vie: le cas de Hallaj, Martyr mystique de l'Islam," *Opera Minora*, II, 174-5; Sourdel, p. 391.

58. Massignon, *Passion* I, 531-3.

59. *Ibid.*, I, 536.

60. *Ibid.*, I, 483, n. 2. citing Subki, and *Recueil*, p. 227, n. 4.

61. Massignon, *Passion* I, 484.

62. *Ibid.*, I, 543.

63. W. Heffening, "Murtadd," SEI, p. 414a; L. Massignon, "Zindīk," SEI, p. 659a. Cf. L. Bercher, "L'Apostasie, le Blasphème et la Rebellion en droit Musulman malékite," *Revue Tunisienne* XXX (1923), pp. 116, 119, 122.

64. Mahdi Naraqi Kashani (d. 1209/1794), in Massignon, *Passion* I, 596.

65. H. Laoust, *Les Schismes dans l'Islam, Introduction à une étude de la religion musulmane*, Paris, 1977, p. 161.

66. *Passion* I, 592.

67. Joseph Schacht, "Ḳatl," SEI, p. 230, quoted by permission of E. J. Brill.

68. Rahim Farmanish, *Ahwal wa Athar-i `Ayn al-Qudat*, Tehran, 1338; Abu al-Ma`ali `Abd Allah ibn `Ali al-Miyanaji al-Hamadani (`Ayn al-Qudat), *Shakwa al-Gharib*, ed. `Afif `Usayran, Intisharat-i Danishgah-i Tihran, 695, Tehran, 1341; A. J. Arberry, trans, *A Sufi Martyr, The Apologia of `Ain al-Quḍāt al Hamadhānī*, London, 1969.

69. `Ayn al-Qudat, *Tamhidat*, pp. 250-1, no. 328; this episode is quoted by Jami, *Nafahat*, p. 415, with an additional phrase, "in an inspired manner." For the date of the *Tamhidat*, see `Usayran, introduction to *Tamhidat*, p. 17.

70. `Ayn al-Qudat, *Tamhidat*, p. 251, no. 329; cf. Farmanish, p. 69.

71. `Ayn al-Qudat, *Tamhidat*, p. 250, no. 327, quoting Qur. 5.110.

72. `Ayn al-Qudat, *Tamhidat*, in Farmanish, p. 10.

73. Taqi Awhadi (ca. 1023/1614) in Farmanish, p. 68; this verse occurs in letter 47 of the Murad Mulla MS of `Ayn al-Quadat's letters (*ibid.*, p. 260).

74. `Ayn al-Qudat, *Shakwa*, in Farmanish, p. 70; trans. Arberry, pp. 30, 32.

75. `Ayn al-Qudat, *Shakwa*, in Farmanish, p. 70; trans. Arberry, p. 34.

76. `Ayn al-Qudat, *Shakwa*, in Farmanish, p. 70; trans. Arberry, pp. 33-4.

77. `Ayn al-Qudat, *Shakwa*, in Farmanish, p. 71; trans. Arberry, p. 38.

78. `Ayn al-Qudat, *Shakwa*, in Farmanish, p. 71; trans. Arberry, p. 54.

79. al-Katib al-Isfahani (6th/12th cent.), in Farmanish, p. 65; Taqi Awhadi (11th/17th cent.), *ibid.*, p. 68; Ma`sum `Ali Shah (12th/18th cent.), *ibid.*, p. 69.
80. Carla A. Klausner, *The Seljuk Vezirate, A Study of Civil Administration, 1055-1194*, Harvard Middle Eastern Monographs, XXII, Cambridge, 1973, p. 55.
81. Farmanish, p. 80.
82. *Ibid.*, pp. 74-5.
83. Abu Sa`id al-Sam`ani, in Sibt ibn al-Jawzi, in Farmanish, p. 76.
84. Farmanish, p. 78.
85. Klausner, p. 55; *Passion* II, 176, for Shirgir.
86. Klausner, p. 73.
87. Abu al-Majd Majdud ibn Adam Sana'i Ghaznawi, *Diwan*, ed. Mudarris Ridawi, Tehran, 1341, pp. 191-23, 561-4; *Makatib-i Sana`i*, ed. Nadhir Ahmad, Intisharat-i Danishgah-i Islami, No. 3, Rampur, 1382 q./1341 sh./1962, letters 5, 6, 14.
88. George Makdisi, "The Hanbali School and Sufism," *Humaniora Islamica* II (1974), pp. 61-72. Ibn al-Jawzi was responsible for transmitting the text of Sarraj's *Kitab al-Luma`* (cf. *Luma`*, p. 1).
89. For examples see David H. Partington's edition and translation of Diya' al-Din al-Sunami's treatise, written in Delhi in the eighth/fourteenth century, "The *Nisab al-Ihtisab*, A Religio-Legal Treatise," Ph. D. dissertation, Princeton University, 1962, ch. 49, pp. 188-198 (text), 366-376 (trans.). Cf. also GAS I, 434.
90. Abu al-Faraj `Abd al-Rahman ibn `Ali ibn al-Jawzi, *Talbis Iblis*, ed. Khayr al-Din `Ali, Beirut, n.d. (1970), p. 186.
91. *Ibid.*, p. 184.
92. *Ibid.*, pp. 185-6, Cf. GAS I, 355 on Muhammad ibn Tahir (ibn al-Qaysarani). Yahya ibn Ma`in (d. 233/847) was an early *muhaddith* and biographer (GAS I, 106-7).
93. Ibn al-Jawzi, *Talbis*, pp. 411-418.
94. Otto Pretzl, "Die Streitschrift des G̱azālī gegen die Ibāḥīja," *Sitzungsberichte der Bayerischen Akademie der Wissenschaften*, Philosophisch-historische Abteilung (1933), vol. 7. Ibn al-Jawzi gives Ghazali's sixth category first, then gives Ghazali's first four categories in order. He leaves out categories 5, 7, and 8 of Ghazali's list.
95. Abu Hamid Muhammad al-Ghazali, *Kitab Faysal al-Tafriqah bayn al-Islam wa al-Zandaqah*, ed. Muhammad Badr al-Din al-Naz`ani al-Halabi, Egypt, 1325/1907, p. 14.
96. `Ali Hujwiri, *Kashf al-Mahjub*, p. 105; trans. Nicholson, p. 131.
97. W. Madelung and M. G. S. Hodgson, "Ibāḥa (II)," EI[2], IV, 662a-b.
98. Abu Ya`la, in Ibn al-Jawzi, *Talbis*, p. 190.
99. Abu Nu`aym X, 321.
100. Ruzbihan, *Sharh*, chs. 116-7, esp. p. 202; cf. Ibn al-Jawzi, *Talbis*, pp. 189-90. Hujwiri presents the story of Abu Hamzah and Muhasibi's goat (here, a peacock) in a very distorted form; he has Muhasibi give an edifying sermon on the evils of theoretical *hulul*, and Abu Hamzah ends up repenting for the sake of seemliness (trans. Nicholson, pp. 182-3).
101. Ruzbihan, *Sharh*, ch. 462.
102. Massignon, *Passion* I, 121.
103. al-Ash`ari, trans. Ritter, *Meer*, pp. 450-1.

104. `Abd al-Qahir al-Baghdadi, trans. Ritter, *Meer*, p. 452; *Luma`*, p. 289; J. Pederson, "Ḥulmāniyya," EI[2], III, 570b.

105. Hujwiri, trans. Nicholson, pp. 260, 416–7.

106. L. Massignon and G. C. Anawati, "Ḥulūl," EI[2], III, 571a.

107. al-Thanawi, pp. 349–352.

108. Ritter, *Meer*, pp. 454–5.

109. *Ibid.*, p. 456.

110. Hallaj, *Diwan*, ed. Massignon, no. 61, p. 96; *in Qur.* 57.3, in Massignon, *Essai*, p. 403, no. 172.

111. `Abd al-Rahman al-Sulami, *Ghalatat al-Sufiyah*, MS 178/8 Majamī`, Dar al-Kutub al-Misriyah, Cairo, fol. 79a. Hallaj's statement is given by Massignon, *Essai*, p. 430. Sarraj, *Luma`*, p. 426. Sufi writings on the "errors (*ghalatat*)" of their brethren evidently began wth Ruwaym (d. 302/915), whose *Ghalatat al-Wajidin* ("Errors of the Ecstatics") Hujwiri mentions as a book of which he was "extremely fond" (trans. Nicholson, p. 135). Cf. the *Ghalatat al-Salikin* by Ruzbihan, of which an excerpt on Hallaj has been preserved in Danish-Puzhuh, *Ruzbihan Namah*, pp. 315–7.

112. Ibn al-Jawzi, *Talbis*, p. 188.

113. *Ibid.*, p. 185.

114. *Ibid.*, p. 187, on Abu Sulayman al-Darani conversing with angels. The same Darani's insistence on the *sunnah* and the Qur'an is quoted on p. 188.

115. Ibn al-Jawzi, *Talbis*, p. 194; cf. GAS I, 622–3 on al-Balkhi.

116. Massignon completely reversed himself on this point, once describing the Hanbalis as opposed to *ibahah* and the Mu`tazilis as opposed to *hulul* ("Taṣawwuf," SEI, p. 581a), and later saying just the contrary ("Zindīk," SEI, p. 659b).

117. Ibn al-Jawzi, *Talbis*, p. 190.

118. Junayd, in Ibn al-Jawzi, *Talbis*, p. 188.

119. Ibn `Ata', in Ibn al-Jawzi, *Talbis*, p. 193.

120. Nicholson, preface to trans. of Hujwiri, p. xiv. Hujwiri's discussion is in book XIV, pp. 137–207 (text), pp. 176–266 (trans.).

121. *Ibid.*, p. 260 (trans.), p. 203 (text). To be sure, Hujwiri blames the theory of the uncreated spirit on Hallaj's disciple Faris, whom these Hallajis cursed.

122. `Ayn al-Qudat, *Tamhidat*, pp. 22, 115; Hallaj, *Akhbar*, no. 6.

123. Reuben Levy, *The Social Structure of Islam*, 2nd, ed., Cambridge, 1971, p. 211, n. 4.

124. Suli, p. 139, lines 2–5.

125. Yahya ibn Mu`adh al-Razi, in Ignaz Goldziher, *The Zahiris: Their Doctrine and History, A Contribution to the History of Islamic Theology*, trans. and ed. Wolfgang Behn, Leiden, 1971, p. 65; Qushayri, in *ibid*, p. 166. Goldziher points out that a number of Sufis found the relatively undogmatic and ritually strict Zahiri school very accommodating to their views, cf. pp. 105–6 (Ruwaym) 169–70 (Ibn al-`Arabi).

126. Massignon, *Passion* I, 566–8.

127. Ruzbihan, *Sharh*, chs. 95 (`*ishq*), 96 (*labbayk*, 249 (witness), 266 (letter).

128. `Ayn al-Qudat, *Shakwa*, ed. `Usayran, p. 32.

129. Ibn al-Jawzi, pp. 387–94; Ruzbihan, *Sharh*, chs. 35, 40, 50, 71, 76, 79, 82 (Bayazid), 140 (Shibli), 466 (Husri).

130. Ibn `Aqil, in Ibn al-Jawzi, p. 386, 393.

131. Vajda, "Zindîqs," pp. 184–5.
132. Massignon, *Passion* I, 558.
133. Arberry, *A Sufi Martyr*, p. 99.
134. Ruzbihan, *Sharh*, ch. 10.
135. `Ayn al-Qudat, *Shakwa*, trans. Arberry, pp. 64–5.
136. `Ayn al-Qudat, *Shakwa*, p. 26; trans. Arberry, p. 53. Cf. Sarraj, *Lumʾ.*, p. 378; Sulami, *Ghalatat*, fol. 78b.
137. Ibn al-Sam`ani, in Subki, in Farmanish, p. 66.
138. Ibn al-Jawzi, p. 189.
139. Massignon, *Passion* II, 235.
140. Mar`i ibn Yusuf ibn Abi Bakr ibn Ahmad al-Maqdisi al-Hanbali, *Risalah fi-ma Waqa `a fi Kalam al-Sufiyah min al-Alfaz al-Muhimah lil-Takfir,* MS 53/2 Majami` Mustafa Pasha, Dar al-Kutub al-Misriyah, Cairo, fols. 35b, 41a. See also GAL II, 369, GALS II, 469, on Mar`i. Joseph Norment Bell observes that Mar`i "left the door open to the influence of Ibn al-`Arabi" in the Hanbali school (*Love Theory in Later Hanbalite Islam*, Studies in Islamic Philosophy and Science, Albany, 1979, p. 185, see also pp. 184–199).
141. *Passion* II, 166–9.
142. Wali al-Din Muhammad ibn `Abd Allah al-Khatib al-Tabrizi, *Mishkat al-Masabih*, Delhi, 1315, Qisas 1 (p. 299), 2 (p. 301), 29 (pp. 307–8).
143. Massignon *Passion* I, 429–30.
144. Kamalpasha-zadah, *Risalah fi Tahqiq Ma`na al-Zandaqah*, trans. Cl. Huart, "Les zindîqs en droit musulman," *Actes du Onzième Congrès International des Orientalists, Paris—1897*, Troisième Section: Langues et archéologie musulmanes, Paris, MDCCCXCIX, pp. 71–77 (not "M. Stuart" as in GALS II, 669/38).
145. Thirty of the eighty episodes of *Akhbar al-Hallaj* refer to his desire to be sacrificed (*Akhbar*, introduction, p. 59). For `Ayn al-Qudat, see *Tamhidat*, pp. 222 (lovers on the gallows and the cross), 230 (law seeks the blood of saints), 235–6 (Hallajian martyrdom), etc.
146. Massignon, *Passion* I, 601.
147. Shams al-Din Mhammad Hafiz Shirazi, *Diwan*, ed. Muhammad Qazwini and Qasim Ghani, Tehran, 1941; reprint ed., n.d., no. 142.
148. Taqi Awhadi, in Farmanish, p. 68.
149. Massignon, *Passion* II, 107–110.
150. Abu Hamid Muhammad ibn Abi Bakr Ibrahim Farid al-Din `Attar Nishaburi, *Kitab Tadhkirat al-Awliya'*, ed. Mirza Muhammad Khan Qazwini, 5th ed. (based on Nicholson), Tehran, n.d. (1336 sh.). Cf. *Passion* II, 370–2.
151. Sarraj, *Pages,* pp. 8–9; Ruzbihan, *Sharh*, pp. 30–32 (adding Husri and discussing Hallaj in detail elsewhere).
152. Sarraj, *Pages,* pp. 7, 11;
153. Ruzbihan, *Sharh*, pp. 26, 29, 32–4.
154 `Ayn al-Qudat, *Shakwa*, p. 39; trans. Arberry, p. 69; Ruzbihan, *Sharh*, p. 32. Cf. Massignon, *Passion* I, 431–3 on this genre. I have not had access to Qushayri's *Mihan al-Sufiyah* (*al-Rasa'il al-Qushayriyah*, ed. F. M. Hasan, Karachi, 1964).
155. Sha`rani, in *Akhbar*, no. 52, apparatus, n. 7; *idem*, trans. Nicholson, *A Literary History of the Arabs*, Cambridge, 1907; reprint ed., 1976, pp. 460–1,

where he adds the names of Nabulusi, Nasimi, Shadhil, and others. Cf. Schimmel, *Dimensions*, p. 395.
156. Jurayri, in *Akhbar*, no. 18.

CONCLUSION

1. Juan de la Cruz, *Subida del Monte Carmelo* II, 28-3, in *Vida y Obras*, ed. Lucinio del SS. Sacramento and Matías del Niño Jesus, Biblioteca de Authores Cristianos, 3rd ed., Madrid 1955, pp. 654-64; trans. Kieran Kavanaugh and Otilio Rodriguez, *The Collected Works of St. John of the Cross*, Washington, D. C., 1973, pp. 202-11.
2. William James, *The Varieties of Religious Experience, A Study in Human Nature*, New York, 1958 (1902), p. 267; Evelyn Underhill, *Mysticism, A Study in the Nature and Development of Man's Spiritual Consciousnes*, 12th ed., New York, 1961 (1911), pp. 429-30, quoted by permission of E. P. Dutton.
3. *Essai*, p. 95.
4. *Ibid.*, p. 119.
5. Meister Eckhart, *Pred.* xcix, in Underhill, p. 420.
6. Gerhard von Rad, *The Message of the Prophets*, trans D. M. G. Stalker, London, 1968, pp. 41-2.
7. *Ibid.*, pp. 32-3, cf. pp. 74-6.
8. Friedrich Heiler, *Das Gebet, Eine religionsgeschichtliche und religionpsychologische Untersuchung*, 5th ed., Munich, 1969, p. 360; trans. Samuel McComb, with the assistance of J. Edgar Park, *Prayer, A Study in the History and Psychology of Religion*, New York, 1958, p. 241.
9. Prof. Hasan Askari of the University of Birmingham in a conversation at Harvard University, October, 1980.
10. Benjamin Walker, "Sayings," *The Hindu World, An Encyclopedic Survey of Hinduism*, New York, 1968, II, 363-5.
11. Henry Corbin, Introduction to *Sharh*, pp. 7-14.
12. Cicero, *De Oratore, de Fato, Paradoxa Stoicorum, de Partitione Oratoria*, ed. and trans. H. Rackham, Loeb Classical Library, Cambridge, Massachusetts, 1942, II, 258, 266, 284 (my translation).
13. Rosalie L. Colie, *Paradoxia Epidemica, The Renaissance Tradition of Paradox*, Princeton, N. J. 1966, pp. 3-7.
14. *Ibid.*, p. 22; cf. pp. 22-30.
15. Underhill, p. 348.
16. Corbin, Introduction to *Sharh*, p. 44, n. 8.
17. Sebastian Franck, *Paradoxa*, ed. Siegfried Wollgast, Berlin, 1966, p. 4.
18. Franck, nos. 220, 226, p. 348: Virum fidelem quis inveniet/Es ist kein glaubender Mann auf Erden; Mundi confidentia vera incredulitatis / Der Welt Glauben ist ein rechter Unglaube.
19. Colie, pp. 27-8.
20. Isshu Miura and Ruth Fuller Sasaki, *Zen Dust, The History of the Koan and Koan Study in Rinzai (Lin-chi) Zen*, New York, 1966, p. 6.

21. Deisatz Teitaro Suzuki, *The Training of the Zen Buddhist Monk,* New York, 1965, pp. 9-13; *idem, An Introduction to Zen Buddhism,* New York, 1964, p. 109; Heinrich Dumoulin, *A History of Zen Buddhism,* New York, 1964, p. 109; Heinrich Dumoulin, *A History of Zen Buddhism,* trans. Paul Peachey, Boston, 1969, p. 130.

22. *Ibid.,* pp. 127-8.

23. Miura and Sasaki, p. 44.

24. Zenkei Shibayama, *Zen Comments on the Mumonkan,* trans. Sumiko Kudo, New York, 1974, p. 22.

25. Dumoulin, pp. 284 ff.

26. Anselm of Canterbury, "An Address (Proslogion)", XIV, trans. Eugene R. Fairweather, *A Scholastic Miscellany, Anselm to Ockham,* The Library of Christian Classics, X, New York, 1970, pp. 83-4.

27. *Tamhidat,* p. 212, no. 271.

28. Hallaj, *Tawasin* XI.26, ed. Massignon.

29. Underhill, pp. 346-57, 367.

30. Ibn Hawqal, *Kitab Surat al-Ard,* ed. J.H. Kramers, Bibliotheca Geographorum Arabicorum, II, 2nd ed., Leiden, 1939, II, 294.

31. Hans Jonas, *Gnosis und spätantiker Geist,* 3rd ed., Göttingen, 1964, I, 234-7.

32. D. L. Margoliouth, trans., "The Devil's Delusion of Ibn al-Jauzi," *Islamic Culture* 12 (1938), p. 239.

33. Mircea Eliade, "Observations on European Witchcraft," *Occultism, Witchcraft, and Cultural Fashions, Essays in Comparative Religions,* Chicago, 1976, pp. 85-8.

34. Firuz Shah Tughluq, *Futuhat-i Firuz Shahi,* ed. Shaikh Abdur Rashid, Aligarh, 1954, pp. 7-8.

35. Carl W. Ernst, "Martyrs of the Delhi Sultanate in the Sufi Biographical Tradition, and the Model of Hallaj" (forthcoming from *History of Religions*); I. H. Qureshi, "Ibāḥatiyya," EI[2], III, 663.

36. Vajda, "Zindîqs," p. 221; Ignaz Goldziher, *Muslim Studies,* trans. C. R. Berber and S. M. Stern, London, 1971, pp. 363-5.

37. Landolt, p. 196, no. 37.

38. Gardet, *Dieu,* p. 368.

39. Edward E. Salisbury, "Translation of Two Unpublished Arabic Documents Relating to the Doctrines of the Ismâ'ilis and Other Bâṭinian Sects," *Journal of the Amerian Oriental Society* II (1851), p. 310. For a comparison of Sufi and Shi`i exegesis, see also Kamil Mustafa al-Shaybi, *al-Silah bayn al-Tasawwuf wa al-Tashayyu`,* 2nd ed., Egypt, 1969, I, 407-25; the latter is partly based on Ignaz Goldziher, *Introduction to Islamic Theology and Law,* trans. Andras and Ruth Hamori, Modern Classics in Near Eastern Studies, Princeton, 1981, pp. 138-40.

40. Massignon, "Ḳarmaṭians," SEI, p. 221.

41. Meister Eckhart, trans. Raymond Bernard Blakney, *Meister Eckhart, A Modern Translation,* New York, 1941, p. 73.

42. Cf. Seyyed Hossein Nasr, "Shi`ism and Sufism," in *Sufi Essays,* Albany, 1972, pp. 113-4.

43. Hallaj, *Tawasin* V.2-5, ed. Nwyia.

Appendix

Ruzbihan's Account of Bayazid's Vision

One of the most celebrated sayings of Bayazid is his narration of a celestial journey filled with remarkable visions, which culminated in his statement that it was all a trick. Some have considered this conclusion an admission of the illusory nature of his experiences. Others have seen this account as forming part of an ascension (*mi'raj*) modelled on that of the Prophet. Perhaps the most extreme example of this interpretation is that of R. C. Zaehner, who stitched together various texts from Sarraj, Sahlaji, Hujwiri, and 'Attar into a composite version of the "so-called 'ascension.'"[1] This procedure was unfortunately arbitrary and attempted to establish literary dependence without adequate foundation. More recent authorities have remained non-committal about the extent to which Bayazid was imitating the Prophet's ascension in this description.[2] It is above all in later popular literature that Bayazid is seen as having an ascension modelled on Muhammad's, as in the imaginative fourteenth-century version published by Nicholson.[3]

Ruzbihan's account,[4] given below, is different from those used by Zaehner, being closest to that of Sarraj. Sarraj became vague at the point when Bayazid approached the heavenly tree, but Ruzbihan explicitly describes how Bayazid ate its fruits. Unlike Hujwiri and 'Attar, Ruzbihan does not conclude his version with praise of Muhammad, nor does he explicitly assimilate Bayazid's experience to the Prophet's ascension. He ends instead on a note of ambiguity, even of obscurity, stressing in his commentary that the realization of the deceptive nature of mystical experience is the prerequisite for the unknowing that leads to gnosis. The most striking part of Ruzbihan's account is his recapitulation of the

whole story, in the first person. This is another example of his interpretive identification with the speakers of *shathiyat*.

342	Abu Yazid says,
343	"In unity
351	I became a bird
352	(with) body of oneness
353	and wings of everlastingness.
354	I was flying in an atmosphere without (*sic*) quality for some years
355	until I entered an atmosphere. After that atmosphere (in) which I was,
356	I flew a hundred million times in that atmosphere,
357	until I entered the plains of pre-eternity.
358	I saw the tree of oneness.
359	It had its root in the earth of eternity and its branch in the atmospherer of post-eternity. The fruits of that tree were Majesty and Beauty. I ate the fruits of that tree.
361	When I looked well, I saw that all was trick upon trick."

(Here follows Ruzbihan's interpretive recapitulation of the narrative:)

This state is higher than the first state,[5] because there gnosis came with the
disposition of *tawhid*, that is,

352	"My soul became the body of gnosis by the soul of gnosis.
353	I flew with the wings of the light of *tawhid* and isolation in pre- and post-eternity. After I became isolated from self and existence, God clothed me with the garment of everlastingness and eternality. He gave me a body from eternity. He caused the wings of oneness to grow Attributes from Him.
356	The bird of eternity flew in the eternity of eternities. It sought union with reality.
357	After reality, I sought the depth of the depth in the deserts of quality. (He) burned my wings with the fire of Majesty. I was consumed in the light of the candle of pre-eternity. He cast the seeing essence into the oyster-shell of primordiality.[6] He cast me in the endless ocean, in the essence of the Attributes. I became subsistent in the Attributes.
358-9	I received the fruits of subsistence from the tree of eternity. My astonishment increased in astonishment. Subsistence took my hand from annihilation. I put on the garment of knowledge. I fell into gnosis with knowledge. I saw the deserts of unknowings with the eyes of gnosis.
369	I knew that everything I saw, all was I. It was not God. It was the deception of manifestation in (apparent) declaration of God's sanctity.[7] Abstraction (of qualities from God) was in fact a ruse. Intimate mystical states were (carnal) thoughts. Thoughts were infidelities. God was God. I was not."

(Now begins the formal commentary):

That which he said in describing the bird and the tree was all symbolic. The meaning of "quality" was "to seek the depths of eternity." "Air" and "space" are greatness upon greatness, "year" and "month" are timeless time, for illuminated consciences. Otherwise, what sort of story is it? Existence is not worth an atom in the beak of the western phoenix of eternity. Temporal bodies are not a (divine) ruse.

He did not display that which he did not give. He did not give that which he did not make known. When the gnostic fell in the ocean of pre-eternity, he became a green drop in the sea of pre-eternity. He becomes (*sic*) colorless in that ocean. A drop from that ocean takes on the color of the ocean, so that it is consumed in the billow of substantiality. The soul that is eloquent without a tongue, the familiar hearing that is deaf, the First Intellect that is confused, the life that is lifeless, the soul that is soulless, see nothing but the wrath of the blow of blows of the luminous oceans of pre-eternity. When that ocean casts the foam of temporality on the temporal, that drop thinks that it has encompassed the ocean—and that is of the nature of apparent clothing with divinity.[8] Otherwise, there are a hundered thousand deserts of waterless mirage on the coast of pre-eternity (giving the illusion of merging with the ocean). That which he mentioned about the eclipse (?)[9] concerns the Attributes; otherwise, he who is of the Essence — Alas!

NOTES TO APPENDIX

1. Zaehner, *Hindu and Muslim Mysticism*, Appendix B.I, pp. 198–218.
2. H. Ritter, "Abū Yazīd al-Bisṭamī," EI[2], I, 162–3 (1960); Qassim al-Sammarai, *The Theme of Ascension in Mystical Writings, A Study of the theme in Islamic and non-Islamic mystical writings*, Baghdad, 1968, pp. 232–40, cf. 186–205, 214–24.
3. R. A. Nicholson, ed. and trans., "An Early Arabic Version of the Miʿráj of Abú Yazíd al-Bistámí," *Studia Islamica* 2 (1926), pp. 402–15.
4. *Sharh*, no. 36, with lines arranged according to the line numbers in Zaehner's *Hindu and Muslim Mysticism*, pp. 214–5.
5. Mentioned in the previous saying, *Sharh*, no. 35, also in Zaehner, p. 212, lines 310–328.
6. Reading *sadaf* for *sarf*.
7. Like Iblis at the creation of Adam, Bayazid had taken his own perception of a form to be the reality, and thus succeumbed to the divine ruse. Satan called his subsequent rebellion a "declaration of God's sanctity" (Hallaj, *Diwan*, no. M 28; also in *Sharh*, no., 344).
8. Reading *talabbus* for the impossible conjecture *tarannus* (see the definition of the former term in *Sharh*, p. 626; this is distinct from actual clothing with divinity, *iltibas*).
9. The text gives *kusuf*, "eclipse," which has no obvious meaning; could this be a mistake for *khudu`*, "deception," in the original Arabic?

Selected Bibliography

Arberry, Arthur J., trans. *A Sufi Martyr. The Apologia of ʾAin al-Quḍāt al-Hamadhānī*. London, 1969.

ʾAyn al-Qudat: see Miyanaji, Arberry.

Badawi, ʾAbd al-Rahman. *Shatahat al-Sufiyah*. Part 1: *Abu Yazid al-Bistami*. Darasat Islamiyah, 9. Cairo, 1949.

Corbin, Henry. *En Islam iranien. Aspects spirituels et philosophiques*. Vol. 3. *Les Fidéles d'amour, Shiʾisme et soufisme*. Paris, 1972.

Dara Shikuh, Muhammad. *Hasanat al-ʾArifin*. Edited by Makhdum Rahin. Tehran, 1352/1973.

Graham, William. *Divine Word and Prophetic Word in Early Islam. A Reconsideration of the Sources, with Special Reference to the Divine Saying or "Ḥadîth Qudsî,"* Religion and Society, 7. The Hague, 1977.

Hallaj, Husayn ibn Mansur. *Akhbar al-Hallaj. Recueil d'oraisons et d'exhortations du martyr mystique de l'Islam*. Edited and translated by Louis Massignon and Paul Kraus. Études Musulmanes, IV. 3rd ed. Paris, 1957.

— — —. *Le Dîwân d'al-Hallâj*. Edited and translated by Louis Massignon. 2nd ed. Paris, 1955.

— — —. *Kitâb al-Ṭawâsîn*. Edited by Louis Massignon. Paris, 1913.

— — —. *Kitāb al-Ṭawāsīn*. Edited by Paul Nwyia. *Mélanges de l'Université Saint-Joseph*, vol. 47. New ed. Beirut, 1972.

Ibn al-Jawzi, Abu al-Faraj ʾAbd al-Rahman ibn ʾAli. *Talbis Iblis*. Edited by Khayr al-Din ʾAli. Beirut, n.d. (1970).

Massignon, Louis. *Essai sur les origines du lexique technique de la mystique musulmane.* Études musulmanes, II. 2nd ed. Paris, 1968.

— — —. *La Passion de Husayn ibn Mansur Hallaj, martyr mystique de l'Islam executé à Baghdad le 26 mars 922. Étude d'histoire religieuse.* 2nd ed. 4 vols. Paris, 1975.

al-Miyanaji al-Hamadani, Abu al-Ma'ali 'Abd Allah ibn Muhammad ibn 'Ali ibn al-Hasan ibn 'Ali. *Risalat Shakwa al-Gharib.* Edited by 'Afif 'Usayran. Intisharat-i Danishgah-i Tihran, 695. Tehran, 1962.

— — —. *Tamhidat.* Edited by 'Afif 'Usayran. Intisharat-i Danishgah-i Tihran, 695. Tehran, 1962.

Nwyia, Paul. *Exégès coranique et langage mystique. Nouvel essai sur le lexique technique des mystiques musulmans.* Recherches publiées sous la direction de l'Institute de lettres orientales de Beyrouth, Serie 1: Pensée arabe et musulmane, vol. 49. Beirut, 1970.

Ritter, Hellmut. "Die Aussprüche des Bayezid Bistami." *Westöstliche Abhandlungen Rudolf Tschudi zum siebzigsten Geburtstag überreicht von Freunden und Schülern.* Edited by Fritz Meier. Wiesbaden, 1954.

Ruzbihan al-Baqli. *'Ara'is al-Bayan fi Haqa'iq al-Qur'an.* 2 vols., with the *tafsir* of Ibn 'Arabi (sc. Kashani) on the margins. Calcutta, 1883.

— — —. *Sharh-i Shathiyat.* Edited by Henry Corbin. Bibliothèque Iranienne, 12. Tehran, 1966.

al-Sarráj al-Ṭusí, Abú Nasr 'Abdallah ibn 'Alí. *The Kitáb al-Luma' fi'l Taṣawwuf.* Edited by Reynold Alleyne Nicholson. "E. J. W. Gibb Memorial" Series, vol. XXII. London, 1963.

Schimmel, Annemarie. *Al-Halladsch, Märtyrer der Gottesliebe.* Cologne, 1968.

— — —. *Mystical Dimensions of Islam.* Chapel Hill, N. C., 1976.

al-Shaybi, Kamil Mustafa, ed. *Sharh Diwan al-Hallaj.* Beirut, 1393/1973.

Index of Qur'anic Citations

Index of Hadith Citations

Index of Names

Index of Subjects and Terms